I LOVE YOU
BUT . . .

I LOVE YOU BUT . . .

Romance, Comedy and the Movies

CHERRY POTTER

Methuen

Methuen

1 3 5 7 9 10 8 6 4 2

First published in Great Britain in 2002 by
Methuen Publishing Limited
215 Vauxhall Bridge Road
London SW1V 1EJ

Methuen Publishing Limited Reg. No. 3543167

A CIP catalogue record for this book is available from the British Library

ISBN 0-413-74990-8

Typeset by SX Composing DTP, Rayleigh, Essex
Printed and bound in Great Britain by
Creative Print and Design (Wales) Ltd, Ebbw Vale

Contents

For Brian and Stephen

Acknowledgements

I owe a huge debt to Brian Clark for his endless support and encouragement at every stage of the writing process, and to both Brian and Stephen Clark for their feedback, which was consistently thoughtful, provocative and fun. I would like to thank my agent, Laura Morris, for her boundless enthusiasm, and my editors; Max Eilenberg for the pleasure he expressed as I delivered him the chapters, which always renewed my energy for the task ahead, and for his humour and warmth; and David Salmo for his meticulous, dependable work. I would also like to thank Michael Earley, who gave me the opportunity to write this book, MovieMail (www.moviem.co.uk) for their excellent mail order video service and Rachel Igel for tracing a copy of *Diary of a Mad Housewife*.

There were times, as I was writing *I Love You But . . .*, when I felt as if I were looking in a mirror, although not the mirror of a life that spans all seven decades, but of a life that began its relationship journey with all the hopeful optimism and belief in the goodness of the fairytale, and progressed, through disappointment, failure, and questioning, although not without fun and adventure, towards a new, different and perhaps more real understanding of love and romance, and yet, without ever quite relinquishing the aspirations of the fairytale. And so, finally, I am indebted to all the love-relationships I have had in my life, which, for better or for worse, have greatly informed my understanding of the relationships I explore in these twenty-eight films.

Introduction

'All tragedies end in death, all comedies end in
marriage'

Lord Byron

There is no value in love that isn't hard won. Whether this is true
in real life is debatable, but it is certainly true in romantic
comedies. The best and most enduring romantic comedies are
exhilarating, witty, sexy, moving and fun. So, with the pleasure
principle as my guide, my first challenge was to write a book that
gives as much enjoyment as the films themselves. That said, the
best romantic comedies are also provocative and complex; they
tell us about ourselves as men and women, sexual desire, love,
relationships, our longings and wishes, our fallibilities and fears.
They show us how our beliefs, about what we 'should' think and
feel and how we 'ought' to behave, are often in conflict with our
sense of self and the burgeoning undercurrents of our wishes and
sexual desires.

These films can be radical, frequently portraying heroes and
heroines who are struggling to push back the boundaries that
confine their and our lives; yet they can just as easily slip into
reactionary mode in their eagerness to resolve at least some of
the problems and arrive at that crucial happy ending. They
reflect the attitudes, assumptions and prejudices about these all-
important aspects of our lives that prevailed when the films were
made and the debates that indicate the changes to come. They

take our wishes and transform them into alternative, imaginative realities where heroes and heroines struggle to make these wishes come true and in most cases succeed. But then the heroes and heroines and their wishes, in turn, become what we emulate; we want to be like them and we want to succeed, as they appear to have succeeded, in our real lives. In this way the imaginative world of romantic comedy and our real-life imaginations have become intriguingly engaged in an endless feedback loop.

This book is a journey through seven decades of romantic comedy, starting with the thirties, a few years after the advent of talking pictures. It is not intended to be a definitive history of the genre. I have selected just four films from each decade, each chosen to illuminate the changing relations between the sexes as, with each decade, a new generation confronts the same questions: What does it mean to be a man or a woman? What are the differences between us, and what are our similarities? What are our proper roles and what are the dangers of straying across the great gender divide and trying on each other's roles? What are our hopes and fears when it comes to love and relationships? What makes a good relationship? What makes us happy? What do men and women really want? These are the questions that have been, and continue to be, the stuff of argument and amusement throughout history and lie at the root of all romantic comedy.

Lord Byron famously said: 'All tragedies end in death, all comedies end in marriage', relishing, one suspects, his ironical juxtaposition of death and marriage. The dictionary defines *romantic* as (amongst other things), ' . . . given to thoughts and feelings of love especially idealized or sentimental love', and *comedy* as both 'the humorous aspect of life' and, in classical drama, a story in which the hero or heroine 'triumph over adversity'. Although whether marriage is, in itself, a triumph over adversity and therefore a happy ending, or whether it is merely a new beginning for the next round of adversity, which may, in turn, become the next comedy or tragedy, is another question. A quick survey of the twenty-eight films in this book reveals that: five end with marriage or living together as if married; thirteen end with either a proposal of marriage or, at least, love is declared in such a way that we assume that marriage or living together will follow; in four the couples are already married or have married earlier in the film but have got dangerously close to being unmarried before managing to save the day and, they hope, live happily ever after; in one the couple were married, divorced and propose to re-marry each other in the end; one ends with the reaffirmation of a marriage although possibly not with the woman of his dreams; another is in every way a classic romantic comedy except that it doesn't end with happily ever after; and finally, three are definitely comedies about love, romance and relationships, although two end with splitting up and the other – well she's still weighing up her options. It is probably no accident that these three films were made in the seventies when new-wave feminism was causing a new wave of confusion in relations between the sexes. Still, Byron was right about one thing; none of the films ends with death.

The pleasure to be gained from stories about the humorous side of love is as old as love itself and 'the battle of the sexes' is undoubtedly the theme that dominates the genre. On the other hand, fairytales, or elements from fairytale mythology, are also detectable in many modern guises. Fairytales, like romantic comedies, are about the pursuit of happiness, which in itself usually means finally finding and securing that ever elusive love. Most fairytales act as a guide to the rite of passage from our childhood dependency and love of our parents to our adult relationships as men and women. Separation from our parents and striking out alone in the world is an event of archetypal significance in all of our lives. However much we look forward to the freedom of leaving home, all sorts of fears or 'separation anxieties' are aroused. As Bruno Bettelheim puts it: 'There is no greater threat in life than that we will be deserted, left all alone . . . The younger we are the more excruciating is our anxiety when we feel deserted, for the young child actually perishes when not adequately protected and taken care of . . . therefore the ultimate consolation is that we will never be deserted',[1] which is implied in the common fairytale ending 'And they lived happily ever after. Therefore, in order to regain the happiness we once enjoyed, or wish we had once enjoyed, in our parents' home, the goal of our journey in the outside world is to find a new equivalent adult security and love.

Cinderella, Dick Whittington, Beauty and the Beast; they are all about leaving home. They are also reminders that the homes we are anxious to leave are not all sweetness and light. Fairytale homes often reflect our secret worries, anxieties and resentments in the form of wicked stepmothers, weak and neglectful fathers and selfish, tormenting siblings, including a common childhood fantasy that these people are not really our relations at all; in fact we are orphans and our real parents, if only they were not lost or dead, would undoubtedly be perfect. If the fairytale is to be at all satisfying, the journey made by the hero or heroine, in order to find this lost perfection, cannot be easy. We must go through all sorts of life tests and trials in the outside world. Dangers will have to be overcome, ordeals endured, decisions made without depending on a parent for guidance or rescue if we are to learn and change and so achieve autonomy, however temporary that autonomy may be, before we are ready for the arms of a new love and can live happily once again.

Such tests of character play a huge part in the fairytale romantic comedies such as *It Happened One Night, Mr Deeds Goes to Town* and *Strictly Ballroom*. The heroes and heroines are always beset by obstacles, they often confront difficult moral dilemmas and they frequently have to make some sort of personal sacrifice in order to prove themselves and finally win the one they love. The underlying message is that only through adversity can we learn and change and only through coming to know ourselves will we be ready and able to love another.

Knights in shining armour appear throughout the films in a multitude of different guises: dissolute newspaper reporters, insurance salesmen, lawyers, high-flying players on the money markets and even the American president. Their female equivalents, princesses, Cinderellas and damsels in distress, also appear in a variety of guises, although they are somewhat more thin on the ground in a century which saw women resisting passivity, determinedly redefining what it means to be 'good' and, in many of the films, working in challenging occupations – which is consistently one of the major causes of conflict between the sexes. Yet despite the many images of strong and successful women, mythological fairytale characters imprinted on us in childhood appear to remain submerged in the private wishing wells beneath our rational adult minds, serving either as a reminder of our failings or our loved one's failings, or, conversely, as an idealized image of what we most desire, which we project on to our future love. And when it comes to what we most fear, the dark and evil characters from fairytales and mythology have an equally powerful hold over our imaginations. Romantic comedies are peppered with dark, selfish, destructive but also, on occasion, sexually exciting women; the whores, sirens and Medusas of mythology and the witches, ugly sisters and wicked stepmothers of fairytales. There is also an abundance of corrupt kings and feckless, philandering men, but they tend to be more recognizably real than their female counterparts!

Romantic comedy and romantic tragedy both involve a tenacious struggle against adversity. The romantic idyll where we meet, fall in love and live happily ever after without any problems may be what we imagine we want, but do we really? A problem-free love story is a contradiction in terms, suspiciously lacking the excitement, complexity and danger of real passion, unless the happy couple are repressing aspects of their own nature and desires, which is in itself a problem. The struggle to repress our instinctive desires in order to be happy – but which also, of course, causes us to be unhappy – could well be the basic contradiction of the human condition. Do we lie to ourselves or to our loved ones? Do we choose hypocrisy or self-denial? This is the central theme of *The Seven Year Itch*, although it also recurs more obliquely in films such as *The Apartment*, *The Graduate* and *Roman Holiday*, which all cater to our eternal fascination with the secret or illicit love and yet are ever mindful that men and women who betray are guilty and must receive their come-uppance. Only *Bob & Carol & Ted & Alice* tackles the theme head on by asking what happens when partners act out their secret fantasies *and* tell each other the whole truth. Whether the film achieves the desired happy ending or simply presents us with a new set of dilemmas is up to each of us to decide.

Which brings us to how the battle of the sexes has been affected by the struggle for women's rights. This also has a long and enduring heritage, although this is often forgotten in our post-modern era with its lazy assumption that feminism began at the tail-end of the sixties, had its heyday in the seventies, and moved into a period of partial equality or backlash, depending on your point of view, in the eighties and nineties. A similar cycle had already taken place earlier in the century when the suffragettes finally won the vote. Their victory was followed in the twenties by a period when women's lives were transformed by new opportunities in the workplace and a new climate of sexual freedom which was enjoyed by both sexes, only to be forced into retreat by the Depression in the thirties. It was then reawakened in the forties by the demands of the war on both sexes and forced into retreat once more by the conservative morality of the fifties. But women have been railing against their lot and demanding their right to express themselves with as much power and fury as men probably for as long as there have been men and women on the planet. Shakespeare, of course, brilliantly reminds us of this in his romantic comedies of the Elizabethan era such as *Much Ado About Nothing* and *The Taming of the Shrew*. Conflicts between our notions of civilization, morality, gender and our sexual desires permeate Shakespeare's comedies and most stories concerning relationships between the sexes. This is irrespective of whether they are considered to be reactionary or visionary or whether the story is tragic or fun. As Shakespeare so skilfully demonstrates, the line between the two can at times be very thin.

Shakespeare was particularly adept at balancing on the precarious tightrope between the light and dark side of relationships, often causing us both to laugh and gasp as the comedy threatens to topple into tragedy. *The Taming of the Shrew* is the most enduring and the most popular romantic comedy of all time. So it is not surprising that its influence is detectable in so many of the films in this book; although most obviously in *It Happened One Night*, *The Quiet Man* and *As Good As It Gets*, which intriguingly reverses some of the familiar gender characteristics of the hero and heroine. Of course there is the famous 1969 film version of *The Taming of the Shrew* starring Elizabeth Taylor and Richard Burton. But Zeffirelli's film misses much of the complexity of the play. For any real insights into *The Taming of the Shrew* and why it has had such an enduring influence we have to return to the original text.

In the play Shakespeare interweaves two love stories: Petruchio and Kate, who by any standards are both outrageously badly behaved; and Bianca, Kate's younger sister, and Lucentio, who in contrast appear to be paragons of virtue. Lucentio is the first to appear in the story when he arrives in Padua as a young student intending to study virtue (no less) at the university. Then he spots the beautiful Bianca, a 'Maid of mild behaviour and sobriety' and falls in love at first sight. Bianca is already surrounded by suitors; a problem which Lucentio quickly resolves by cleverly changing places with his servant in order to secure a job as Bianca's tutor and so to get ahead of the competition and woo her in secret. The major, and seemingly insurmountable problem is Bianca's elder sister, Kate. Bianca's father is adamant; Kate must be married before Bianca, but Kate is renowned for being mad, wild, violent and angry. No man can get near her without quaking with fear, despite the large dowry her father has offered to whoever agrees to take her off his hands. Enter Petruchio who, unlike lovesick Lucentio, claims to have no romantic ideals or delusions. He has come to Padua with the specific purpose of finding himself a fortune in the form of a wealthy wife.

Lucentio and Bianca clearly represent the ideal of romantic love; an attentive, chivalrous, learned young man who woos the modest, virtuous, innocent maiden by becoming her teacher, which enables him to mould her still further into his ideal of perfection. This is also a theme which recurs in many later romantic comedies; men do like the opportunity to teach women about life, and women are adept at playing the role of the good pupil. Petruchio and Kate, on the other hand, appear to represent, at least at the outset, the traditional arranged marriage where property and money are the primary considerations. Just as in many twentieth-century romantic comedies, the controversy at the heart of the play reflects a contemporary debate; which in Shakespeare's England was whether arranged marriages or marriages based on romantic love were the basis for happiness. (The dowry system is also tackled in *The Quiet Man* and the characterization of the heroine, Mary Kate, is clearly influenced by Kate, much to John Wayne's consternation.)

For modern women it is not difficult to understand why Kate is in such a rage with her lot as a woman. Her future lies in the hands of her father who intends to pay a man to take her off his hands, although preferably a man Kate loves. But whatever his 'good' intentions, Kate feels that she has little choice but to suffer the humiliation of being treated as goods in a financial transaction. To make matters worse, Kate's father clearly prefers her paragon of a sister, which only serves to incite Kate's fury still more. She mercilessly attacks her sister, her father and all men who she sees as wanting to imprison all women in her sister's stifling image. But whatever the cause of her violent rages, and however justified they may be, when we first meet her they have become so out of control that she is driving herself mad, as well as intimidating any man or woman who tries to come near her. It seems there is no man strong enough to stand up to a woman as wilful as Kate, except, perhaps, Petruchio.

Petruchio is an adventurer. He has sailed the raging seas, hunted wild animals and fought on the battlegrounds of war. Rather than be put off by Kate's temper tantrums, he is positively stimulated into action; she is his latest challenge. In fact he 'loves her ten times more' for being such a 'lusty wench' and putting up a good fight. He never actually hits Kate, although he threatens to when she hits him. But instead of striking her back he demonstrates his superior strength by holding her tight. This of course infuriates Kate but as she struggles to free herself, their close physical contact is arousing, as the sexual innuendo in their verbal sparring suggests: 'What is your crest – a coxcomb?' she taunts him. 'A combless cock, so Kate will be my hen,' Petruchio jests. 'No cock of mine, you crow too like a craven,' Kate replies. This is the all-important moment when we see and feel the electric sexual chemistry between Kate and Petruchio, long before they are prepared to admit to it to each other. (This moment of sexual chemistry is emulated in most of the romantic comedies in this book, although of course in each case it manifests itself in a completely different guise.) It also leads to a moment of weakness on Kate's part, when despite herself she agrees to marry Petruchio.

Petruchio's plan for 'taming' Kate, which he carefully explains to the audience, is as audacious as Kate herself. He intends both to deliberately outdo Kate with his own displays of ill-temper and capriciousness and, however outrageous her behaviour becomes in response, he will also praise her by telling her the things that deep down every woman wants to hear about her beauty and charm. His method is similar to that of taming a wild falcon; depriving it of food and sleep and watching it continually until eventually it gives in. Apparently this treatment also makes the falcon 'very loving to the man, which is exactly how Petruchio wants Kate to be'.[2] He proceeds to starve his new wife of food and sleep, to tear up the clothes she wants to wear to her sister's wedding and generally coerce her into obeying his every whim.

But when they finally travel together to attend her sister's wedding, rather than appearing unduly angry or intimidated by Petruchio's bullying, for the first time in the play Kate seems in good spirits. She agrees to admire how brightly the moon is shining, if Petruchio wishes it to be the moon, even though it is the sun. And when Petruchio insists that an old man they meet on the road is, in fact, such a fair and lovely women that 'stars do spangle heaven with her beauty', Kate agrees. She even compliments the bewildered old man still further by telling him how happy the man will be who takes 'thee for his lovely bedfellow'. It is as if the scene itself is enchanted by the many allusions to age-old archetypes such as the masculine sun, the capricious feminine moon, the romance of moonlight, the multitude of stars in the night sky, nature which buds like a virgin 'fair and fresh and sweet' – in short all the pleasures Kate has discovered beyond the confines of her childhood home, including the delight to be found between 'lovely bedfellows'. In other words she is changing, and what better place to mark her transition than the natural world where atavistic forces have always had, and continue to have, a magical effect on the progress of love.

The climax of *The Taming of the Shrew* has probably caused more argument amongst men and women than any ending in the history of romantic comedy. When Kate and Petruchio attend Bianca and Lucentio's wedding feast, while the women have retreated to the parlour, the men make a bet on which of their wives will come when summoned by their husband, thus proving who is the most obedient wife. Bianca, the paragon of virtue at the outset of the play, has since demonstrated how she compensates for her lack of real power as a woman by skilful manipulation. Now she is securely married to Lucentio she no longer needs to play such games and she sends him a message saying she is too busy to come. Kate, on the other hand, not only comes when sent for, but proceeds to make a brilliant if enigmatic speech on what it means to be a woman and a wife. 'Thy husband is thy Lord, thy life, thy keeper, thy head, thy sovereign, one that cares for thee . . .' Ever the rebel, her speech challenges the prejudices held against her by the very same people she was in rebellion against at the outset of the play – in this sense Kate's speech is one of triumph. They would lock her into her role as a man-hating shrew; now she asserts herself as a more whole, feminine and loving woman than their own wives. But the lingering questions remain. How can it be that Kate has changed so? Has she been brainwashed by Petruchio's 'taming' methods? Does she really mean what she says or is she using irony to confound her audience?

Of course, resorting to physical or mental violence in the battle of the sexes is even more unacceptable now than it was in Shakespeare's time. Although men have traditionally been required to demonstrate their physical strength or their 'brilliant left hook' as proof of their manhood and superiority over other men, there is a very real problem when men's strength shifts its focus from being a positive asset for a 'knight in shining armour' to becoming a threat to the damsel whose heart is being won. This is an issue which recurs in a variety of scenes in this book, although never without threatening to reveal unpalatable truths about the inequality underlying the battle of the sexes and threatening to topple the comedy into tragedy.

There are, of course, many possible interpretations of Shakespeare's play. But whatever each of us decides to make of Kate's speech, there is no doubt that she has changed. At the beginning of the play, in her father's house, she is angry with her lot as a woman, but she is also lonely. She may not understand exactly what it is that she wants in life, but we can see how she needs a new role to play, if for no other reason than that she is miserable in the old role. Through meeting a man who is strong enough to stand up to her and who at the same time values her fiery temperament, who can equal her blow for blow in wit, passion and fury, Kate's spirit as a woman has not so much been tamed as liberated. As Kate's speech demonstrates, her fire still burns, but now it burns for Petruchio, as his wife and lover. And the energy Kate and Petruchio generate between them is undoubtedly sexy; as confirmed at the very end of the play when

Petruchio says admiringly, 'Why, there's a wench! Come on, and kiss me, Kate.' Could it be that Petruchio has been as much 'tamed' or liberated by Kate as she by him? For at the outset he was an adventurer and now he is a married man.

The battle of the sexes is just one theme in romantic comedy. Not all prospective lovers are sparring partners and there are as many different problems besetting the path of love as there are kinds of lovers. Shyness, fear of commitment, apparently incompatible occupations, age differences, class differences, cultural differences, being married already, or divorced and afraid of being hurt again, are just some of the many vicissitudes that threaten love. As our attitudes to gender change so do the kinds of problems we encounter. This was particularly marked in the seventies when relations between the sexes were thrown into crisis by feminism.

In *Diary of a Mad Housewife*, *An Unmarried Woman*, *Annie Hall* and *Starting Over*, each of the heroines, although they have different personalities, are struggling to redefine their identity as women. As the title *Starting Over* suggests, the effect of feminism on relationships was dramatic, leaving both sexes to pick up the pieces in an attempt to start again. While films such as *Crocodile Dundee* vainly attempted to reinstate the traditional 'Iron John' concept of masculinity, the more common result for both sexes was a degree of gender confusion and what has been more recently described as the 'crisis in masculinity', such as that revealed in *Four Weddings and a Funeral* and *As Good As It Gets*. On the other hand, a new kind of friendship between the sexes, united by their mutual confusion and liberated by the growing sense of equality, was also beginning to emerge. This is particularly apparent in the much loved *When Harry Met Sally*.

But whatever our temperament and circumstances and the obstacles to be overcome, change is, in essence, what most of us seek in love-relationships – we want change, and love changes us. Initially we want to change from being our parents' child to becoming our lover's spouse or partner. Then as our long and often complicated lives proceed many of us find ourselves alone again, and again we want to change and be changed by love. Which is why our quest to find love, what we learn from love and how we are changed by love, often in the most unexpected ways, is such an enduring topic.

Finally a note about my selection of films, which will undoubtedly be contentious, particularly if I have left out some favourites. My selection was guided not by popularity – although most were popular at the time of their release – but by the themes and ideas portrayed in each film, and how, as a group of four, they best illuminate the major shifts in relations between the sexes which appeared to arise in each decade and provide new insights and different points of view. As well as being interested in the individual stories of each film, I have also been aware of the developing 'big picture', or the story of the seven decades as a whole. Therefore I have not included historical romantic comedies such as *Shakespeare in Love*. I also reluctantly decided to restrict my selection to American, British and Australian films. Although there have been many brilliant European romantic comedies, particularly from France, Italy and Spain, these countries also have distinct cultural backgrounds and histories of sexual relations, and to include them would have been beyond the scope of this book.

As I progressed through the book I became increasingly aware that all the films, except *Crossing Delancey*, were directed by men, and most, with the exception of *Crossing Delancey*, *Adam's Rib*, *Diary of a Mad Housewife* and *When Harry Met Sally*, were also written by men. This dearth of women's voices behind the scenes itself says something about the battle of the sexes in the film industry. On the other hand, I don't think this gender imbalance prevents us from detecting the very real shifts that were taking place between the sexes. After all, each film has a heroine as well as a hero and for the film to be popular it had to appeal to a large female audience. Also the gender of a writer or director doesn't necessarily prevent them from providing very real insights into the experience of the opposite sex, although sometimes it is necessary to take their gender into account when attempting to decode the many, often conflicting messages and meanings embodied within the film. Of course this would also apply to me, as the female author of this book!

One
It Happened One Night in the Thirties

'America at the close of the Great War was a Cinderella magically clothed in the most stunning dress at the ball,' Ann Douglas was to write about the twenties.[1] Europe was devastated and Russia was in the throes of revolution. America seized the initiative and, with the emergence of mass consumerism and popular culture, became the economic leader of the modern liberal world. 'Culture', as F. Scott Fitzgerald famously said at the time, 'follows money.' And in the twenties the consumer was bewitched by money and the new and bewildering array of material and cultural artefacts, such as cars, radios, phonographs and household appliances, which they could buy with easy credit and instalment plans. Popular music and dance crazes spread like wild fire across the country. With jazz, the blues and dances like the Charleston, for the first time Black America was impacting on mainstream cultural life. The first mass-market tabloid newspaper was published. The popularity of films went from strength to strength and in 1927, the first talking picture, *The Jazz Singer*, was released.

Social barriers were falling, assisted by prohibition and the popularity of Speakeasies where the classes mingled for alcohol and entertainment. Prohibition and the consumer society also provided ample opportunities for exploitation and the notorious interplay between the suckers and the racketeers.[2] As F. Scott Fitzgerald put it, 'The parties were bigger, the pace faster, the shows were broader, the buildings were higher, the morals were looser.'[3]

At the end of the Great War the suffragettes finally won the vote in Britain, and in America a few years later. Dress hemlines rose from the ankles to the knees. Pre-war Victorian attitudes to sexual morality were joyfully thrown out by the young. A whole generation began dating instead of courting on the back porch. Marriage manuals such as Marie Stopes' *Married Love,* which proclaimed that 'the single bed was the enemy of marriage', and Theodore van de Velde's *Ideal Marriage,* which stressed the importance of 'love play', 'after glow' and 'the simultaneous orgasm', including instructions on how to achieve it, were worldwide bestsellers.[4] Trojan condoms made their first appearance.

There was a huge expansion in the job market for 'women's work': stenographers, typists, switchboard operators and sales assistants. With financial independence single women could afford to live away from home. In America 10 per cent of young women went to college and began entering the predominantly male professions of medicine, teaching, journalism and law. Female 'firsts' were enthusiastically reported in the newspapers: the first woman deep-sea diver, the first woman kettle drummer, the first woman to crew a plane and cross the Atlantic.[5] And of course there were the glamorous billboard images of successful film actresses with star billing alongside their male counterparts.

The popularity of the stock market was unparalleled. 'Everyone was a broker, more or less,' wrote John Steinbeck. 'At lunch hour, store clerks and stenographers munched sandwiches while they watched the stock boards and calculated their pyramiding fortunes. Their eyes had the look you see around the roulette table . . . Then the bottom dropped out.'[6] In 1929 Wall Street crashed, pitching America and Europe into the greatest depression the world has ever known. The editor of *Nation's Business* described the mood of the time as 'Fear bordering on panic, loss of faith in everything, our fellow man, our institutions, private and government. Worst of all no faith in ourselves or the future.'[7]

The big domestic issue of the thirties was male unemployment

– men's primary role as breadwinner was at stake and by extension his very claim to manhood as provider and protector. Although many women continued to work, the issue of women's equality was demoted in importance. Working wives in particular were frowned upon and concern focused on the potential negative effects of women's freedom on men's job opportunities and men's self-esteem. Eleanor Roosevelt who, as First Lady, became one of the most influential women in the country, campaigned tirelessly for equal rights, although she, like many politically active women, believed in equal rights for all; the poor and ethnic minorities, not just women. She believed passionately that women should be fighting alongside their men, not against them.

Organized feminism was in retreat. Feminism, so the argument went, was synonymous with being lonely and unmarried. Dorothy Dunbar Bromley complained that modern young women had contempt for feminists, 'who antagonize men with their constant clamour about maiden names, equal rights, a woman's place in the world, and many other causes.'[8] The new-found sexual freedoms enjoyed by both men and women in the twenties, which had gone hand in hand with women's greater freedom generally, were under attack.

1930 saw the enforcement of the Hays Production Code, set up by the American motion picture industry as a form of censorship laying down what characters could and could not do on screen in the sexual arena. The code reflected the fears of the puritanical moralistic right who were clamouring for a re-establishment of traditional family values. This pervading fear of sexuality went under the guise of the need to protect vulnerable women from footloose men whose very biology as males caused them to have primitive sexual urges, which, unless restrained, would threaten the edifice of civilized family life.[9]

The popularity of the cinema, however, continued unabated, particularly as the new talking pictures offered some escape from the unrelenting gloom. Frank Capra's *It Happened One Night* was released in 1934 and, with its enormous popularity, the film genre of romantic comedy was born. *It Happened One Night* was a fairytale romance and, with its sparkling, witty dialogue, it brought the hugely entertaining spectacle of the battle of the sexes to the screen. In the film Clark Gable at first appears to be just the kind of footloose male that vulnerable women may well have needed protection from, but in Claudette Colbert he has more than met his match.

In 1932 Franklin D. Roosevelt, known as FDR, had been elected president. At the time, national income had been cut in half and more than 15 million people were unemployed, but his election, accompanied by his theme song, 'Happy Days Are Here Again', was met with dancing in the streets and jubilation. As one of his aides said, 'FDR was like the fairytale prince who did not know how to shiver . . . He lacked the capacity even to imagine that things might end up badly . . . He gave the nation a hopeful, and hence creative, stance toward the future.'[10] The journalist Martha Gellhorn said of the way Roosevelt related to ordinary people: 'He is at once God and their intimate friend; he knows them all by name, knows their little town and mill, their little lives and problems. And though everything else fails, he is there, and will not let them down.'[11] In the days before television the fact that FDR had been crippled by polio had very little impact on his popular image. A newspaper editor is reputed to have told FDR, 'For box office attraction you leave Clark Gable gasping for breath.'[12]

The fairytale is, in essence, a story told to reassure children (or the child within all of us) that, despite all the bad in the world, good can win through in the end. The fact that FDR's popular appeal was likened to that of a fairytale prince (although, with his fireside radio talks to the nation, his persona was closer to that of the wise king or archetypal good father), reflects the contemporary desire for such reassurance. Capra's *Mr Deeds Goes to Town,* which was released in 1936, not only captures the essential moral quality of the fairytale, but his hero, Gary Cooper, also reflects the icon of masculinity epitomized by FDR. Longfellow Deeds is strong, courageous, morally upstanding, confident, at ease with himself, yet burdened by the evil of the Depression and seeking a way for goodness to win through. Unlike FDR, who was married to Eleanor with whom he had six children, Deeds really was the epitome of a modern-day fairytale prince; handsome, romantic, eligible and living in hope of meeting and rescuing his damsel in distress.

The thirties was a decade with a thirst for precise ideas and role models when it came to sexual morality and gender roles. This was partly a reaction to the immorality of the twenties and to the threat of feminism, as perceived by traditional women as well as by many men. But it was also a desire for certainty in a climate of economic instability and growing anxiety about the rise of fascism in Europe as Hitler and Mussolini came to power. In the thirties men were men, women were women and, even if they didn't understand each other, at least the boundaries between the genders were clearly defined. The ever-popular marriage manuals were quite clear about the differences between men and women, and how their roles should be respected if the couple were to achieve marital bliss, just as they were equally certain that romantic heterosexual love followed by marriage was the only route to happiness.

According to the manuals the husband should be older than the wife; the husband should be the initiator, the wife his pupil; when they marry the husband should be sexually experienced but his bride should be a virgin; the husband should provide for and protect his wife and she should nurture and look up to him; and because the man is subject to vigorous animal urges 'his job is to keep his head; his wife's job is to lose hers'.[13] With so many 'shoulds' and 'oughts' everyone was of course fallible, and it is surely no accident that the 'Screwball' genre emerged to release the tension.

Screwball is anarchic farce portraying not so much 'the battle of the sexes' as an endless series of bewildering and hilarious misunderstandings as the sexes puzzled about what each other wanted, or attempted to manipulate each other to get what they wanted themselves. Which just about sums up the problems encountered by Cary Grant and Katharine Hepburn in *Bringing Up Baby*, one of the most enduring of the many thirties Screwball comedies.

But finally in 1939 people's worst fears were realized; war broke out in Europe, although for the time being America remained on the sidelines. Throughout the twenties and thirties increasing numbers of European artists, writers, actors and film-makers had emigrated to America, partly lured by the exciting cultural climate and wealth of opportunities but also to escape fascism. Amongst the European arrivals were Greta Garbo, Ernst Lubitsch and Billy Wilder. Together they made *Ninotchka*, which still clung, if somewhat tenuously, to the fairytale form, although by the time the film was released in 1939, the conviction that good would triumph in the end was beginning to seem a little hollow.

It Happened One Night (1934)

Directed by Frank Capra; screenplay by Robert Riskin; based on a short story by Samuel Hopkins Adams; starring Clark Gable and Claudette Colbert

'You're just the spoilt brat of a rich father . . .'

Frank Capra's *It Happened One Night* was a huge success when it was released in 1934. Although it is one of the earliest romantic comedies, with its perfect combination of fairytale conventions and its feisty portrayal of the battle of the sexes, it continues to be one of the most memorable and most loved. It's easy to see how the story structure resembles that of a fairytale. Ellie, the heroine (Claudette Colbert), is the spoilt princess, used to a pampered life in her father, the king's castle, where she wears fine clothes, gives orders, has temper tantrums and generally does as she pleases. The story is about what happens when she defies her father, leaves his castle and sets out for a life of her own. And like all the best runaway princesses, once she is alone in the outside world she has to go through all sorts of life tests and trials before she has grown up enough to be ready for the arms of a new protector and can live happily ever after.

The film opens on board a millionaire's luxury yacht at anchor. Ellie, a beautiful young woman dressed in a satin evening gown, is locked in a furious row with her father over her secret marriage to a man called King Westley. Ellie's father is so angry with her he has imprisoned her on his boat while he arranges to have the marriage annulled. Ellie, in retaliation, has gone on hunger strike. Her father is convinced that she only married Westley because he told her not to. Ellie points out that her father has been telling her what *not* to do ever since she can remember. 'Quit being such a stubborn idiot,' Ellie's father tells her, impatiently. 'I come from a long line of stubborn idiots,' Ellie retorts, proving that she can give as good as she gets. But the sight of her father settling down to eat so infuriates her (no doubt he knows that a hunger strike might not be his daughter's strongest card) that she runs out of the cabin, jumps overboard and swims for the shore. Ellie's father immediately dictates a wire to a detective agency: 'Daughter escaped again. Watch all roads . . .'

As Ellie herself observed, in this power struggle with her father, they have genes in common. Just as he is determined to control and dominate her life, she is equally determined to fight him with the same degree of fire, spunk and stubbornness. As for her secret marriage to King Westley, we have the sneaking suspicion that her father may be right; she did marry Westley only to spite him.

We next see Ellie waiting in a bus station by a sign: 'Night Bus to New York'. Somehow, since jumping into the ocean, she has managed to swim to shore, get out of her wet satin dress and find a very elegant travelling outfit; skirt, blouse, fitted pullover and a neat little beret. (We learn later that she sold her jewellery to buy the clothes.) In another part of the bus station a group of drunken newspaper hacks crowd around a telephone booth. Inside the booth we meet Peter Warne (Clark Gable), who is talking to his editor on the phone: 'Hey listen monkey face, when you fired me you fired the best news hound your filthy scandal sheet ever had.' What a brilliant first line for the male lead! Peter Warne is the kind of man who can call his boss *monkey face* and his paper a *filthy scandal sheet* . . . or at least he's the kind of man who can say these things to his boss when he's drunk after being fired. The hacks look impressed as Peter lurches out of the booth: 'Is my chariot ready?' he asks, grabbing a slug of whisky. 'Your chariot awaits, Oh my king,' jokes one of the hacks. 'Make way for the king. Make way for the king,' the hacks chant as they walk in mock procession to the New York bus where they take their leave of him.

So Peter Warne is not just one of the hacks, he's special. Apart from standing out because of his playful roguish good looks, having the hacks jokingly refer to him as 'the king' immediately associates him with King Westley, Ellie's new husband, who we haven't yet met. What if Warne were to be Ellie's king, not Westley? Could it be that, in fairytale terms, both 'kings', her father and King Westley, will have to 'Make way for the king', Peter Warne? With this in mind we come to the all-important first meeting.

On the crowded bus, while Peter is engaged in an argument with the driver over the only remaining seat, Ellie slips quietly past him. Peter turns to see her sitting innocently in his seat. 'Excuse me lady, but that upon which you sit is mine,' he addresses her, like a slightly drunken knight at arms. Ellie sweetly appeals to the driver who, of course, backs her claim for the seat. Annoyed, Peter establishes that the seat accommodates two people, instructs her to move over and squeezes in next to her. Ellie looks at him coldly and then stands up to put her bag on the rack. At this moment the bus starts up, she is thrown off balance, Peter catches her and holds her comfortably on his lap, smiling at her playfully. Suddenly furious and humiliated, Ellie pushes him away.

In this brief tantalizing moment of physical intimacy our sense of a potential relationship between them has been aroused, yet there are so many obstacles both in their life circumstances and their difference in characters that it seems nearly impossible that they could ever overcome them. Peter is a sacked newspaper hack, desperate for a good story to get his job back, and Ellie, a runaway heiress, is a news story waiting to break. This makes Peter's potential as Ellie's knight in shining armour a little suspect. On the other hand, we have seen certain intriguing aspects of Peter's character that offer some hope: he's not just one of the lads he's the one they all follow; he's funny, he's original, he's capable of standing up to his boss, he's his own man. But how will he react when he finds out who Ellie really is? Whose side will he be on, Ellie's or her father's? Also, whatever Ellie's motives for marrying King Westley, the fact of her marriage is a huge obstacle.

But the most immediate obstacle is Ellie herself. Her attitude is typical of a spoilt princess. She is proud and condescending and when her first test arrives – in the form of a thief who steals her bag – she fails miserably. She's too annoyed with Peter for failing to catch the thief to appreciate his gallantry (an essential requirement for knights in shining armour) or to thank him for his efforts. And despite the fact that she now has only four dollars in the world, she proudly insists that she doesn't need his help, refuses his offer of breakfast and issues orders to the bus driver to wait for her as if he is her personal chauffeur.

The bus, of course, doesn't wait for her but Peter does. He shows her a newspaper – her father is offering a reward for information about her whereabouts. Ellie, who has taken to condescendingly calling Peter 'young man', assumes that he's the kind of man who will want the reward. She tells him she will pay him more than anything her father offers to keep quiet. Peter responds like a gallant knight ought to; he's insulted: 'You're just the spoiled brat of a rich father. The only way you get anything is to buy it . . . Haven't you ever heard of the word humility? I guess it never occurred to you to say "please Mister, I'm in trouble, will you help me?" No, that would bring you down off your high horse for a minute.' The film's theme is beginning to bear a marked resemblance to *The Taming of the Shrew*. Ellie, like Kate, with her temper tantrums and arrogant pride, will have to be knocked off her pedestal and taught a few lessons in humility if she is ever to make a 'good wife'. And who better to teach her than Peter who, like Petruchio, with his manly experience of the world, wit, self-confidence and rough manners, assumes that he knows better than she does what's good for her.

Peter's lessons in humility begin almost immediately, assisted by a fortuitous storm which forces their bus to stop at a motel for the night. Without consulting Ellie, Peter checks them into a double room on the pretext that they are husband and wife. Although their financial circumstances are such that Peter had little choice, Ellie is outraged. She stands outside in the rain rather than go in to face what she is convinced Peter has in mind.

But when eventually she plucks up the courage to enter the room, Peter bluntly tells her that if she thinks he's interested in her, forget it. All he wants is a deal: if she lets him have her story, he will help her get to King Westley; if she doesn't co-operate, he will tell her father where she is. To prove his total lack of interest in her sexually he tosses a pair of pyjamas at her, hangs a blanket up between the two single beds, and proceeds to get undressed for bed while Ellie watches in horror. Totally humiliated, she flees to her side of the blanket. 'Still with me brat?' Peter calls to her from his bed. 'You've got nothing to worry about. The wall of Jericho [the blanket] will protect you from the big bad wolf.'

By affectionately giving her the pet name 'brat' and evoking the idea of bedtime stories with himself playing the big bad wolf, Peter has made their situation safe by de-sexing their relationship and turning it into a game. The game continues through the next day. By assuming the role of the father figure to Ellie's child, Peter has touched on a powerful dynamic in her psyche. His brusque, commanding, almost paternal manner infuriates her, but at some level she delights in being the child, just as Peter is having fun playing the parent. This becomes even more apparent when they are forced to spend the following night outdoors – a passenger recognized Ellie from the newspaper and it became too dangerous to remain on the bus.

They come to a river and Peter lifts Ellie, fireman style, over his shoulder in order to carry her across. Ellie claims that her father was a 'great piggyback-ride giver'; Peter insists that her father can't have been so great because 'this is no piggyback ride, wrong position'. Ellie protests – she is allowed to criticize her father but no one else is – at which point Peter gives her a slap on her bottom causing her to cry out with an ambiguous mixture of delight and pain. This hint at the notion that what a recalcitrant woman needs is a spanking to bring her into line is a sudden and awkward reminder that stories about the battle of the sexes often threaten to reveal difficult truths about ourselves and the darker side of the dilemmas underlying the sexual politics of male and female relationships.

We next move even closer to the idea that there are certain basic, primitive characteristics governing the roles of men and women, which lie buried just beneath the surface of our psyches. Given the right conditions – particularly a moonlit night outdoors in the open countryside reminiscent of how our ancestors once lived – our atavistic nature will rise to the surface and penetrate our veneer of sophistication. Peter selects a place to spend the night, a field with a couple of haystacks. He makes Ellie a bed of hay and in response to her complaints about being hungry, goes to find something to eat. Ellie lies down to rest, bathed enticingly by the moonlight – the moon has long been associated with romance, lunacy and all things feminine. Suddenly she screams in panic. Peter runs back to her and she clings to him, furiously demanding to know where he has been. Capra's point here is clear: women want their independence *and* their male providers and protectors, they want it both ways – a contradiction which, as Peter says in exasperation, is guaranteed to 'drive a man crazy'. Nevertheless, he gently places his raincoat over Ellie to keep her warm. She looks up into his eyes. Their faces are just inches apart in the moonlight; their need to kiss is imperative; the moment is breathtaking. But Peter manages to drag his eyes away from hers.

He turns his back on her, walks away to the fence, lights a cigarette and gazes at the dark countryside. As an honourable man he must resist his desire to take advantage of her. Ellie watches him thoughtfully; no longer the petulant child, now a grown-up woman. She asks him what he is thinking about. 'You,' he replies, 'I was wondering what makes dames like you so dizzy.' Here Peter finally voices the question that has, according to much poetry and literature, perplexed men through the millennia: what makes women so difficult to understand, so contrary, so touched by the irrational magic of moonshine? What do women want?

The theme of the differences between the sexes continues the next day although in a more down-to-earth manner. This time we focus on the male compulsion to educate the female on subjects supposedly beyond her experience or understanding. The situation is so familiar that most women know the rule is to feign a greater ignorance than they actually have and to be a good audience; absorbed, entertained, and impressed by whatever the man says or does. When Ellie appears to be ignorant about hitch-hiking, Peter leaps at the opportunity to give her a lecture on the subject, demonstrating his repertoire of thumb movements and claiming that he knows so much he could write a book about it. Ellie sits dutifully on a fence and listens. Finally, when Peter's method fails to stop a single car, she acts. She goes to the roadside, lifts her skirt and bends to fix her suspender, revealing the beautiful lines of her thighs and calves elongated by her high-heeled shoes. The next car immediately screeches to a halt. Once settled in the car Peter goes into a sulk: 'Why don't you take off all of your clothes. Then you can stop forty cars,' he snaps at her. 'I'll remember that when I need forty cars,' Ellie responds, demonstrating that she can be as witty as he when the mood takes her.

They are now just a few hours from New York, where Peter has promised to hand Ellie over to King Westley. Their mood takes on a new seriousness as once again they check into a motel for the night. Ellie sits on the edge of her bed and stares wistfully at her side of the 'wall of Jericho'. She asks Peter if he has ever been in love. He concedes that he hasn't been able to find the right girl yet although he's 'been sucker enough to make plans'. If he could find the right girl his dream would be to take her to a Pacific island: 'She'd have to be the kind of a girl who would jump into the surf with me and love it as much as I did. You know, nights when you and the water and the moon all become one and you feel you are part of something big and marvellous.' Unconsciously he is describing a night very like the one they have just spent together in the hayfield – but without the ocean which represents the irresistible passion of their sexuality if they were to unleash their desire. Suddenly Ellie appears on Peter's side of the 'wall of Jericho': 'Take me with you Peter . . . I want to do all those things you talked about.' She kneels by his bedside. She loves him, she says, nothing else matters. Peter gruffly tells her that she should go back to her bed. Humiliated and ashamed she says she is sorry and hurries away to cry alone. 'Hey brat,' Peter says eventually, 'Did you mean that? Would you really go?' From his side of the 'wall of Jericho' he doesn't realize that Ellie has cried herself to sleep.

Ellie has come down off her pedestal, she has learnt from the tests of real life beyond her father's castle walls, and now she has truly fallen in love. She has also awakened Peter's own dream of love, although she doesn't yet realize this – which we shall see is crucial to the final drama. Whilst she sleeps, Peter secretly gets up and goes to his newspaper's offices to sell his story about Ellie. For an awful moment we think that Peter is betraying her, until he says to his disbelieving editor, 'A guy can't propose to a girl without a cent in the world can he?' Meanwhile, back at the motel Ellie wakes to find herself thrown out on to the street – she has no money to pay for the room. Believing that Peter has run out on her, she dejectedly walks to the police station to phone her father. As Peter happily drives an old jalopy back to the motel to propose, he is overtaken by Ellie's father and King Westley with Ellie seated miserably between them. They are being driven at top speed in what looks like a royal cavalcade with a police escort. Peter gives chase but the jalopy's engine overheats and the tyre gets a puncture. As we watch the tyre deflate we get a fair idea of how Peter feels as his dream disappears into the distance – he's just been a sucker again, Ellie obviously didn't love him after all.

Peter goes to his editor's office, grimly tears up the article he wrote about Ellie's escape and gives back the money, thus proving that he is a moral man, not the kind who can be corrupted by money. Newspaper headlines reveal that Ellen Andrews is to be remarried today at the request of her father who wants a proper society wedding. In the fairytale castle the princess listlessly awaits her fate. Her father wants to know what's wrong – never has a bride-to-be, even an already married one, been less enthusiastic about her own wedding. Ellie cries like a child in his arms and tells him she's in love with another man. Her father can't understand why Ellie doesn't marry this other man instead of King Westley, whom he has never liked. Ellie tells him that it's no use: 'Peter says that I'm spoiled and selfish and pampered and thoroughly insincere. He doesn't think so much of you either, he blames you for everything that's wrong with me . . .'

We can see how, as a result of her relationship with Peter, Ellie has changed. She now sees herself through Peter's eyes and doesn't want to be the person she was at the beginning of the film. We also see Ellie's father in a new light; at the outset of the film he appeared to be a tyrant, now he is a typical wise old 'fairytale king' who loves his daughter and only wants her to be happy. Although when Ellie tells him Peter's name, he feels obliged to reveal to her that he has received a letter from Peter asking him for money. For Ellie this is the last straw – not only does Peter despise her for everything that she is, but all he wants now is her father's reward for finding her. This, combined with Peter's belief that Ellie has 'made a sucker out of him and taken him for a ride', makes the chances of a happy outcome look very bleak. Left to their own devices, how will Ellie and Peter ever overcome the blind fury and hurt that fills the void left by what they believe to be their spurned love? A cupid figure is needed – a catalyst or someone to 'fix it' – as Ellie's father suggests, offering himself for the role.

Who better to have on the lovers' side than the most powerful man in the kingdom? But Peter and Ellie's obstinacy proves hard even for her father to tackle. He is still trying to 'fix it' at the very last minute as he walks down the aisle with his daughter on his arm and the bridal march playing for her official wedding to King Westley. He has established that Peter didn't want the reward, all he wanted was $39 to cover his costs when looking after Ellie. This for Peter is 'a matter of principle' and necessary to re-establish his self-esteem which Ellie's father, as a fellow man, thinks is very laudable. Ellie remains obstinately unconvinced as she listens to her father's final attempt to change her mind. The marriage ceremony begins. But it is not until it is Ellie's turn to say 'I do' that she runs. (The first of many romantic comedy runaway bride scenes.)

The film ends outside Ellie and Peter's motel room. We hear the sound of trumpets and cut to a shot of the 'wall of Jericho' falling to the floor. In fairytales, as Bettelheim suggests, 'if one remains true to oneself and one's values, then, despite how desperate things may look for a while, there will be a happy ending'.[14]

Mr Deeds Goes To Town (1936)

Directed by Frank Capra; screenplay by Robert Riskin; based on a story by Clarence Budington Kelland; starring Jean Arthur and Gary Cooper

'He's got goodness . . . we've forgotten what that is.'

In *Mr Deeds Goes to Town* Frank Capra takes on board one of the major social issues of the decade, the Great Depression. His concern is with the moral dilemmas underlying the extremes of poverty and wealth caused by mass unemployment on a scale never before seen. In the film Capra poses a deceptively simple question: Why don't rich people, with far more money than they need or know what to do with, simply give it to the poor and so alleviate the problem of poverty? Capra is not concerned with the Victorian concept of charitable donations, or self-serving foundations to aggrandize the giver, he is talking about an individual giving away *all* of his wealth except what he needs to live a modest life. His question leads quite naturally to another, equally deceptive in its simplicity: What does an individual need to be happy?

In order to explore this theme Capra chooses another kind of fairytale, described by Bettelheim as 'the story of the unnoticed boy who goes out into the world and makes a great success of life'. Bettelheim tells us that although the details may differ, the basic plot usually remains the same: 'the unlikely hero proves himself through slaying dragons, solving riddles and living by his wits and goodness until eventually he frees the beautiful princess, marries her and lives happily ever after'.[15]

We identify with 'the unlikely hero' because the story acts out one of our most common fantasies. Like most of us, the hero begins by living in anonymous obscurity but one day he frees himself from the shackles of ordinary everyday life and sets off on a journey which involves many wonderful exploits, enabling him to prove himself to the world and gain the recognition he justly deserves. Such worldly recognition is also the key to finding the thing we most crave, which is of greatest value of all; the one great love that is meant for us and us alone. Although merely finding the loved one is not enough – in order for the hero to be fully appreciated as a knight in shining armour, the damsel must be saved. The degree to which his act will be deemed heroic depends on the degree of distress assailing the damsel and the degree of difficulty in saving her. The bigger the dragon the greater the heroic deed.

Longfellow Deeds is just such a potential 'unlikely hero'. Until the story begins he has been perfectly content with his life in the small backwater town of Mandrake Falls. He is a simple, honest man who happens to be played by handsome, laconic Gary Cooper. He is also somewhat eccentric: he plays the tuba in the local brass band, he earns a living by writing sentimental poems for greetings cards and if he hears a fire engine pass by outside he is seized by a childlike desire to rush to the window and watch. Although his parents have long since died, he is well looked after by a homely housekeeper who tells us that Deeds is not married because 'he has a lot of foolish notions about saving a lady in distress'. Gary Cooper's shy, embarrassed smile when she says this alone would be enough to raise the spirits of most distressed damsels.

So, when we first meet Longfellow Deeds, he is apparently untainted by life's dark side and still believes in the primacy of human goodness. The fact that he is an orphan without siblings or any sort of family life, far from leaving him damaged or in a state of self-pity or rebellion, has freed him from those family relationships which, although they give us the foundations for our experience of love, also provide the bedrock for a mass of complications such as resentment, envy or jealousy as we compete for our loved one's attention in what Freud called 'the family romance'. In fairytales, being an orphan positively enhances the hero's status, providing us with the perfect blank on which to project our own longings for innocence and goodness, free of guilt, particularly the kind of guilt associated with the fantasy of rescuing a damsel in distress. Bettelheim notes that in fairytales 'the most desirable female is kept in captivity by an evil figure'.[16] He suggests this is because in families the boy-child's fantasy desire is to rescue the mother from the father, a fantasy which involves conflicting loyalties and a considerable amount of guilt and confusion, hence the attempt to cast the father as an evil figure. In this respect orphans have a distinct advantage.

The story begins in the small town of Mandrake Falls when two dark-suited strangers arrive from the city bearing the news that Deeds has inherited a fortune from a Mr Semple, a relative of Deeds' mother. Deeds, who has never before left Mandrake Falls, is to accompany these men – Cedar, a lawyer, and Cobs, a bodyguard, whose job it is to keep the inevitable publicity at bay – to New York where he is to begin his new life as one of the richest men in America.

The question at the forefront of our minds is: How will Deeds' innocent goodness be able to withstand the forces of greed and corruption, which we know accompany vast fortunes (although that knowledge doesn't appear to stop us buying lottery tickets in the hope that we might win). Sure enough, as soon as Deeds arrives in New York he is surrounded by liars, cheats, people who want his money and people, like the lawyer, Cedar, who has already been cheating old Mr Semple out of vast sums of money (and now that Semple is dead is anxious not to have his crime discovered).

The newspapers are also desperate to cash in on Deeds' notoriety. At one newspaper office we see an editor haranguing his reporters for not giving him the stories he needs. The hacks complain that Cobs has got Deeds under lock and key – they can't get at him to get the stories. The editor dismisses them all in disgust. The last to leave is petite blonde Louise Bennett (Jean Arthur), known on the paper as Babe, the only female member of the reporting team. The editor offers her a month's holiday with pay if she will bring him something on Deeds. Louise accepts the challenge.

Our first impression of Louise is that of a hard-bitten news reporter and an independent woman who knows what she wants – hardly Deeds' fantasy of a damsel in distress. Conversely our innocent, straightforward, gullible hero is hardly the kind of man to attract a worldly woman like Louise Bennett. But inside his palatial mansion, like the innocent boy who dares to say that the emperor in fact has no clothes, Deeds is beginning to show that he is not such a pushover as everyone assumes. He refuses to be hoodwinked into providing sponsorship for an opera company that is losing money; he objects to the absurdly deferential manners of his valet and butler; he picks up a crooked lawyer by his shirt-collar and has him thrown out of the house; and he manages to deceive his bodyguards by locking them in a cupboard when he wants to go out at night for a walk alone. This is precisely the opportunity Louise has been waiting for. Outside the mansion gates, dressed in a plain old-fashioned hat and coat, she stumbles slowly along the street and when she is quite sure Deeds has seen her, she collapses on to the pavement. Deeds instantly rushes to her aid.

Unwittingly, or perhaps not so unwittingly, Louise has struck at the most vulnerable part of Deeds' psyche. He is away from home for the first time, alone in a great city, needing intimacy more than he ever has before and a beautiful woman collapses at his feet, conforming absolutely to his fantasy of rescuing a damsel in distress. Louise tells him in a humble, shaky voice how she collapsed because she hasn't eaten, she's been out all day searching for work. She says her name is Mary – as if to enhance her virginal credentials. Deeds offers to take her out for a meal and help her in any way he can.

He takes her to the Literati Café where he's heard that celebrated writers and poets meet. Louise watches with embarrassed fascination as the famous writers make fun of Deeds for writing greetings card poems. But Deeds does not allow these eminent men to deflate his ego. 'Maybe if you went to Mandrake Falls,' he tells them 'you would look just as funny to us, only nobody would laugh at you and make you feel ridiculous because that wouldn't be good manners . . . I guess I found out that all famous people aren't big people.' He finishes his speech by punching the noses of two of the most offensive literary gentlemen. But one of the writers is so pleased to meet 'a poet with a straight left and a right hook' that he offers to take Deeds and Louise out on the town.

Each of these episodes – the condescending opera committee, the fraudulent lawyers, the obsequious servants, the snobbish literati – is a 'dragon to be slain', a test for the hero to prove his wit, goodness and courage and thus gain his manhood. Proper manhood is not just about mental strength or standing up for values such as honesty, kindness and justice. A real man, a hero, does not shirk from punching or fighting other men if the situation justifies it. But Deeds does have a problem with 'knocking men's heads together' in front of a lady, so he politely seeks Louise's permission before he throws his punches. Also real men are not prudes, they don't have a problem with having fun and going out on the occasional drinking binge.

Louise remains true to her promise to her editor and the next day the headline in the newspaper is 'Cinderella Man's Night on the Town'. But as her relationship with Deeds develops on further dates she finds that, despite her cynicism, she likes him more and more. Deeds talks to her about the stuff the newspapers are writing about him, never for one moment suspecting that she is the culprit. 'What puzzles me,' he says, 'is why people get so much pleasure out of hurting each other. Why don't they try liking each other for a while?' As Louise listens to him we can see how her disingenuous situation is becoming increasingly excruciating. When Deeds describes his experience while looking up at the New York skyscrapers, he quotes Theroux to her: 'They created a lot of grand palaces here but they forgot to create the noblemen to put in them.' Here he shows that he's not the simpleton so many city people assume him to be; beneath his apparent innocence there is wisdom based on learning, and Louise, as a writer, is impressed and moved. She tells him about the small town where she grew up before leaving home to come to New York. She says that Deeds reminds her of her father – 'he was a lot like you, talked like you too'. We can see from the wistful expression on Louise's face that she has forgotten about her fictional persona, Mary, and her reporting assignment, she is simply being herself and speaking the truth.

In a Capra film, as we have already seen in *It Happened One Night*, if a woman sees a similarity between her father and the man she is with she must be falling in love. At home Louise expresses her growing confusion to her flatmate: 'That guy's either the dumbest, stupidest, most imbecilic idiot in the world or else he's the grandest thing alive . . . He's wholesome, fresh. To us he looks like a freak . . . He's got goodness . . . we've forgotten what that is. We're too busy being smart alecs, too busy in a crazy competition for nothing.' Here she is giving voice to what the film is about. She is expressing her deep desire to believe in simple goodness, without embarrassment or feeling the need to denigrate it with irony or cynicism, which is also necessary if she is to be free to love Deeds. But the more she falls in love with Deeds the worse her situation becomes. The label 'the Cinderella Man' and her newspaper articles about him have made him a laughing stock. Louise is both crucifying him and falling in love with him at the same time. Her conflict is becoming unbearable. At the beginning of the film she pretended to be a damsel in distress but now her distress is real and Deeds knows nothing about it.

The last straw for Louise is when Deeds proposes to her by giving her a poem. She goes to talk to her editor, who we now see is her father substitute. Although earlier he was the bad father, trapping Louise in the corrupt world of tabloid journalism, now he becomes the good father; more concerned for her happiness than his self-interest. Louise resigns from her job and resolves to tell Deeds the truth. But she is too late; Cobs has found out her secret. 'You've been making love to a double dose of cyanide,' he tells Deeds and presents him with a photograph of the *Mail*'s star reporter Babe Louise Bennett. Gary Cooper's performance here is quite brilliant. The shock he feels, when he discovers that the woman he has fallen in love with is also the woman who has been making a laughing stock of him in the press, is palpable. His pain is silent, understated and terrible. Even the archetypal tough guy Cobs is moved.

For a man in the thirties, showing extreme pain is a major problem. Tests for manhood are about courage in the face of adversity, they don't include expressing emotional pain or loss or failure. Tears are for wimps or women, not for heroes. Consequently, either the pain is turned inward, to remain trapped rather than be expressed, or some form of sublimation is needed into which to channel the energy in ways that are more socially acceptable for men, such as violence or work. In the case of a hero, an opportunity for more valiant action is needed than for most ordinary mortals, such as the opportunities presented by feats of bravery in war or the kind of selflessness required on the fringes of civilization amongst the poor, the down-and-outs and the disenfranchised.

In response to a desperate, unemployed farmer who breaks into his mansion and begs for help, Deeds decides to channel his energy into good work by giving away all his money. As mentioned earlier, at the time of making *Mr Deeds Goes to Town*, the plight of the unemployed was desperate, exemplified by the destitute farmers of the dust bowl who had lost everything. But Deeds' attempt to give them all his money turns out not to be so easy. While two thousand destitute farmers crowd around his mansion clamouring for their share, the police arrive and arrest Deeds on a charge of insanity. This is the responsibility of Cedar, who has been scheming with some distant relatives of Deeds', to put an injunction on the money.

Alone in the mental hospital, having now lost his only form of sublimation, Deeds sinks into a deep depression. He is quite simply heartbroken. Louise tries desperately to get to see him, but Cobs turns her away accusing her of having 'crucified Deeds for a few stinking headlines'.

Louise has to do penance for her badness – she has to be shut out, rebuffed, excluded. She has to believe that she has lost him forever and thoroughly regret the error of her ways before she can be purged of her guilt and free to be happy once again. This is one of the lessons of the story – for each of us our dragons come in many different guises.

At the 'insanity hearing', which is conducted like a trial, Deeds refuses to speak or have a lawyer to speak for him. Cedar leads the prosecution, twisting everything Deeds has done in order to misrepresent him, using Louise's articles to back up his case and paint a portrait of Deeds as a violent man and a liar, finishing with the suggestion that Deeds' attempt to give away his money will foment social unrest in the nation. Just as Deeds is being sentenced to a life in a mental asylum, Louise, at great personal risk of being held in contempt of court, pleads with the judge. Cedar points out that her testimony is of no value because she is obviously in love with Deeds. Louise admits that she is in love with him. On hearing her words, for the first time since he discoved that Louise deceived him, Deeds perks up. At last he agrees to speak in defence of his sanity. His speech ends by addressing Cedar's assertion that by giving away all his money he will rot the foundations of the entire system of government: 'What does Mr Cedar expect me to do with it? Give it to him and a lot of other people who don't need it?' Deeds punches Cedar on the nose, to cheers from everyone in the courtroom, and is carried out into the street on the shoulders of the celebrating farmers. Louise is left crying alone in the almost empty courtroom until Deeds comes running back to take her in his arms.

As a reward for outwitting the biggest dragon of all – the established order and social system as represented by the courtroom – Deeds finally does get to rescue his lady in distress, although never in his wildest dreams would he have imagined that her distress would be caused by guilt over the harm she has done to him. His ability to forgive her, despite what she has done, simply because he realizes that she really does love him as he does her, is heroic, although again his is an emotional bravery, not normally associated with manly heroism. One of the strongest themes in the film has been how Deeds' personality has perplexed all the characters he meets. They have variously attempted to pigeonhole him as a simpleton, a small-town hick, an old-fashioned man with traditional values, or just 'pixilated' – as he is referred to in the courtroom by two old ladies from his hometown. But what is so remarkable about Deeds is his emotional sensitivity and openness – character traits normally assumed to be feminine. Deeds' character confounds many of the typical male stereotypes that constrict men – in this sense he is as much a man of the future as of the past.

Finally, the idea that if rich people would only give away their money to the poor, then the power of wealth and the malevolent forces of capitalism would be overcome (and we would have a simple solution to some of the world's ills) has a childlike innocence about it, like Deeds himself. But *Mr Deeds Goes to Town* is not about politics, it is a story about how innocence is pilloried by a sophisticated, cynical and corrupt society. Innocence, like love, is something many of us long for but have spoiled or lost or never found. But in fairytales, as we all know, wishes, or those things we most long for, are granted in the end.

Bringing Up Baby (1938)

Directed by Howard Hawks; screenplay by Dudley Nichols and
Hagar Wilde; starring Katharine Hepburn and Cary Grant

'When I take my hands down you will be gone.'

The attraction of opposites is a scientific principle frequently
cited as applying not only to the poles of a magnet but also to
the magnetic attraction between two lovers who might at first
appear totally unsuited to each other. *Bringing Up Baby*,
directed by Howard Hawks and released in 1938, is about a man
and a woman who have diametrically opposed personalities,
causing sparks to fly as their radically different temperaments
continuously clash. But finally it is the energy generated by their
opposing natures that attracts them to each other – or is it that
they unconsciously recognize in each other the missing aspects of
their own personality, which they need in their lives to enable
them to be happy?

At the time of its release, *Bringing Up Baby* was a box office
disaster. Reviewers said it was 'screwball gone too far . . . too
silly and crazy'.[17] It has been recognized since as one of the
funniest and most durable of the early screwball comedies –
which is perhaps a welcome reminder that audiences don't
always get it right at the time of release. Screwball comedy or
farce employs a quite different narrative structure from the
fairytale romantic comedy. The moral dimension is largely
absent, as is the requirement for the protagonists to be on a
journey involving a series of experiences from which they learn
and change, although their circumstances will have changed
quite radically by the end of the film. In screwball our engagement with the story and the humour relies on the fun in
recognizing typical mannerisms and behaviour patterns rather
than our emotional identification with the protagonists. We are
simply swept away by the anarchic craziness of it all and the

frissons of sexiness that emanate from the fun. While the classic romantic comedy often makes us feel a whole gamut of emotions, from laughter to tears, with screwball we rarely feel moved to tears, unless they are tears of laughter.

One of the reasons *Bringing Up Baby* has proved so durable is the universal nature of the film's underlying conflicts, such as those between duty and pleasure, order and anarchy, intuition and reason, sexual repression and sexual fulfilment. These are oppositions that affect us all both as individuals and within our relationships. Another reason is the brilliant performances of Cary Grant and Katharine Hepburn, who imbue their characters with a magical vitality, particularly Hepburn who sweeps Grant off his feet, both metaphorically and literally – as a result of meeting each other they fall over flat on their backs or their faces fourteen times in the course of the film, which brings a whole new meaning to the idea of falling in love.

The first image we see of Professor David Huxley (Cary Grant) is in the museum where he works, sitting high up on scaffolding near a dinosaur's tail puzzling over where a particular bone fits into a reconstructed brontosaurus skeleton. The image immediately suggests that here is a man used to living at a higher level with his head so full of facts – or at least the knowledge of how dinosaur bones fit together – that he has become somehow disconnected from his body and the earthly world below. Cary Grant's good looks have been disguised by heavy round glasses and an unflattering overall, which he wears tied high across his chest making it look like a garment his mother might once have made him wear to stop him getting his clothes dirty.

The childlike aspect of David's character is further empha- sized when he hears the news that the very last bone he needs to complete the brontosaurus is arriving the next day, the same day he is due to be married. He is so excited he spontaneously kisses his fiancée who also works at the museum, a smart, formidable woman tightly buttoned up in a business suit. Instead of sharing his excitement she reprimands him – the museum is not a place for unseemly shows of affection. She also reminds him that when they are married she doesn't intend to allow their 'domestic entanglements' to interfere with his work and she certainly doesn't think there will be room in their marriage for children. She looks up at the huge dinosaur skeleton and earnestly declares, 'This will be our child.' Poor David is crestfallen and thoroughly deflated when he sets off for the golf course where, at his fiancée's insistence, he must meet with Mr Peabody – a lawyer with a client who is planning to make a million-dollar donation to the museum.

In other words Professor David Huxley's character not only fits the commonly held view of a typical academic; brilliant in his own field but absent-minded, clumsy and inept in the world outside the museum. But he is also the archetypal long-suffering, put-upon man: women dominate him, he moans, complains, tries to stand up for himself, usually fails and easily accepts defeat. And as this opening scene also makes clear, he is a man on the threshold of a potentially miserable marriage, unless he is somehow rescued in time.

At the golf course we soon find out exactly how inept David is when he has the good fortune – or misfortune depending on how you look at it – to accidentally bump into Susan Vance (Katharine Hepburn) and as a result misses his meeting with Mr Peabody. Susan's character appears to be the complete opposite to David's. Her beauty, like her bush of thick curly hair and her entire personality, is wild and vivacious. Typical of a certain kind of woman born into wealth and privilege, she doesn't work, she has no apparent worries and she treats the world as if it were an adventure playground built just for her. She loves having fun, playing games, talking fast and she has a way of causing mayhem wherever she goes. Susan is also the kind of woman who is used to getting what she wants – and what she wants, she soon realizes, is David.

Susan meets David for the second time that evening in a nightclub. David is not the kind of man who would normally go to a nightclub but due to the chaos Susan caused at the golf course he is still trying to find Mr Peabody. He walks past Susan just as the barman is teaching her how to flip an olive up in the air and catch it in her mouth. Susan misses the olive; David slips on it and falls flat on the floor. Susan laughs at him, she can't help it, but this is also the moment she falls in love. As David ruefully inspects his squashed hat he is completely unaware of how stunningly handsome he looks in his bow-tie and dinner jacket or how his vulnerability, exacerbated by his discomfort in such glamorous surroundings, makes him even more attractive. Susan's problem now is that the more she pursues David the angrier he becomes. In the voice of a long-suffering parent he suggests to her that they play a game. She is delighted – she loves playing games. 'I'll put my hands over my eyes,' David tells her, 'and you go away. And I'll count to ten and when I take my hands down you will be gone.' Susan is hurt. Finally it seems that David has got the message through. He doesn't want her. But as she turns to walk away from him his foot accidentally catches the back of her satin evening dress and an entire panel of the skirt tears away. However much David wants to be rid of her he can hardly allow her to be humiliated in public. He quickly puts his arms around her from behind, presses his body against hers to conceal the offending sight of her exposed stockinged legs and silk knickers, and frogmarches her out of the nightclub. The scene is hilarious, very sexy and reveals how beneath David's fuddy-duddy persona there lies a gallant heart.

The storyline of *Bringing Up Baby* is woven around David's earnest pursuit of the million-dollar donation for the museum, which is constantly disrupted by Susan who, although she insists that she is only trying to help David find Mr Peabody, is really intent on getting David to fall in love with her. The story becomes even more complicated by the arrival the next morning of two items through the post. Just as David is in his apartment unpacking the all-important dinosaur bone, Susan receives a special delivery of her own; a tame leopard called Baby, which her big-game hunter brother has sent her from Brazil. She immediately seizes the opportunity to disrupt David's wedding day by pretending on the telephone that she is being savaged by the leopard in order to get David to rush to her apartment to rescue her. She then ensnares him into helping her take Baby to her aunt's country cottage by telling him that if he doesn't go with her she will leave the leopard with him.

David insists on carrying the dinosaur bone under his arm everywhere he goes until he loses it – another of the many disruptions to his life caused by Susan – and becomes obsessed with finding it again. Literally, the bone is the final piece of the brontosaurus skeleton that David needs in order to complete four years' dedicated work. Metaphorically, the bone represents David; inert, dusty, out of date – in fact a fossil in need of bringing back to life by a woman like Susan. Similarly Susan's character is metaphorically represented by the leopard, which for much of the film she is either transporting or losing and trying to find again. Like the leopard, it is doubtful if Susan's personality can ever be fully tamed. She is the epitome of an archetypal image of womanhood: a loose cannon, hedonistic, self-centred, dizzy, irrational, spontaneous and totally out of control. David's personality is conversely governed by the principles commonly associated with civilized man: order, rationality, logic, reason and most importantly, self-control. Susan is just the kind of woman who terrifies men like David. Although, like many of us, David is fascinated by what he is most afraid of.

David is clearly so completely under his fiancée's thumb that it will take a woman as determined as Susan to prise him free. But the film never raises the question of whether for David this could be a case of out of the frying pan, into the fire – if his fiancée gets her way by straightforward domination, Susan gets her way by employing a whole multitude of so-called feminine wiles, rendering David equally powerless. Susan is instinctively manipulative and will resort to anything to get what she wants, as she demonstrates when, as soon as she has David ensnared in her aunt's cottage, she steals his clothes while he is in the shower in order to prevent him going to his own wedding. This is also the moment when Susan's aunt arrives unexpectedly at the door, only to be confronted by David, who is wearing Susan's flimsy feminine bathrobe. Susan's aunt demands to know not only who he is but why is he dressed like that? David's frustration at being misunderstood suddenly erupts and he leaps into the air shouting 'I just went gay suddenly'. (This moment is particularly funny for a modern audience.) He then literally puts his foot down by stamping on Susan's toe in order to shut her up. The meaning here is complicated. On the one hand it would appear that only when dressed as a woman can David finally assert his power – he does succeed in shutting up Susan, if only for a minute. On the other hand the effectiveness of his power relies on an act of violence, however small, and it is this that enables him to get his own way. Susan is impressed and (as she later secretly tells her aunt) even more determined that he is the man she is going to marry – reinforcing a traditional notion that when the chips are down a woman likes a man who can take control in a manly fashion, even if he is dressed as a woman at the time.

Susan may be impressed by David but her aunt definitely is not. This is a serious blow for David as Susan's aunt, it turns out, is also Mr Peabody's mystery client who intends to give a million-dollar donation to the museum (although if she finds out that David works for the museum she may well change her mind). Susan's aunt is such a battleaxe, her authoritative tone and withering looks even intimidate a retired army major who shortly arrives to dine with them. The director, Howard Hawks, has here created a world where one of the biggest problems for men, and in particular David, is that all the female characters are in their own way threatening, forceful, dominating and impossible for men to control.

David's moment of getting his own way by stamping his foot was short lived. His problems now rapidly go from bad to worse: he misses his wedding because of Susan, Susan's aunt's dog steals his precious dinosaur bone and buries it and the leopard, Baby, escapes into the woods in the dead of night. As we saw in both *The Taming of the Shrew* and *It Happened One Night*, moonlit nights in the lonely countryside can release atavistic tendencies in the human psyche, which is particularly good for raising the sexual temperature and falling in love. Susan, governed as she is by her feminine intuition, which is traditionally associated with the mysterious forces of nature, lures David into the dark woodland, insisting that if he follows her they will find his precious bone and the lost leopard and then everything will be all right. David protests with his now familiar repertoire of frustration, repressed rage and helpless confusion but nevertheless he ends up following her lead. The brilliance of Cary Grant's performance here lies in his ability to portray David's deeply serious, dutiful, long-suffering nature and yet, at the same time, to communicate the exciting sexual potency underlying all that is happening to him. The shape of the story also echoes this – as it has now become a journey from the civilized order of the museum where dead things are preserved for posterity, to the freedom and exciting chaos of the natural world as reflected in the wild wood at night, a place where a dangerous escaped leopard lurks. (Coincidentally a second leopard has escaped from a local circus on the same night as Baby has escaped from Susan.)

In the penultimate scene of the film David finally redeems his manhood. He saves Susan from the vicious man-eating leopard and through his display of gallantry he becomes a classic hero in Susan's eyes – even though he faints as soon as the dangerous leopard is safely locked away. The cautious, overly cerebral professor, as a result of meeting Susan, has discovered an aspect of himself that he didn't know was there – he *is* capable of being a courageous knight in shining armour who rescues his damsel in distress. He's also quite proud of himself for what he has done. But this brief fairytale moment is certainly not convincing enough to stand as a satisfactory ending to the story.

In the final scene when David is back at work in the museum, Susan brings him the lost dinosaur bone, which she has found. David's initial response to seeing her is fear – he climbs up to his platform high above the brontosaurus to get away from her. We can understand David's deep ambivalence: his problem is that what he most fears is also what he most desires. As if suddenly realizing this he overcomes his fear and announces that the time they spent together was the best day in his whole life and exultantly declares that he loves her. Susan, who by this time has climbed to the top of the ladder on the other side of the bronto-saurus in order to reach him, is so overcome by his declaration of love that she begins swaying wildly – a wonderful reflection of the way their emotions are also oscillating bewilderingly from one extreme to another. The ladder suddenly falls. Susan saves herself by clinging to the back of the brontosaurus. Just as the whole skeleton collapses and smashes to the floor beneath them, David manages to grab hold of her and pull her on to the plat-form with him. He has saved her once again, but beneath them lies the destruction of what has taken David four years to create.

Is this what being in love with Susan and everything that she represents means? Just as David oscillates here from extreme fear to extreme desire, so he is likely to remain oscillating for their entire future relationship together. Susan has lied, black-mailed and cheated to get her own way and she has disguised all her manipulative actions with feigned innocence, childlike playfulness and flirtatious charm. She has stolen David from his fiancée on his wedding day without any qualms of guilt. In short Susan is a monster. No wonder men are frightened of her. She is the epitome of a privileged society woman who, in the absence of real power – that is the kind of power, usually male, that comes with status and influence in worldly matters – has devoted herself to the art of subterfuge in order to get what she wants in the domestic arena.

Whether, in reality, a man like David would be more likely to live happily ever after with a woman like Susan than his original fiancée, with whom he had far more in common, is questionable. But her free spirit has brought a new life-force into his overly controlled world and she may well benefit from his discipline and reason in order to give her life a sense of meaning and direction. And, despite all her failings, Susan is definitely more fun.

Ninotchka (1939)

Directed by Ernst Lubitsch; screenplay by Charles Brackett, Billy Wilder and Walter Reisch; based on the story by Melchor Lengyel; starring Greta Garbo and Melvyn Douglas

'Don't make an issue of my womanhood . . .'

Wouldn't the world be a much nicer place if seduction and laughter were our tools for resolving international conflicts instead of threats and bombs? This wonderfully naive sentiment, which underlies Ernst Lubitsch's *Ninotchka*, struck a chord with many people when the film was released in 1939, just as Hitler's armies began marching through Europe. In such a climate who wouldn't long to escape, if only for an evening in the cinema, into a fairytale solution to the world's ills? As Ninotchka, the eponymous heroine (played by Greta Garbo with her inimitable misty-eyed passion), pleads earnestly in the film, no doubt voicing the feelings of numerous young lovers at the time: 'Bombs will fall, civilization will crumble . . . but not yet please, wait . . . what's the hurry? Give us our moment, let us be happy.'

Lubitsch had emigrated to America from Berlin in 1923. A few years later Garbo left her native Sweden to pursue her career in Hollywood, and a decade later in the mid-thirties Billy Wilder, a key member of *Ninotchka*'s writing team, arrived from Vienna via Berlin and Paris. With their combined personal experience of sophisticated, cosmopolitan Europe they must have seemed ideally suited to take a light-hearted, insightful look at the subject on everyone's mind, although the resulting film suggests that the looming political crisis was almost too overwhelming to handle.

It's not difficult to understand why a love story uniting nations with incompatible ideologies seemed like a good idea at the time. Neither is it difficult to fathom why the film-makers decided to hone their matchmaking skills on the rival ideologies of western capitalism and Soviet communism. After all what nation, apart from Germany, would have wanted to see a romantic comedy with a Nazi heroine? Unfortunately 1939 turned out also to be the year when Stalin made a pact with Hitler, which lasted until Germany invaded Russia in 1941.

The many problems posed by *Ninotchka*'s release in this momentous year are hinted at in the opening caption which informs us: 'This picture takes place in Paris in those wonderful days when a siren was a brunette and not an alarm . . . And if a Frenchman turned out the light it was not on account of an air raid.' In fact a brief appearance early in the film of a middle-aged Nazi couple greeting each other with the 'Heil Hitler' salute suggests that 'those wonderful days' were already coming to an end. But the caption's wisecracks invite us to turn away from this uneasy fact and escape into the crazy anarchic world typical of screwball farce. At the same time it gets Lubitsch off the hook of dealing with the quagmire of shifting wartime alliances and frees him to play with sexual innuendo, national and gender stereotypes, and even to risk straying into the sensitive area of political caricature. He takes on the daunting task of portraying capitalism's seduction of communism through a Cinderella romance: a fun-loving western playboy's seduction of a serious-minded, dutiful, female Russian commissar.

In the film Count Leon D'Algout (Melvyn Douglas) is given the formidable task of personifying western capitalism. He's in his mid-thirties, tall, suave, urbane, wears a sharp double-breasted pinstriped suit and has a tiny, immaculately trimmed moustache. Within minutes of his arriving at his lover, Swana's, luxurious Parisian apartment we learn that his chief pursuit in life is pleasure and he makes his money by gambling and living off well-connected women such as the Grand Duchess Swana, who is in exile from communist Russia. His latest idea for making money is that Swana should write a book about her exotic life and love affairs and use the profits to buy *him* a diamond watch. Hardly a laudable ambition for a romantic hero whose super-smooth appearance, self-satisfied demeanour and somewhat worn-out flirtation routine is more reminiscent of a used-car salesman. But, we must remember, this is a fairytale and given the right trials and tests of character and the opportunity to meet the right woman, it may be possible even for a worm like Leon to redeem himself. We assume that the right woman is not Swana, whose main interests in life, apart from Leon, appear to be her fading beauty as she approaches middle-age and her jewels, which were 'stolen' or 'nationalized' (depending on your point of view) when the Bolsheviks took power in Russia.

The story of *Ninotchka* ostensibly revolves around Swana's jewels. At the outset of the film three elderly Russians, dressed for a Moscow winter and clutching a battered old suitcase, gaze in awe at the plush foyer of a sophisticated Parisian hotel. They quickly retire to the street outside to anxiously debate the pros and cons of good communists staying in such a luxurious hotel: on the one hand, if Moscow finds out they might get sent to Siberia; on the other hand, as the Royal Suite has the only room with a safe big enough to hold the suitcase (which, we soon learn, contains what used to be Swana's jewels), surely they have the perfect excuse to stay there? They finally reassure themselves by imagining that if their hero, Lenin, were alive he would certainly tell them to take the room and not to be such fools. After all, 'for once in your life you are in Paris . . .'

Sasha, Sergei and Misha are stereotypical emotional, ebullient Russians. They are also, like the dwarfs in *Snow White*; good hearted, gullible, innocents. They are no match for the smooth-talking Leon when he strolls casually into their hotel room – Swana has heard that the Russian government, in need of hard currency, is selling her jewels in Paris and Leon's mission is to retrieve them for her. Leon's chief technique for getting what he wants in life, whether with Swana or these three susceptible innocents abroad, is to manipulate and seduce. He introduces his 'new friends' to a few capitalist delights, such as unlimited champagne, exotic food and the solicitous attentions of the hotel's cigarette girls who wear dinky little skirts and bows in their hair. 'Leon, why are you so good to us,' they drool, as he dictates a telegram, supposedly from them, informing Moscow of Swana's claim to the jewels and suggesting that a fifty-fifty deal is the best solution. Naturally, Moscow does not take kindly to the news and immediately dispatches an 'envoy extraordinary' to Paris to take charge of the situation. Panic-stricken, the three Russians rush to the station to meet their new boss, who they assume will be a man.

Whether in real life or romantic comedy, the moment when we first encounter someone special imprints itself on our consciousness with a particularly powerful resonance, as we attempt to work out who they are and whether we like them or not. Of course, in real life as well as in films we all too often get it wrong, but the first impression nevertheless stays with us. The Moscow train has already arrived when Sasha, Sergei and Misha rush into the station.

As the last passengers depart we see Ninotchka's small figure standing alone on the empty platform waiting with two small suitcases at her feet. For an all-important moment she appears vulnerable and lonely. Then, as we observe her more closely – her dowdy military-style suit, sensible shoes and felt hat which is pulled down over her ears – we see that she has a fixed expression of solemn severity and eyes that gaze with a steady and disturbing directness beneath arched critical eyebrows. She is just the kind of woman who would terrify many men, not least poor Sasha, Sergei and Misha, whom she greets with a manly handshake. Misha attempts to soften the formality of the moment by nervously suggesting that it was 'a charming idea' for Moscow to surprise them by sending a lady and if they had known they would have brought flowers. But Ninotchka is not impressed: 'Don't make an issue of my womanhood, we are here for work, all of us. Let's not waste any time.' She then instructs the station porter to leave her bags alone; his business is 'no business, it's social injustice'. She picks up her own bags and marches out of the station. 'How are things in Moscow?' Misha asks anxiously as he struggles to keep up with her. 'Very good,' she replies, 'The last mass trial was a great success. There are going to be fewer but better Russians.'

In short, Ninotchka is the epitome of a brainwashed Communist Party apparatchik and she also has the demeanour of a woman who merely by raising her eyebrow is capable of turning to stone anybody who attempts to interfere with her certainty and clarity of purpose. This impression is reinforced when she stops to stare at a ridiculous hat on display in a shop window. 'How can such a civilization survive if it permits their women to put such things like that on their heads?' she declares, shaking her head. Invoking the spectre of the fall of capitalism, she adds darkly, 'It won't be long now comrades.' These brilliant one-liners, which Garbo delivers with complete sincerity, set the tone for the whole film. And it's not difficult to imagine what fun Lubitsch and his writing team had when creating this caricature of a repressive communist as the super-ego standing in judgement on the self-indulgent egos of the pleasure-seeking capitalists. The major problem confronting Lubitsch is how to turn this political satire into a fairytale romance and make us believe that the formidable and sincere Ninotchka could also be susceptible to the charms of a superficial playboy and, conversely, that Leon himself is capable of transforming from a womanizer into a romantic hero.

Ninotchka first meets Leon when they are both stuck on a traffic island outside her hotel where she is studying a map of Paris, searching for the Eiffel Tower. 'Good heavens, has that been lost again?' Leon quips, but she doesn't get the joke, or if she does she doesn't show it. Ignoring her cold, withering looks Leon persists with his flirtation routine. Finally she takes the bull by the horns: 'I have heard of the arrogant male in capitalistic society,' she informs him dryly. 'It is having a superior earning power that makes you that way. Your type will soon be extinct.' With that she turns and walks away, leaving Leon to gaze after her, as if her condemning him to extinction were the most exciting thing to happen to him for a long time – thus reaffirming the old adage that there is nothing womanizers find more exciting than women who are hard to get. Spurred on by her indifference he immediately rushes to the Eiffel Tower and follows her to the top. He becomes even more stimulated when she suggests that he show her his apartment. Although she makes it clear that she's not stupid enough to believe in his attempts at romantic poetic banter, as a 'product of a doomed culture' he should prove to be an 'interesting subject of study'. She examines his apartment with the curiosity of a museum visitor and informs him that she does not believe in love, although she does believe in 'chemical processes'. She doesn't appear to have learnt the usual protocol; that it is the man, not the woman, who should take the sexual initiative. In fact, if the scene in Leon's apartment is to be believed, it is her manliness not her femininity that Leon finds most enthralling as, stripped down to the Cossack's tunic under her jacket, they lie together on the floor while she tells him of the time when, as a sergeant in the Red Army, she killed a Polish lancer. She even offers to show Leon her war wound, although sadly for him this turns out to be on the back of her neck.

But before we stray too far along this potentially dangerous path of gender reversal, S&M or the even more subversive prospect of communism seducing capitalism (instead of the other way around), the phone rings. Misha is calling Leon to tell him that a special envoy has arrived from Moscow. When Leon writes down the special envoy's name both he and Ninotchka realize the problem: regarding the all-important matter of Swana's jewels, they are enemies. Ninotchka hurriedly leaves.

This fortuitous phone call also gives Lubitsch the opportunity to steer the story away from the tricky area of political and gender subversion and to attempt to instate the increasingly elusive fairytale romance. Leon must stop being so enchanted by Ninotchka's masculinity (which is a curious and potentially disturbing insight into the nature of an incorrigible womanizer) and prove himself as a politically correct 'prince' who is morally worthy of her. He must also get the political message back on track by persuading Ninotchka to appreciate the many joys of capitalism: to take life less seriously, to relax, to have fun and, of course, to believe in love. (Possibly Lubitsch thought this mission would also solve Europe's ills?) The joke about Ninotchka's outlandish behaviour as an emancipated woman is also in danger of getting seriously out of hand. In order for her to be a suitable romantic heroine she must now begin to behave like a proper woman.

Ninotchka's first lesson in the art of western womanhood is to laugh at her suitor's jokes, even if they are not at all funny. In what Ninotchka believes to be a politically correct working-class restaurant, Leon pursues his mission to make her have fun by bombarding her with jokes. This is the scene that made *Ninotchka* famous as the film where 'Garbo laughs', although her side-splitting laughter is a result not of Leon's jokes, which are truly awful, but of the fact that he finally gives up trying and in exasperation falls backwards off his chair on to the floor. Ninotchka's laughter is pivotal in her transformation as a woman and it is also the moment when she falls in love. To prove it she buys the very silly hat, which she had earlier declared should cause the demise of civilization, and reveals that underneath her mannish exterior there lurked a real woman all along. At last she is free to express her 'feminine side'; she becomes simpering, shy, unsure, a little skittish and very jealous of her rival, the Grand Duchess Swana.

Garbo's portrayal of Ninotchka in love is a weirdly incongruous mixture of her former communist mannerisms and the affectations adopted by the kind of upper-class women who frequent elite Parisian circles. One night, drunk on love and champagne, she takes Swana's jewels out of the hotel safe and adorns herself with a glittering diamond tiara. She turns to Leon with radiant eyes and declares those immortal words: 'The revolution is on the march, I know. Bombs will fall, civilization will crumble . . . but not yet please, wait . . . what's the hurry? Give us our moment, let us be happy. We are happy aren't we Leon?' This is the moment when the film finally encapsulates the audience's dream of an escape from the fearful reality of war-torn Europe. And the moment is quite magical, not because of the success of the love story but because of Garbo's remarkable performance. As Molly Haskell put it, 'Garbo is sex spiritualized . . . it's no accident that her leading men were weak or became invisible, for as a figure who combined elements of both sexes, and the essence of love itself, Garbo usurped the whole screen.'[18]

In other words, unlike the thirties films we have looked at so far – where our fascination lies in both the fairytale and the dynamic sexual and emotional chemistry between the man and the woman – in *Ninotchka* our fascination lies with Garbo alone. At this crucial moment in the film Ninotchka appeals directly to us, the audience, and Leon is effectively redundant or invisible.

Despite Prince Charming's shortcomings, Lubitsch struggles valiantly to find a fairytale resolution for the story. Swana, acting like Cinderella's wicked stepmother, forces Ninotchka to leave Paris by offering her the jewels in exchange for Leon. Ninotchka, like Cinderella, is too morally good to act in her own self-interest; so she has no alternative but to sacrifice her love for Leon for the higher calling of her duty to her country and the poor people of Russia who she believes rightfully own the jewels. She duly returns to her spartan communal living conditions in a grim Moscow apartment, her dull uniform as a working woman and her regimented work in a man's world. There she must wait passively until Leon, as her Prince Charming, finds a way of saving her. Leon does this by tricking the Russian government into once more sending her to the west as a special envoy. On her arrival he manages, with a little smooth talking, to convince her that she will be a better Russian by deserting her country and marrying him than by going home. Ninotchka smiles radiantly and with total sincerity enthuses, 'No one, will be able to say Ninotchka was a bad Russian.'

The central problem at the heart of *Ninotchka* is why such a sincere, passionate, morally upright, intelligent, emancipated woman should fall in love with a superficial playboy. It is equally difficult to believe that a womanizer like Leon is capable of loving her, let alone remaining faithful for long after the thrill of the chase has worn off. As we all know, strange and unlikely liaisons do happen in life, but whether they lead to lasting happiness is another matter.

Finally, one of the most fascinating aspects of *Ninotchka* is the film's portrayal of a western male fantasy of dealing with an emancipated Russian woman – and by extension what life for men might be like if and when women in the west begin looking and acting like Ninotchka. As we shall see, women working in male occupations was to become the most pressing issue for the battle of the sexes in the war-torn forties.

Two

The Taming of the Shrew in the Forties

At the outset of the forties the Second World War was on everyone's mind, although America remained on the sidelines until the end of 1941 when Japan and Germany declared war on her. War is, of course, a serious and tragic business, and the popular demand was naturally for more serious romances such as *Gone With the Wind*, which was released in 1939. Nevertheless romantic comedies remained popular and some of those made in the forties are the most interesting and challenging of the genre.

War is about extremes; the life-force struggling to survive in the face of human madness, injustice, separation, loss and death. War is also the great upholder of traditional models of masculinity, providing a multitude of opportunities for men to prove their steadfastness and heroism in the face of danger. At the top were Winston Churchill and Franklin D. Roosevelt, who remained President of America until his death in 1945. Beneath them were the generals, air marshals and admirals masterminding the campaigns; then the fighter-pilots, commandos and parachutists spearheading the action; the vast numbers of foot soldiers, sailors and airmen steadfastly obeying orders; and, of course, the lone undercover agents or resistance fighters pursuing their missions in the dead of night. All were reinforcing the masculine archetypes of physical and mental strength, loyalty, courage, heroism, brotherly love and unity in the face of enemy fire.

On the other hand, the erosion of the traditional feminine archetypes that had begun in the Great War twenty-five years earlier continued. The angels in the house; the long-suffering, ever-loving mothers, the lonely wives, the virginal sisters and daughters, all waiting passively for their male providers and protectors to come home, were no longer sufficient. In the Second World War more women than ever before were required to prove their abilities in every conceivable kind of men's work: from farm labour to shipbuilding and 'manning' the munitions factories. Many women joined the armed forces, although they were usually placed in the softer occupations such as secretarial back-up, driving or nursing. But, like the men, they were a long way from home, frequently in danger and also required to be courageous and heroic in the face of the enemy. Women entertainers, such as 'the forces' sweetheart' Vera Lynn, went to the front to perform for the troops. Some women became as dauntingly powerful as their male counterparts, such as the heads of the WRENs, WRAFs and FANYs, who were known as the 'Queen Bees'.

Others demonstrated the kind of courage in the face of danger commonly associated with male heroes. Martha Gellhorn, a *Time* magazine war correspondent, regularly braved the dangers of the front line to send her reports home, while for much of the war, according to Martha, her second husband, Ernest Hemingway, languished off Cuba fishing. (After husband number three Gellhorn famously wrote: 'For me, marriage is a terrible institution and it should be suppressed.'[1]) Lee Miller, already celebrated as a *Vogue* fashion model and for her affairs with various surrealists in Paris, confounded prejudices about the innate weakness of the fairer sex by becoming *Vogue*'s front-line photo-journalist. Not only did she risk her life daily but she also photographed some of the most terrible sights of the war, including the liberation of Dachau concentration camp. Odette Hallows, a British housewife who was born and brought up in France, became a clandestine Special Operations Executive courier, although when she was interviewed for the job there were some doubts about her suitability: 'Would she be able, as a mother of three young daughters who might be constantly on her mind, to undertake missions requiring steely nerves and an ability to concentrate on the task in question to the exclusion of all else?'[2] She proved, not only that she could, but also that she was tough enough to withstand torture and the horrors of Ravensbrück concentration camp.

In peacetime, lovers had usually conducted their relationships at a leisurely pace; their choice of partners was often restricted to the narrow confines of their local community and governed by conservative attitudes to sexual morality and courtship. In wartime, young men in the armed forces were regularly moved around the country and billeted overseas, as were the young women who had joined up. Many women who worked in the auxiliary occupations were also living far from home and even those women who remained at home found, with the frequent movement of troops, that their opportunities for meeting the opposite sex were greater than ever before and so was the range of partners to choose from. Add to this heady brew the excitement and danger of war; dance bands such as Glen Miller's playing 'In The Mood' in the local dancehalls, the fun of the jitterbug and, when the dances were over, the inevitable coupling and walks home through the blacked-out streets or country lanes, and it is not difficult to understand why many men and women decided to throw conventional peacetime morality out of the window. Seize the day for tomorrow we may die.

Exciting, brave, strong-willed women, particularly if they also happened to be beautiful, were, of course, tremendously attractive to men. But when it came to the kind of woman men wanted to marry, most still clung to the idealized fantasy of the soft, feminine woman who would be there waiting for them when they got home. This dichotomy is manifest in *Gone With the Wind*. Scarlett's strength and courage surpasses that of many men, as do her survival skills in the Civil War, but it is her saintly cousin Melanie whom Ashley chooses to marry. This sentiment is also exemplified in *Annie Get Your Gun*, a huge hit in the forties musical theatre. The hero rejects gun-slinging Annie for being too masculine and sings, 'The girl that I marry will have to be, as soft and as pink as a nursery. The girl that I call my own, will wear satin and laces and smell of cologne . . .'

Of course many women continued to nurture an image of their future loved one as the ultimate masculine man who would be their provider and protector, but at least for women their fantasy aspiration was, if anything, reinforced by the war effort. It was the men's cherished fantasy of their women that appeared to be under threat. After all, if the women, who were now proving their abilities by doing the men's peacetime jobs, became too like men what would be the effect on their love affairs and relationships? Given such confusion deep within the male psyche it is easy to see why the dominant themes of the forties romantic comedies were the battle of the sexes and the conflicts arising from women working in a man's world.

The problem of self-sufficient and strident women had begun to emerge in romantic comedy even before America joined the war in 1941, most notably in such films as *Philadelphia Story* and *His Girl Friday*. Although in *His Girl Friday* the heroine's character, as a brilliant news reporter, is redeemed from the outset of the film by her declaration that what she really wants is to be a 'proper woman', a housewife and mother. The irony is that her ex-husband, who is also her editor and boss, didn't want an angel in the house, he wanted her to be his girl Friday. In this way the film neatly addresses the subject yet manages to sidestep the threat the New Woman poses to the contemporary male.

In contrast, *Woman of the Year* tackles the threat head on. The heroine of *Woman of the Year* (released in 1942), played by Katharine Hepburn, is one of the most outspoken, strident and intellectually powerful women to be portrayed in the entire history of romantic comedy. Katharine Hepburn herself wasn't short of role models. Her real life mother had been a suffragette and ardent campaigner for birth control. And Eleanor Roosevelt continued to be a formidable role model for women of the period. Like the heroine of *Woman of the Year*, Eleanor Roosevelt spoke at national conventions, she wrote a syndicated column, she delivered lectures and was a radio commentator. Throughout the war years she continued to speak out on civil rights, racism and equality for women. She held press

conferences, which she restricted to women journalists, knowing
that papers would be forced to hire their first female reporters in
order to have access to the First Lady. During the war she
recruited women to work in the factories with the words, 'If I
were of debutante age, I would go into a factory where I could
learn a skill and be useful.' She also cautioned young women
against marrying too early before they had a chance to expand
their horizons.

'Can't you muzzle that wife of yours? . . . Do you have lace on
your panties for allowing her to speak out so much? . . . Why
can't she stay home and tend her knitting?' were some of the
questions put to FDR about his wife's unrelenting
outspokenness.[3] This question indicates the outright hostility
engendered in many men by women like Mrs Roosevelt. Such
deep ambivalence is also apparent in *Woman of the Year*,
causing the film to be one of the most curiously disturbing and
emotionally confusing of all romantic comedies.

The theme of *No Time For Love*, released in 1943, is also
imbued with the pressing concerns of the time, although the only
signs of the actual war lie in a few background details, such as
an occasional poster for war bonds. But the character of the
film's heroine, an artistically inclined fashion photographer who
finds herself lured into working in the tough masculine world of
photo-journalism, may well have been influenced by Lee Miller's
war reports for *Vogue* magazine. In contrast to *Woman of the
Year*, the film positively praises women who venture into man's
domain and prove themselves to be, if not as physically strong as
men, equally dedicated, courageous and mentally tough. But
implicit in the film's message is a serious warning to such
women: be careful or you may undermine your man's sense of
his own masculinity – and that's not good for you or for your
man; nor is it good for the war effort.

The Second World War finally ended in 1945. Following the
initial euphoria, two conflicting moods prevailed as people
began to return home or to welcome their loved ones home and
pick up the pieces of their normal peacetime lives. On the one

hand, the end of war had generated a tremendous mood of optimism and political idealism about the future. Many people, particularly those on the left, were convinced that a more egalitarian and enlightened society would replace the pre-war social structures and that each person would have a part to play in building the brave new world. The war had further eroded old class divisions, and working men, who had offered their lives for their country, now expected their country to value and respect them in return. Women who had proved their abilities in the war effort had discovered a new sense of fulfillment, self-confidence and freedom, which they hoped would continue in peacetime. On the other hand, men had been away from home for too long. They may have wanted to play a part in building a brave new world, but they also wanted a life of certainty and security with a place in the community and, if they were married, to follow their father's example as head of their own family. Women too had been yearning for their men to return and the peacetime domestic harmony they imagined would automatically follow. They had also been longing to start their own families – the result was the soaring birth rate known as the post-war bulge.

Pregnant or not, most women were unceremoniously fired at the end of the war, which came to some as an enormous blow. Eleanor Roosevelt, as outspoken as ever, insisted that what women workers needed was the courage to ask for their rights with a loud voice. But, just as in the Depression years of the thirties, men's work was again the priority. The arguments about equality for women were to continue until the end of the decade, when *Adam's Rib* was released, with Katharine Hepburn again playing the part of a strident, outspoken heroine. But *Adam's Rib* was to be the last of the 'battle of the sexes' romantic comedies to openly acknowledge the fierce struggle for equality that had been rekindled by the war, at least for the time being.

His Girl Friday (1940)

Directed by Howard Hawks; screenplay by Charles Lederer
(from the play *Front Page* by Ben Hecht and Charles
Macarthur); starring Rosalind Russell and
Cary Grant

'Tell me, is the Lord of the Universe in?'

His Girl Friday contains no hint of fairytale fantasy. Instead
Howard Hawks plunges us straight into the two dominant issues
of the forties: the battle of the sexes and the issue of a woman
working in a man's world. The film relies on the realism of the
gritty, hard-bitten world of journalism to punch its message
home. The film is about love, but this is a hard, tough look at
love, raising difficult but fascinating questions about what
makes us love the kind of people we choose; about compatibility; conflicting wants and needs; and the devious ploys some
people will resort to when attempting to get what they want.
These themes are a natural follow-on from Hawks' earlier film
Bringing Up Baby, only then the devious manipulator was
Susan, who used all her wit, intelligence and feminine wiles in
order to trap her man. In *His Girl Friday* Hawks reverses the
roles, making the devious manipulator the man, and the result
feels altogether more serious and more dangerous. (In *Front
Page* – which was both a play and a film, the latter directed by
Billy Wilder – the two main characters were men. It was Hawks'
idea to rewrite one of the parts for a woman and so turn the
story into a romantic comedy.)

When the film opens, Hildy (Rosalind Russell) walks into the
offices of the *Morning Post* wearing a truly amazing coat: slim-
fitted waist, wide padded shoulders, a bewildering array of
diagonal stripes that bump into each other and a matching
pillbox hat (it's altogether an outfit to put eighties power-
dressing to shame). 'Tell me is the Lord of the Universe in?' she

asks the telephonists. On learning that he is, she tells Bruce, the bashful fiancé she has in tow, to wait. She's come to see Walter Burns (Cary Grant), the editor of the paper, who is also her ex-husband. She walks into Walter's office just as he is plotting how to get a reprieve for a man condemned to hang in the morning. 'Well,' Walter says to Hildy, 'it's the first time I ever double-crossed a governor, what can I do for you?' Hildy sits cross-legged on his desk, Walter tosses her a cigarette and they soon slip into a familiar combative banter. 'Been seeing me in your dreams?' Walter asks. 'No,' Hildy replies, 'mama doesn't dream about you any more Walter, you wouldn't know the old girl now.'

Within minutes of Hildy walking into Walter's office we have got a picture of the entire history of their relationship leading to their present situation. Five years earlier Walter had taken 'a little college girl from the school of journalism . . . a doll-faced hick . . . and made a great reporter out of her.' His comments are deliberately chosen to rile Hildy and she instantly rises to the bait, pointing out that he wouldn't have taken her if she hadn't been 'doll-faced'. Walter doesn't see anything wrong in that – hers was the only face in the office he could look at without shuddering. Anyway, once he had made her what she is they became a team, 'I need you, you need me, the paper needs both of us and everything would have been fine if you hadn't made me marry you and spoil everything,' he finishes with a broad grin. 'I suppose I proposed to you?' Hildy demands, outraged. 'Well you practically did, making goo-goo eyes at me for two years until I broke down,' Walter replies, pretending to be the aggrieved party. Hildy is so speechless with fury she hits him.

Walter is the kind of man who will only show weakness if he is pretending. He's not the kind of man to risk expressing anything as banal or sentimental as a real emotion. For Walter feelings are like ideas; things to be tossed around and played with. Hildy knows him well enough to know that's his game and, although she gets infuriated by the way he twists everything to his own advantage, she also clearly enjoys the energy, stimulation and competitive nature of their banter almost as much as he does. This is Hildy's problem; she got sucked into Walter's world once and unless she's very wary she might get sucked in again. Ever since she left him Walter has been relentlessly trying to get her back, phoning her 'twenty times a day' and inundating her with telegrams. His masterstroke was when she was getting her divorce; he sent an airplane to write in the sky above the courthouse, 'Hildy, don't be hasty. Remember my dimple, Walter', which apparently delayed the divorce for twenty minutes while the judge went outside to take a look. The sheer audacity, as well as the charm, of such a gesture might have melted most women, but Hildy's determination to break free of him is stronger than that.

She finally tells him what she has really come to see him for – she's quitting the paper and getting married again, tomorrow. For the first time Walter looks shocked and genuinely worried as he racks his brains trying to think of a way out of this one. He tells her she can't quit the business, 'she's a newspaper man'. This, as Hildy points out, is the essence of her problem. She doesn't want to be a newspaper man, she wants to be a woman with a normal life, a home and children. Bruce, the man she is marrying tomorrow, is good, kind, considerate, the kind of man who forgets the office when he is with her, and he doesn't treat her like an errand boy. 'Sounds like I ought to marry him. What's his name?' Walter wisecracks.

The irony here is that, whereas most men would want their wives to be a woman first and a reporter second, if at all, Walter wants her to be like a man, or as the film's title suggests, to be 'his girl Friday'. Not that he wants her to be his equal. When it comes to power Walter is boss, he is the lord of his universe; as Hildy pointed out in her opening line. Just how devious, manipulative and utterly ruthless Walter is prepared to be when it comes to getting what he wants, becomes clearer as the story progresses. He has no qualms about lying and cheating. He will say anything to anybody to get a story or to keep Hildy – in Walter's world these two things are of paramount and equal importance. The crucial difference between Hildy and Walter is that, although she's as bright, clever and witty as he is, and she can put up a good fight, she's also honest, straightforward and speaks her mind; Walter keeps his mind to himself and says what he thinks will get him what he wants. This means Walter knows exactly where he is with her and Hildy never knows where she is with him. Therefore, although they both like to think they know the other well enough to handle each other, Walter has the edge on Hildy, as he demonstrates when he says he wants to meet Bruce, whom he refers to as 'her paragon'. Hildy doesn't think this is a good idea but, as soon as Walter suggests she is afraid to introduce them, she rises to the bait – of course she's not afraid.

Walter steamrollers the couple into letting him take them out to lunch. In the restaurant he patronizes poor earnest Bruce mercilessly. 'Where are you going to live? At home with your mother, that will be nice.' He grins at Hildy as he scores yet another point and she kicks him under the table. Unsuspecting, Bruce talks happily about his insurance business, how his work 'really helps people. Not when they are alive of course, but afterwards, that's what counts.' 'Oh really?' Walter raises his eyebrow in amusement. This time Hildy kicks the waiter by mistake and the poor man cries out in pain. The implications of Hildy's choice are becoming clearer by the minute: a dull life with cautious, honest Bruce where the future is more important than the present, or an exciting life with dishonest Walter who is rude and cavalier and lives for the excitement of the moment.

Finally Walter plays his trump card. He talks emotionally about the injustice of the case of the poor man who is due to hang in the morning. If Hildy would agree to write about the case she could 'save that poor devil's life' and still get the six o'clock train with Bruce. She refuses, so he decides to work on Bruce: 'You'll be going into your marriage with blood on your hands. All through the years you will remember that a man got hanged because she was too selfish to wait two hours.' Bruce is impressed and Walter grins – he's won! But it would be simply too much for Hildy to concede total defeat (leaving aside the fact that she secretly wants to do the story), so she makes Walter agree to take out one of Bruce's life insurance policies as a quid pro quo.

Much of the remaining film takes place in the press room above the courthouse, where Hildy is warmly welcomed by all the hard-nosed reporters who are busy playing cards while the gallows are being built outside in the courtyard below. Hildy is immediately at home in their company and excited and stimulated by what she insists will be her last assignment. As soon as Hildy leaves to go to interview the condemned man, the hacks begin taking bets on how long Hildy's next doomed marriage will last. They just can't see her as a housewife, having babies and changing nappies. Neither do they believe that Walter Burns, the man who had one of his journalists thrown into jail for merely threatening to quit, will let her get married.

There is an interesting parallel here between the two countdowns: one to the hanging of the condemned man in the morning; and the other to Hildy's marriage the next day which, by implication, for Hildy will be another kind of death. Also the moral issues underlying the story have become more complex, as have the conflicting forces behind Hildy's decision to quit journalism and make a bid for a more wholesome, rounded, feminine lifestyle. When she interviews the condemned man it is soon clear that he is a stooge, an innocent victim of corruption on the part of local politicians. So although Walter is a schemer and a conniver, his cause is ultimately honourable. At heart Hildy is an idealistic journalist strongly motivated by her desire to uncover the truth, but the world of journalism is full of cynicism, dirty tricks, lies and false intrigue, and it is incompatible with her desire for a family life. In both of the important aspects of her life she is pulled in opposing directions: she's trying to quit the work she clearly loves and to get away from the powerful dominating attractive man, whom we suspect she loves.

The fact that Bruce is also dumb sways the odds in Walter's favour, until Hildy hears that Bruce is in jail (he's been stitched up by Walter to get him out of the way). Hildy flies into a rage and phones Walter to tell him, 'I wouldn't cover the burning of Rome for you if they were just lighting it up.' She dramatically tears up the story she has written for him and announces to her audience of impressed hacks that she's leaving, she's going to be a woman, not a news-making machine, she's 'going to have babies and take care of them, give them cod liver oil and watch their teeth grow'. But no sooner does one part of her warring self make a decision than another part of her self snatches it away. Outside there are sounds of gunshots: the condemned man has broken out of jail. The hacks all grab the phones to call their editors with the news, and Hildy phones Walter – she can't resist it, the excitement of a breaking story is too much for her. In other words she may want to be a good wife and mother but the thrill and stimulation of her work is going to be hard to give up.

After still more twists and turns in the plot, as is usual in farce, all the strands come together in a penultimate scene before the climax. Hildy is alone in the press room when the condemned man rushes in like a pathetic frightened animal. She hides him in a huge leather-bound desk. All the reporters come back having given up their hunt for him. Bruce's surprisingly aggressive mother turns up to reprimand Hildy for how badly she is treating her son, who is once more in jail on a trumped-up charge of Walter's. (The suggestion here, that behind every weak man there lurks a dominating woman, is reminiscent of Hawks' theme in *Bringing Up Baby*.) Walter turns up just as Hildy is about to go and find Bruce. Once more Walter demonstrates how he knows her better than she knows herself. 'How many times she has got a murderer locked up in a desk?' he asks her. This is a once in a lifetime story, she's got the outcome of the election in the palm of her hand, this is front-page stuff: 'Never mind the European war, we've got something bigger than that.' Walter is like Mephistopheles tempting Faust, and it works, Hildy is flattered. When Bruce arrives she's too busy writing her story to talk to him. 'Hildy, I don't think you ever loved me at all,' Bruce tells her plaintively and leaves with his mother to catch the train.

Finally, when Hildy and Walter are celebrating their achievement – the condemned man's reprieve and the nailing of a couple of corrupt politicians in the process – Walter plays his trump card. He tells Hildy she had better get going to find Bruce. At first Hildy doesn't know what to make of his apparent about-turn. But Walter insists that he is trying to be noble for a change; he might have made fun of Bruce but that's because he was jealous. He now realizes that Bruce can give her the kind of life she wants, and he can't. Hildy is devastated and begins to cry. She's crying because, now that he's sending her away to be with Bruce, she's realized that she doesn't want to go. For a brief moment Walter appears genuinely concerned by her tears, but the next minute he is on the phone to his deputy triumphantly telling him Hildy's coming back to the office and the good news is they are going to get married again! He's forgotten to pop the question directly to Hildy but she's delighted anyway. She wants a proper honeymoon this time – they spent their first honeymoon down a coal mine covering a story. At that moment the phone rings for Walter, another big story is breaking; there goes their second honeymoon.

Through superior manipulative skill, Walter has won. He has got Hildy back and entirely on his own terms. If he has learnt anything at all from the course of events portrayed in the story, it only reinforces what he knew already; that he's good at getting what he wants. Hildy on the other hand, when she finally allows herself to listen to her real feelings, realizes that marrying Bruce as an antidote to Walter isn't the answer to her problems. But other than acknowledging that she has really been in love with Walter all along, she's no nearer getting the changes she wanted in their relationship and in her life; nothing has altered.

His Girl Friday is a brilliant portrayal of the dilemmas faced by many women, past and present, as they try to juggle their desire for marriage and children with the demands of a challenging career, and the additional problem of accepting that many men just don't have these choices to make. It also brilliantly explores that other perennial problem; although many ambitious women know they ought to prefer men like Bruce who are good, kind and caring, they are more attracted to powerful men like Walter. Like the mental equivalent of a good judo match, a battle of wits with a powerful partner is stimulating and exhilarating. It's great to be stretched to our limits both physically and mentally; it's fun and it's sexy. The problem is that in many power struggles, particularly those between men and women, the partners are not equal. And, if the woman attempts to fight for her corner in a man's world, playing a game he has been in training for all his life, the battle so often ends with women like Hildy feeling confused and cross because something about the battle just wasn't fair. Maybe she wasn't ruthless enough or her femininity got in the way? If only she could put her finger on precisely what it was, then maybe she can win next time.

We are left with the uneasy feeling that Hildy is back where she was before she divorced Walter. This ending is completely believable as far as their relationship is concerned and it certainly doesn't resort to sentimentality. Hildy's story is uncomfortably familiar – we think we are making a break for freedom and a fresh start, only to find ourselves back in the same old predicament, repeating the same old pattern. This, it seems to me, is especially true of love stories.

Woman Of The Year (1942)

Directed by George Stevens; screenplay by Ring Lardner and
Michael Kanin; starring Katharine Hepburn and Spencer Tracy

> 'The outstanding woman of the year isn't a woman
> at all!'

What are the essential requirements for a successful relationship?
This question appears to be eminently reasonable and most people
would probably agree that the ideal is for both parties to be
equally loving and caring for each other and not to take each other
for granted. Although given the complexities of many people's
lives this ideal is not always easy to achieve. This is the question
posed by *Woman of the Year* and the story invites us to share in
the difficult journey a couple makes when attempting to achieve
the ideal, particularly as the relationship appears to be threatened
by the woman's ambition and success. The disturbing aspect of
the film is how the story invites us to share unquestioningly in an
at times almost savage attack on its heroine, Tess Harding
(Katharine Hepburn), and by implication all women who aspire
to taking their place alongside men on the world stage.

The subtlety, and consequently the insidious nature, of the
attack is that it is not led by the hero, Sam Craig (Spencer Tracy),
who is a kind, considerate and tolerant man. It is precisely
because we like Sam so much and we recognize his vulnerability
that we identify with him and hate to see him hurt, particularly
by a woman like Tess. This is how the film's criticism of Tess
becomes enmeshed in the very texture and structure of the story
– it seeps out of the pores of almost every scene. The more Tess
hurts Sam, the more angry we become with her. The fact that
Sam is slow to fight back on his own behalf makes us want to
fight back for him. Implicit in the story is the unassailable
message that Sam is behaving well and Tess is behaving badly
and she needs her comeuppance.

All this may suggest that we could simply discount *Woman of the Year* for being a bad film – but, frustratingly, the film has too many good qualities to enable us to dispose of it so easily. One of these qualities, which is crucial to redeeming Tess's character from the self-centred egoist that she appears to be, is the fact that Sam loves her, and through his eyes we too see Tess as loveable, despite what the film presents as her obvious flaws. The casting is important here. When Katharine Hepburn and Spencer Tracy are together on screen they appear to light up in each other's eyes. Theirs is not just a sexual chemistry; the feelings they emanate when they are together are more profound – we feel that they really do love each other. We now know that these two actors were involved in a secret, powerful and enduring real-life love affair, which may in some part explain the sense of love and compatibility that seems to unite them on screen. Although, as two brilliant performers, they would both be perfectly capable of acting as if they hated each other, if the script called for it. But in *Woman of the Year* the aspiration of love, as represented by Hepburn and Tracy, appears to transcend the characterizations of Tess and Sam and even the storyline of the film itself.

Woman of the Year was released in 1942, the year after America entered the war, and through the character of Tess Harding the film quickly reminds us of the international political situation. Tess uses her boundless energy, formidable intellect and talent as a writer and public speaker to express her opinions on subjects as wide ranging as Hitler and the war in Europe, international politics generally, numerous humanitarian causes, women's rights and how sport is a waste of time and energy. Sam Craig, a humble sports correspondent, happens to hear her air this last opinion on the radio and retaliates by attacking her in his sports column. Tess responds and very soon they are conducting a very public acerbic argument via their respective newspaper columns, until Sam's editor decides to broker a peace between them and summons Sam to his office to meet Tess Harding in person. Sam's first sight of Tess, and ours, is via a slow pan up her very beautiful leg to where she is bending over to fix her stocking top. Their eyes meet, they soften, their mutual attraction is instant. Could this be love at first sight? And if so will such a love prove to be strong enough to overcome their differences?

The first part of the film concerns their dating and courting problems. Sam takes Tess to a baseball match where, although she tries hard, she is clearly not very interested the game. In return she invites Sam to her apartment for drinks. He turns up, smartly dressed and carrying a large bouquet of flowers, touchingly anticipating a romantic evening, only to find Tess in the throws of a crowded party made up largely of foreign intellectuals. Sam finds himself ignored, snubbed and lonely. To make matters worse, Tess's work schedule – organized by Gerald, her condescending male secretary (which in itself is an interesting role reversal) – is so busy that the only way Sam can get to see her at all is by offering to chauffeur her from one meeting to the next. The point of view of the film becomes blatantly clear when Sam arrives at a community meeting hall in time to catch the end of Tess's speech on the subject of women's rights. 'Our place is no longer only in the home, it is also in the first line of battle,' she rhetorically pronounces to her large all-female audience, while trying to ignore their laughter as Sam, consumed with embarrassment, accidentally stumbles on to the stage behind her.

Many men at the time might have taken flight after such a public declaration of her views on the role of women, but not Sam. In contrast to Tess's very public and extrovert ambition, Sam is an absolute sweetie. He doesn't ask for much, or certainly nowhere near as much as many men would demand from a relationship. He could even prove to be the perfect man for a woman like Tess precisely because he is so tolerant and understanding. This is what Tess's Aunt Ellen thinks. When Sam seeks her advice about his relationship with Tess, Aunt Ellen unhesitatingly advises Sam to ask Tess to marry him. Aunt Ellen was herself once a women's rights activist but now she is an ageing, lonely spinster. The suggestion here is that unless Tess gets her priorities right she (and by implication all women actively involved in the women's movement) will end up sad, lonely and full of regrets, like Aunt Ellen.

George Stevens' brilliance as a director (as displayed in his earlier films such as *Alice Adams*) lies in his strong identification with sensitive people and his ability to portray every nuance of how their feelings are continually hurt by the insensitive people to whom they are invariably, perhaps inevitably, attracted. Consequently, each time Sam is snubbed or taken for granted by Tess, and the way she invariably assumes that her own work and interests are more important than his, makes her seem more monstrous and makes us feel Sam's hurt as if it were our own. But if the story were simply a study of how an insensitive person hurts a sensitive person the audience would quickly lose patience with Sam for being weak and foolish and start hoping that he quickly finds another woman who will love him properly. For any love story to work we have to want it to succeed, which in this case means that we have to see 'the good' in Tess as well as 'the bad' and we have to want 'the good' in her to overcome 'the bad'.

Sam takes Tess to a local bar, a place that is a part of his simple unassuming world, in stark contrast to Tess's social circle of the rich, powerful and well connected. There he mentions how much he likes the freckles on her nose. Tess is moved, no one has mentioned those since she was twelve. He also plucks up the courage to tell her that he loves her. 'Even when I'm sober?' Tess jokes. 'Even when you are brilliant,' Sam replies. Although we don't doubt Sam's sincerity when he says this, it's clear that for him the more loveable side of Tess is the non-threatening, vulnerable, fun-loving child within her; the problem for Sam and their love story is Tess's stunning success. If only she would stop being brilliant all the time and allow herself to once more be that ordinary freckled kid, then everything between them would be all right.

The second half of the film is about their marriage. The wedding itself is a hurried ceremony in order to fit it into Tess's busy diary. The wedding night is even worse. While Sam eagerly changes into his brand-new pyjamas and dressing gown (we can see the label still pinned to the back), a refugee friend of Tess's turns up on the doorstep, having recently escaped from a European concentration camp. Rather than telling him to go away because it is her wedding night, Tess is eager to hear all about his experiences in war-torn Europe. 'Isn't this the most thrilling night of your life?' she breathes to Sam when he shyly enters the nuptial bedroom only to find her ensconced in conversation with the refugee, who is sitting on their bed with no intention of leaving. Knowing what we now know about the concentration camps, Tess's interest in her refugee friend, even though it is her wedding night, is understandable. But George Stevens again focuses our attention on the way Sam is hurt, however inadvertently, by Tess who always puts her self and her work first.

As their marriage settles into a routine, things go from bad to worse. When Sam arrives home from work, Tess is too busy to notice that he is tired and hungry and anyway she can't cook. Gerald, the secretary, treats Sam as if he's little more than a servant and Tess doesn't even notice when Sam buys himself a new hat. But the incident that precipitates the real crisis in their relationship is when, at breakfast one morning, Tess asks him how he feels about having a child. Sam assumes she is pregnant and is beside himself with delight, confessing that he hopes it will be a boy. 'It is a boy,' Tess assures him and fetches from the hall a small frightened Greek refugee boy who speaks no English. Tess explains that she was addressing a meeting of the refugee committee and they asked her to adopt a child. How could she refuse? She would have looked idiotic. In other words she cares more about her public image than she does about the child.

Tess, of course, has no idea how to look after and love a husband, let alone a child. Her final condemnation arrives just a few days later when she is to be awarded the title of America's Woman of the Year. Sam's long-suffering patience with her snaps when it becomes clear that she intends to go to the awards ceremony, leaving the little boy alone in their apartment. 'The outstanding woman of the year isn't a woman at all,' Sam tells her in a fit of anger. He refuses to accompany her to the ceremony and instead takes the boy back to the refugee orphanage where the child joyfully greets his old friends. On the orphanage radio Sam hears Tess being introduced at the awards ceremony as a woman 'who so magnificently symbolizes the full and rounded life, the glorious emancipation of womanhood in this country'. The irony of these words in the face of Tess's obvious failure as a wife and a mother couldn't be more clear. Sam returns home, packs his bags and leaves her.

Tess's redemption comes when she realizes what she has lost. Tess's father, a widower, and Aunt Ellen are getting married – Ellen's long spinsterhood is over. Tess is shocked. 'I never thought of you as being anybody's wife . . . I always felt you were above marriage,' she tells her aunt, who has also been her mother substitute and role model as a woman. But Ellen is radiantly happy for the first time in the film. Tess plays the wedding march on the piano for them and listens to the words of their marriage ceremony with tears in her eyes: 'Let the joys of each be the joys of both, the sorrows of each be the sorrows of both, be not moved in your devotion, believe in the ideal . . .' Tess resolutely drives to Sam's new house.

The final sequence, with Tess trying to cook Sam breakfast, is hilariously funny because of her total ineptness in the kitchen; the coffee boils over, the waffles bubble out of control, the toast burns, but she is determined to prove to Sam that she has seen the error of her ways – she can change and be a good wife. Sam watches her antics with amusement but finally tells her that he doesn't want her to be 'that kind of woman', he just wants her to be Tess Harding Craig. We are still trying to work out what this means for Sam when Gerald, Tess's secretary, turns up with a champagne bottle. He's come to tell her she's scheduled to launch a new battleship that morning. Sam now demonstrates a side to his character we have never seen before: he loses his patience with Gerald and physically throws him out of the house. A few moments later Sam comes back indoors with the broken bottle in his hand. 'I've just launched Gerald,' he announces triumphantly. The film then ends as the happy couple kiss.

It is tempting to sit back in satisfaction and enjoy this ending at face value. Tess has changed, she has learnt that she must move her husband to the top of her list of priorities in life. Sam, by ejecting Gerald (the unacceptable feminized man) from the house, has demonstrated that he is capable of asserting his masculinity in the time-honoured way. Now they have established at least a semblance of the proper gender balance; they are free to be happy. At least that was the conventional mythology. The film also redeems itself because, irrespective of gender, the ideal – that both parties in a relationship need to be equally loving and caring of each other – is so clearly sound. Even at the very end Sam tells her that he doesn't want her to be the kind of woman who can cook amazing breakfasts, he just wants her to be Tess Harding Craig, in other words, herself and his wife.

And yet, although the tone of the film may have seemed eminently reasonable to a contemporary audience, particularly as Tess is so insensitive, I remain disturbed by the journey we have been on to arrive at the ending. Imagine how the story would play if Tess were the man – his work would appear important, impressive, exciting and intellectually stimulating. The fact that he had a busy and somewhat domineering secretary might prove irritating but it would also be normal. If he were also as handsome as Tess is beautiful and as fun to be with, he might appear to many women a perfect husband. There would be problems of course, probably somewhat similar problems – his wife might feel that there is not enough time for her in his busy schedule and that their relationship is suffering as a consequence. For many women there might also be the problem of her lacking in confidence or feeling slighted by his brilliant friends, or indeed by refugees turning up in the bedroom on their wedding night. Her job may appear less important than his and they would have the usual issues concerning housework, cooking and wanting a baby. All of which are Sam's problems. But if the roles were reversed, if Tess were Tom and Sam were Samantha, would we care so much about Samantha's problems? Would Samantha want Tom to be Tom Harding Craig, himself and her husband? Would anyone even bother to make a film about them?

What is good and what is bad in any of us is not merely a matter of objective morality, it is also a question of our individual judgement, priorities and preferences. At no point in *Woman of the Year* are we invited even to consider the possibility that Sam might be good, but somewhat unimaginative, even dull for a woman as intellectually lively as Tess. Our judgement of Tess's bad character traits is so expertly steered by George Stevens' seductive directing skills that we find ourselves caught up in the conventional value system of the film almost despite ourselves.

No Time for Love *(1943)*

Directed by Mitchell Leisen; screenplay by Claude Binyon;
starring Claudette Colbert and Fred McMurray

'Superman saved by a lady!'

No Time for Love falls easily into 'the battle of the sexes'
category of comedy, but into its heady brew it pours a further,
equally contentious and hotly debated issue of the period – the
class struggle. Two themes bob to the surface of the mixture –
pride and prejudice. In fact the weakest thing about *No Time for
Love* is its eminently forgettable title. Far better to have called
the film *Pride and Prejudice*, if Jane Austen hadn't already
snapped it up.

At the outset of the film we meet Katherine (Claudette Colbert),
one of the foremost photographers in America, although she
prefers her photographs to be aesthetically beautiful rather than
getting her hands dirty dealing with the pressing issues of real life
– which is why her editor at *Mirror* magazine gives her the
toughest, dirtiest assignment he's got. He sends her to take
pictures of a gang of Irish American 'sandhogs' who are building
a massive tunnel under the river. The men are stripped to the
waist and covered in dirt and sweat, in stark contrast to Kate
who arrives smartly but appropriately dressed in trousers and
shirt, donning the regulation hardhat and insisting on carrying
her own equipment. The men's immediate reaction to her is to
complain; it's bad luck to bring a woman into the tunnel. Kate
responds by imperiously telling them not to be so childish. Her
attention is then attracted by a magnificent naked male torso.
She wants to take its picture but its owner, Ryan (Fred
McMurray), refuses to pose for her despite his foreman telling
him the president of the tunnel project has instructed the men to
co-operate with Kate. 'Maybe she's his type,' Ryan throws back
at him dismissively, demonstrating what he thinks of Kate's

arrogance and that of the rest of her class. He goes back to his work and Kate sets about taking her pictures accompanied by a chorus of wolf-whistles. Suddenly she sees Ryan fall: a heavy machine is about to crush him to death. Kate throws down her camera and leaps to push him out of the way.

Has the men's premonition of bad luck come true? A more likely explanation is that the accident was caused by their lack of concentration with a woman around. Whatever, Ryan's humiliation amuses them. 'Superman, saved by a lady,' they jeer at him mercilessly. He reacts furiously and a fistfight breaks out. Kate, the intrepid professional, takes pictures. On their way back to the surface of the tunnel Kate informs the sulking Ryan that he's got a chip on his shoulder. This, of course, is a classic insult to a working-class man, particularly one who is still nursing his injured masculine pride. He retaliates by attacking her most vulnerable spot, her feminine pride: 'You've been on the prowl ever since you met me. Aren't you old enough to know it?' Kate boils over at his implication, that he knows she finds him attractive: 'You conceited ape! You are living proof that men can exist without mentality . . . at home in my bedroom I have an inanimate object, a chair, that has ten times more quality and character than you.' She stalks off, forgetting that she has left her tripod behind. The causes for the outbreak of war are now clearly in place.

The next move is Ryan's. He turns up at Kate's apartment with the ruse of returning her lost tripod, but he also has a score to settle. 'When a guy gets to feeling he knows a little about women and then along comes something like you, it puts him back in short pants,' he complains and demands to see this chair that's better than him. He picks the chair up, compares it to his reflection in Kate's dressing-table mirror and informs her that there is a crucial difference: 'If you want to get away from a chair you get up and walk away from it. Try getting away from me.' He suddenly picks Kate up. She wriggles and threatens to scream if he doesn't let her go. So he kisses her. 'You coward, kissing a woman,' she hisses at him, furiously. 'What am I supposed to kiss?' he asks, picking up his hat. 'I feel better now. Got my long pants back on.'

This scene epitomizes traditional assumptions about what women, and men, really want. Ryan kisses Kate by force; she wriggles and struggles but really she enjoys it. When he's made his point – that he's the masterful man, the boss, he wears the pants – he puts her down. And she, at least on the surface, is furious, but secretly she liked it; secretly what a woman really wants is a man who wears the pants. The disturbing problem here is the small step between this position and the old adage that when 'a woman says no she means yes', which is, of course, a much more serious matter.

So, having re-established his masculine pride Ryan appears to have won this round, but he hasn't won the war. He still has the rest of her class to contend with, as he discovers when he meets her society friends on his way out. They excitedly gather around him, as if this 'sandhog' is a freak in a side show. They plead with him to entertain them by acting out the fight they have seen in Kate's photos. One of Kate's friends, a composer called Roger, strikes up a few chords on the piano to give the show a musical accompaniment. For a moment it looks as if the upper-class dilettantes may well succeed in making a fool of Ryan, but suddenly he acts out the fight for real and smashes two of the men's heads together – one of whom is Kate's fiancé.

We discover the effect on Kate of this display of raw masculinity in one of the funniest dream sequences in cinema history. As she tosses and turns in her sleep we see a huge dressing-table chair flying through the air. Kate, wearing a diaphanous dress is fighting off the attention of a wicked man who looks suspiciously like her fiancé. She breaks free from him, falls through the air and is caught by Ryan, dressed in the comic-strip costume of Superman. He flies with her back to the chair. There Kate's fiancé tries to shoot Ryan, but to no effect as the bullets merely bounce off his manly chest. Ryan throws the hapless fiancé off the chair, adopts the classic Tarzan pose and triumphantly beats his chest. Kate is now writhing in her bed as if in some kind of sexual ecstasy. The meaning of Kate's dream could not be clearer, not only to the audience, but also to Kate herself. Her unconscious is obviously telling her she's attracted to Ryan. But how can an educated and sophisticated woman like her be attracted to a muddy man who works in a tunnel and is not even capable of an intelligent conversation?

The idea that it is not just men whose base sexual appetites are controlled by their hormones, but women can also be similarly afflicted without anything so pure as love to justify their feelings, is markedly different from the more sexually reticent heroines of the thirties comedies. It also reflects the greater sexual permissiveness generated by the war. The reality of the lives of many women in the audience was that when men were leaving for the front, perhaps never to return, love affairs were frequently short, passionate and highly sexually charged – there simply isn't time for the niceties of a fairytale romance when tomorrow you may be alone or dead. Although what couples did privately and what they were prepared to admit to publicly was quite a different matter.

But whatever was really going on between couples in war-time, Hollywood still believed that it was necessary to position itself very carefully between what was publicly acceptable and privately desirable. Hence Kate, while acknowledging her fantasies, must valiantly resist her dangerous sexual feelings. In order to do this she devises a wonderfully convoluted plan, which she explains to her sister who arrives for breakfast the next morning. She has decided to get to know the real Ryan, to counteract her ridiculous dream version of him. Then, she asserts confidently, she is bound to become bored with him because he's merely a not-very-bright manual labourer. In other words, if she uses her rational powers to quell her inconvenient sexual urges, she will be cured of her obsession!

At that moment the object of her obsession turns up on her doorstep. Ryan's boss has suspended him (as a result of *Mirror* magazine's publication of Kate's photos) and he's come to complain. Seizing the opportunity to put her plan into action, Kate offers to hire him as her assistant, as if to make amends for his misfortune. Amused by the prospect of working for a woman, Ryan, unsuspectingly, takes the job. But soon, although he conforms to Kate's prejudices about his brawn, his brains prove more difficult for her to pigeonhole. He continually out-manoeuvres her. On a photo shoot in a vaudeville theatre he convinces one of the showgirls not only that he is Kate's boss but also that he owns *Mirror* magazine. Kate is forced to jealously stand aside while Ryan borrows her car to take the showgirl out on a date. He also skilfully sabotages her photography session with the man voted to have the most beautiful body in America. The two sequences both play deliciously with the idea of stereotypical sex symbols, male and female, and how, despite ourselves, we measure our own powers of sexual attraction against such stereotypes. 'Brazen, bleached and not a brain in her head, just the type for Ryan,' Kate declares angrily to her sister, when she prints the photos of the showgirl – deliberately reinforcing her prejudice in an attempt to ward off the threat to her self-esteem.

Kate confesses her despair of her ill-conceived plan ever working to her composer friend, Roger, who suggests, as a new tactic, that she should play the class card. If she takes both him and Ryan to a posh restaurant, the kind of place where the average working man 'could be thrown into a panic by a waiter's squeaky shoes', then Ryan's lack of social graces and amusing conversation will be starkly revealed. The problem is the reverse happens: in Ryan's company it's the restaurant that seems boring and when he suggests they go to 'a joint with decent food' Kate jumps at the chance to get away.

Murphy's is a rough Irish American eating house and the back room is full of sandhogs from the tunnel project. The backroom also has a rule – 'no women'. Despite, or because of, her plan being spoiled Kate is clearly enjoying herself as she ignores their rule and sits down. Very soon a fight begins to break out between the men. Kate, ever the intellectual, tries to persuade them that if fights are their way of establishing who is boss, they could find that out without anybody bleeding to death. Her solution is a game of musical chairs. She busily arranges the chairs as she explains the rules to the bemused men. Very soon they are marching obediently around the chairs, concentrating hard and eyeballing each other aggressively, while Roger plays the piano. The music stops, they each try to grab a chair and pandemonium breaks out. The scene is, of course, an hilarious metaphor for the major issue on the minds of the contemporary audience – men fighting as a means for resolving disputes or establishing who is leader is the very essence of war. It is also becoming apparent that Kate is wrong about Ryan being all brawn and no brains. At the end of the scene he is the one left calmly sitting on the only unbroken chair. He has not only outwitted her, he has also won the game. He grins at her, 'You're right, this is a lot better than fighting.'

Afterwards they drive to Kate's apartment and sit talking in the car. The mood between them has mellowed considerably. 'If you say "Ryan I'm nuts about you" you might find out I feel the same way about you,' Ryan tells her. And at last Kate confesses, 'I'm nuts about you Ryan.' But just as they begin a passionate kiss, Kate's sister rushes angrily out of the apartment block to save Kate from 'the apeman'. She tells Ryan about how Kate has been trying to make a fool of him in order to get over her adolescent attraction. And she sternly reminds Kate of her commitments, she is after all already engaged to be married to another man. The idea that Kate has deliberately made a fool of him is too much. Ryan angrily walks away and their relationship appears to be over.

The theme of pride now overtakes the theme of prejudice. Also the whole tenor of the film changes as it begins to address more serious issues: the need for brave and courageous men in times of war, and the danger women like Kate pose to men's sense of their own masculinity.

A newspaper headline introduces the final part of the film: 'Cave-ins Block Tunnel Project'. The article goes on to say that only one man can save the tunnel and that man is Ryan. *Mirror* magazine assigns Kate to cover the story. Once in the tunnel with all the other reporters, Kate learns the truth about Ryan. He only worked as a sandhog in order to familiarize himself with the tunnel's construction problems. In fact he is a skilled engineer and has invented a tunneling machine – the very machine that is now about to be tested in order to save the tunnel. Ryan tells the press pack that he's sorry they can't photograph his machine in action but it's too dangerous for them in that part of the tunnel. On hearing this Kate realizes there is something she can do for Ryan to make amends. She hides under the tarpaulin that covers Ryan's machine. When Ryan and his men start work on the tunnel, Kate slips out from her hiding place and begins to photograph the machine in action. But her flashbulbs distract the men's concentration, the tunnel walls begin to crumble and the tunnel rapidly fills with mud. The men have no alternative but to abandon their work in order to save Kate's life. As a result Ryan's machine is declared a failure. It appears that the men are right; it is bad luck to allow women in the tunnel.

But Kate refuses to accept defeat. Back in the collapsed tunnel lies her camera with film in it that could prove that Ryan's machine did work. Without Ryan's knowledge she bravely risks her life by wading back through the river of mud to find her camera. The next newspaper headline is 'Ex-Sandhog Saves Tunnel Project'. We know that it is in fact Kate's bravery and her photographs that have saved both the tunnel and Ryan's career, but Ryan doesn't know this. Kate has sworn to secrecy the only two people who know the truth, the director of the tunnel project and her friend Roger. She insists that she doesn't want Ryan to feel indebted to her. The same newspaper announces her engagement to the publisher of *Mirror* magazine.

'Romantic marriage went out with smelling salts,' Kate tells her sister dejectedly as she prepares for her engagement party. 'Today it's a common sense institution. If you don't have intelligence enough to better your position, you deserve to fall in love and starve to death.' 'Okay,' her sister says wearily, 'I'm on your side, what do you want from me?' Kate looks at her despairingly, 'An argument you dope!'

There is a distinct similarity here to the ending of *It Happened One Night,* when Ellie (also played by Claudette Colbert) was prepared to settle for a man she didn't love for rational, rather than emotional, reasons, and an intermediary or cupid figure was needed to 'fix it'. In this case cupid is Kate's friend, Roger. He goes to see Ryan in his brand new office, reflecting his new status as a celebrated tunnel-saver, and tells Ryan straight that he is the one who should be marrying Kate. Roger also breaks his promise to Kate by telling Ryan that it was Kate's photographs that really saved the tunnel project. 'Why can't she leave me alone,' Ryan responds angrily, 'I've got pride. Just once in his life a guy likes to feel he's getting somewhere on his own.' Roger finally tells him the kind of truth that a man like Ryan can only take from another man, that he's a goof.

The film ends with Ryan charging into Kate's engagement party and, much to her relief, claiming her for his own by picking her up, slinging her over his shoulder and carrying her away with him.

The message of the film is clear: men have to be men for the war effort and women's job is not to undermine them, but to support them in the difficult, highly skilled, dirty and often dangerous work they have to do. But the film also takes up the baton on behalf of strong-minded and courageous women, although here the message is more convoluted. Kate's action, when she goes back into the tunnel, which is filling perilously with mud, in order to find her camera, is undoubtedly as brave as any deed we have seen performed by a man. But she has also learnt that a man and a woman can't have a proper relationship if the man feels indebted to the woman. In this sense the film is both presenting a radical new role for women and at the same time incorporating this new role within the traditional framework of the necessity for a woman to sacrifice any glory she has earned from her own achievements for the sake of the primacy of man's masculine pride. The final image, with 'caveman' Ryan carrying happily submissive Kate over his shoulder, of course simplifies this somewhat by resorting to the idea that beneath our superficial sophistication we all really want to be 'me Tarzans' or 'you Janes' in the jungle of life.

As far as the class struggle is concerned, the outcome is even more ambivalent. Ryan is not and never has been an average manual labourer, although Kate declares her feelings for him before she knows this. Kate's upper-class male friends are in no way presented as better than Ryan but, in order to give the future of their relationship real credibility, the story conveniently side-steps the class problem. By transforming Ryan into, not just an educated, highly skilled and innovative engineer but also a leader of men – just the kind of hero needed in times of war – the story finally re-enters the world of the fairytale where it takes just such a knight in shining armour to win a princess.

Adam's Rib (1949)

Directed by George Cukor; screenplay by Ruth Gordon and
Garson Kanin; starring Katharine Hepburn and Spencer Tracy

'What do you want, to give her another shot at him?'

Adam's Rib, released in 1949, presents an enviable and very
modern picture of a happily married couple – friends as well as
lovers, they both work and both enjoy sharing everything at
home. (There are no children, although this doesn't appear to be
an issue.) The film also captures the initial post-war optimism
for change and the confidence that, just as the suffragettes had
won the vote for women at the end of the First World War, so
the issue of women's rights would once more be high on the
agenda for debate. The question *Adam's Rib* poses is: Will the
push for women's equality threaten even the most modern
compatible relationships? With hindsight the very directness of
the film's subject matter, although now appearing somewhat
naive, also seems to be at least two decades before its time. It is
interesting to note here that the screenplay was written by a
male–female partnership.

Like *Woman of the Year*, made seven years earlier, *Adam's
Rib* stars Katharine Hepburn and Spencer Tracy, and again
captures the extraordinary essence of a couple ideally suited to
each other. But in contrast to the one-sided attack on the
successful working woman in *Woman of the Year*, which made
no bones about inviting us to identify with the man, and
therefore see the woman's behaviour as 'bad', George Cukor in
Adam's Rib attempts to explore both sides of the argument
about sexual equality. In fact much of the film, which could be
described as both a romantic comedy and a courtroom drama, is
structured around a court case where the issue of equality is
central and the audience is placed in a similar position to the
jury in that we have to weigh up the merits of both sides of the

argument in order to decide where we stand. Cukor also provocatively probes into the subtext of the theme by exploring the differences between the sexes in our techniques for winning arguments – as manifested in all sorts of subtle and not so subtle behaviour such as sulking, flirting, flattery, wheedling and crying in order to get our own way.

The film opens with a young woman, Doris Attinger (Judy Holliday), who, almost out of her mind with hurt and fury, shoots wildly at her husband because he is having an affair. A married couple, Adam (Spencer Tracy) and Amanda (Katharine Hepburn), read about the shooting in the morning papers while having breakfast in bed. Amanda immediately takes the wife's side and rails angrily against what she believes to be a double standard: how it's far more acceptable for men to have affairs and how much more sympathy there would be for a man who shot his wife for having an affair than there is for this poor woman who was probably only trying to keep her home intact. Adam scoffs at her – how do you keep your home intact by knocking off your husband? Amanda points out that the woman didn't knock him off. 'Okay,' Adam says, 'She tried, she missed. What do you want to do, give her another shot at him?' They are still annoyed when they arrive at work in their respective offices and we discover not only that they are both successful attorneys, but that Adam has been appointed to represent Mr Attinger's case for the prosecution. He phones Amanda to tell her the news and unwisely laughs at her furious response, saying 'you sound so cute when you get causey'. Amanda slams down the phone and without his knowledge she goes to see Doris Attinger to ask if she can be her defence attorney at the trial.

The battle lines between husband and wife are drawn. And so are their very different character portraits. Adam's character conforms to a set of standard masculine archetypes: cool, rational, solid, down-to-earth, in control – of himself at least. Amanda in contrast is typically feminine: hot-headed, passionate and somewhat out of control or 'causey' as Adam calls her. On the other hand, she is a qualified attorney, which would suggest she also has skills in rational argument and matters of law. But their approach to this case is very different. This is partly because Adam works in the District Attorney's office and therefore takes the cases that land on his desk, whereas Amanda works for a private law firm, which means she can 'ambulance chase' or go after the cases she wants. But Amanda is also the active one and Adam is more passive, which might suggest that the archetypes with which we traditionally define masculinity and femininity are not necessarily located in the separate genders – at least not in this household.

Their first interviews with their new clients are revealing. We know, because we saw the shooting, that Mr Attinger is a liar when he denies having an affair and paints a portrait of his wife as a calculating murderer and a 'fruitcake'. But Adam takes his account at face value. Amanda, in contrast, probes far more deeply into Doris Attinger's character and her statement about what happened. She learns that Doris is a simple, uneducated, working-class housewife and mother of three, whose husband started 'batting her around' eleven months before when his affair with the other woman began. Of course she wanted to kill him but only because she wanted him back. The irrationality of Doris's statement comes across as charming, amusing, sad, utterly honest and (dare I say it) deeply feminine, and she immediately arouses our sympathy – largely due to Judy Holliday's brilliant performance along with Cukor's directing. As Doris herself says, on the day of the shooting she was just 'doing everything in a dream, I was watching myself, but I couldn't help it', which is the legal lynchpin of Amanda's case – malicious intent is necessary to establish proof of attempted murder and Doris is just too guileless to be malicious.

That evening we are given an insight into the potential havoc the case might wreak on Adam and Amanda's marital bliss. Adam brings home a pretty flowery bonnet for Amanda to win back her favour after the morning's argument. It is not until they are in the middle of a dinner party that Amanda casually mentions she will be defending Doris Attinger. Adam is so shocked he drops the tray of drinks he's carrying and then goes into a sulk for the rest of the evening. Finally a full-scale row erupts in the bedroom. Adam demands that she drop the case. Amanda refuses. Adam retaliates by throwing down the gauntlet – 'I am going to cut you into twelve little pieces and feed you to the jury.' Amanda hugs him – at last he's accepted that she's taken the case.

It soon becomes clear that Adam may not find it so easy to carry out his threat. On their first day in court the judge overrules Adam's objections when Amanda quizzes potential male jurors and throws them off the jury selection if they appear to be prejudiced against women. In an attempt to show there are no hard feelings, Adam knocks his pen off the table and signals to Amanda that she should do the same. Their eyes meet under the table, Amanda flirtatiously lifts her skirt to show her white petticoat and Adam pretends to be shocked. Beneath the table is sexy and fun and uniquely theirs, free from whatever is going on in the world above, or so they would like to believe.

The case is portrayed in the newspapers as a *cause célèbre*, with Amanda as Doris Attinger's heroine in shining armour. At home in the evening Amanda tries extra hard to be the most perfect, loving wife in order to assuage her guilt and make Adam feel better – he is after all in many ways a perfect husband: attentive, sharing all the chores, loving. But she is in a dilemma; she's blossoming with her success, which she tries to tone down because she can see it hurts Adam, but she can't help it, she loves it. Adam on the other hand tries not to show that his ego is hurt, but it is. The truth of their situation is that neither one of them can win without the other failing. At this level the film is about the clash of their two egos.

Back in the courtroom Amanda establishes that Mr Attinger was having an affair and also that he hit his wife, frequently stayed out all night and despite all this still claims to be 'a good husband'. Amanda smiles knowingly at the jury and shrugs to underline the irony of his ridiculous claim. In retaliation Adam attempts to prove that Doris also behaved badly in the marriage by scolding her husband and making him a 'nervous wreck'. But the emotional impact of the testimony of the 'poor suffering husband' is nowhere near as powerful as Doris's tears when she talks about how she has three children and how the 'other woman' was threatening to break up her home. Adam then accuses her of being a shrew and an unstable irresponsible mother, which only makes her tears worse. From Adam's point of view this is a big mistake – nobody likes to see a man make a woman cry, least of all a jury. He appears cold and unfeeling and the jury look at him very disapprovingly. Amanda is now so angry with him she completely loses her temper and, ignoring the judge's attempt to bring the court to order, passionately quotes the playwright Congreve: 'Heaven has no rage, like love to hatred turned, Nor Hell a fury, like a woman scorned.'

Whether it's the verse that ennobles Amanda's case or merely the heat of her passion in contrast to Adam's cold attack, the press are unanimously on her side. At home in the evening, while the couple attempt to return to the normality of their married life and give each other a massage, Amanda can barely contain her delight that she has scored yet another triumph. Their neighbour, Kit, has even written a song about her which she sings along to as it plays on the radio. Adam suddenly slaps her bottom hard. He immediately feigns innocence but Amanda is angry: 'Typical, instructive, masculine brutality. It felt not only as if you meant to but as if you had a right to!' Adam admits that he is 'sore at her', she's having fun at his expense and to make matters worse she is 'shaking the law by the tail' and he doesn't like it: 'I'm ashamed of you, Amanda.' Amanda suddenly dissolves into tears. Adam doesn't buy it and walks away, but then he begins to feel guilty and tries to cajole her. Amanda shakes her head childishly at whatever he offers her until suddenly, when she's got him where she wants him she kicks him hard. 'Let's *all* be manly!' she announces and marches out of the room.

It's easy to see how the issues they are arguing about in court are being mirrored in the microcosm of their married life. They are both using their respective masculine and feminine character traits – Adam resorting to high-handed paternalism and Amanda to emotional petulance – in order to assert themselves and get their own way, and they are both furious with each other for doing so. They are playing the same game but by different rules and it's simply not fair – or to use courtroom language, it's not just.

In the next court scene Amanda doesn't pull her punches. In order to prove that women are equal to men, she calls as witnesses a variety of women who have equalled or outshone men in their professional lives. Her argument reaches its climax when she calls a middle-aged woman who looks more like a member of the women's temperance movement than the circus weightlifter and acrobat she professes to be, until she performs three backflips in front of the jury and then tells the judge she also 'does an open pyramid' where she supports five men. 'Surely you are not the only woman who does that,' Amanda wisecracks. Adam objects on the grounds that Amanda is insulting the dignity of the court. Amanda gestures to the strongwoman who proceeds to take hold of Adam's ankles and lift him high above her head, ignoring both Adam's and the judge's instructions to put him down. The court is in an uproar of laughter.

That evening when Amanda sees Adam packing his bags to leave her, she realizes she's gone too far and begs his forgiveness. But Adam is adamant; he accuses her of having contempt for the law, and what is marriage if it isn't a law? 'You get yourself set on some dimwitted cause regardless. And you don't care what it does to you, to me, to anybody . . . I'm old fashioned. I like two sexes. I want a wife not a competitor. If you want to be a big he-woman go and be it, but not with me.' We feel for Adam because he is vulnerable and with her strongwoman stunt Amanda did go too far (despite the fact that it was very funny) and Adam's case was certainly not being helped by a weak judge. On the other hand, Amanda's 'cause' is not dimwitted. She is carrying out her professional duty to defend a woman who, if she is not innocent of the deed, is innocent if Amanda can prove that Doris's action was an unpremeditated crime of passion and can further persuade the jury to judge her as they would a man. In this sense Amanda is showing as much respect for the law as Adam, whose own argument is based on an emotional assumption – that as a man his understanding of the law is superior to hers, rather than simply a different or an alternative interpretation.

On the final day in court Amanda eloquently sums up her case for the jury. She reminds them that men have killed and been set free, in wars and in self-defence. She asks them to look at Mrs Attinger and imagine her as a man; a good husband whose callous wife has betrayed him and who was only trying to defend his home. To aid the audience's imagination Cukor cuts to Doris Attinger sitting in her usual place in court, but now she is dressed as a man and as such she appears handsome but ineffectual. He then cuts to Mr Attinger whose gender has been similarly transformed, only he appears mean and unscrupulous as a woman. Amanda finally points out that each and every one of us is capable of attack if provoked, and concludes that there has been no murder attempt here, only a pathetic attempt by a neglected, maltreated wife to defend her home. In contrast Adam makes a complete mess of his summing-up speech. He starts by losing his temper with Amanda, as if they were at home having a domestic argument. He then becomes so flustered he mixes up the words in his sentences. He finally loses his thread entirely by accusing Doris of performing for the court and putting on a sweet face 'crowned by a tenderly trimmed bonnet . . . I haven't been taken in, ladies and gentlemen, because I happen to be the fellow who paid for the bonnet!' He is now so cross by the sight of Doris wearing the bonnet he gave Amanda at the outset of their conflict, that he forgets himself completely, reaches over and snatches it from Doris's head. The jury's verdict is 'not guilty'.

As is so often the case, particularly in forties films, if a woman wins in the world she loses her man at home. That evening alone in their apartment Amanda appears to have well and truly lost her man and she is upset. (Little does she know that Adam is lurking in the dark street outside the apartment building.) She goes to visit her neighbour, Kit, and pours out her troubles. Kit seizes the opportunity to confess his love for her. Amanda doesn't take him seriously but from where Adam is standing in the street, their two silhouetted figures look suspiciously intimate in the light behind the curtained window. Just as Kit takes the reluctant Amanda into his arms, Adam bursts into the apartment brandishing a gun: 'You said anyone is capable of attack if provoked – including me!' Amanda and Kit are terrified. 'You have no right,' Amanda tells Adam, 'No one has the right to . . .' She suddenly stops, realizing what she has said. Adam grins triumphantly, puts the gun barrel into his mouth and pulls the trigger. Just as Amanda screams in horror, Adam bites off the gun barrel – it's made of liquorice!

In the shock of the moment it suddenly appears that Adam has finally won his argument; no one has the right to threaten and terrify another person with a gun – reason and principle must triumph over passion. After all if Amanda were the victim would she defend him for shooting her? Adam's point here is very compelling. But it is also academic. As Aristotle said, when deciding whether a deed is morally good or bad we have to take into account 'the occasion, the means and the reason'. In other words there are no moral absolutes, only human stories that need to be known and understood before they can be judged. Adam is attempting to prove an absolute without the complex circumstances of a story to give it context. In this sense his pretended action can not be assumed to be a proper parallel to Doris Attinger's story.

Amanda is, of course, furious with him and their ensuing fight is destructive and violent and they are both the losers. But a few weeks later, when they are discussing their financial assets with their accountant and their marriage appears to be finally over, Amanda sees with amazement that Adam is crying. Her anger with him melts and she instinctively goes to comfort him lovingly. Later, when they are in their country cottage where they have come to patch up their marriage, Adam confesses to his trick. He shows her how he too can 'do what women do when they are losing'. He concentrates hard, looks distressed and as the tears begin to trickle down his cheeks, he grins with satisfaction. Amanda is impressed, until it occurs to her that his point only serves to demonstrate her case; there is no difference between men and women . . . although 'maybe there is a *little* difference', she finally, tentatively admits. '*Vive la différence,*' Adam announces and takes her to bed.

Adam's Rib works because it is not a polemic or merely an illustration of clever arguments. It works because Adam and Amanda's relationship works. We enjoy their relationship; we don't want their marriage to be destroyed by this dispute. All the little details of their compatibility give us hope in the face of the huge public argument they have about men and women. They may be equal but they are clearly not the same. Amanda is a successful attorney but at the same time she is playful, frequently confused, full of life and vitality, and she is feminine. Adam may lose the case but he has all the qualities of a loveable man – he's warm, affectionate, fun, easily hurt but unashamed to show his feelings. We may not go along with his arguments but we rarely stop liking him. We don't want to see him humiliated or hurt. Although one of the reasons we feel for him is because he always appears more vulnerable than she, and more fallible – this is partly because Cukor is using his directing skills to make sure we feel this way. But there is no doubt that when Amanda has the strongwoman actually lift Adam up in the air in court, she has gone too far. That really was humiliating.

But should we care for Adam so much? Shouldn't we feel more cross with him for not once seeing her side of the argument, for sticking uncompromisingly to his rigid views and principles, for never questioning his assumption that his supposedly logical, rational argument is superior to Amanda's, for never doubting himself or wondering if his own views might be based on emotions such as hurt pride or injured masculinity, and for finally winning his argument by picking out what he assumes are typical female tricks and blowing them up into a big deal.

When Doris cried in court it was not fake, it was real. Adam's failing is that he never allowed Doris's deeply human story to touch him. And he never understood or appreciated that his wife might be valiant, even heroic in taking up and fighting for a just cause. Somehow the film lets him get away with this by seducing us with his apparently reasonable approach to life, his humour and his charm.

Just as Amanda plays the role reversal card in court, can we reverse Amanda and Adam (as the similarity in their names seems to invite us to do)? Amanda is very concerned about his ego and she tries her best to give him extra love and attention to make up for the hammering he's getting in the courtroom. But if Adam were the one trouncing her in court and she was getting hammered by his brilliant arguments would it matter so much? Or would she, rather than feeling humiliated and angry, be filled with admiration for him, as her husband, and bask in her reflected glory as his wife – which is how things should be? I suspect she would and there wouldn't be a story to tell if their roles were reversed. Just as if the roles were reversed in *Woman of the Year*, Amanda's story would also simply be normal life.

Although it is amusing to see a man being made fun of by a woman, finally he has to be reinstated in his manly role, and her redemption as a woman depends on her being punished for humiliating him. Will the push for women's equality threaten even the most modern compatible relationships? This is the question posed by the film. And the answer has to be a resounding *yes*. As with the other films of this decade, the dignity of man is sacrosanct and certainly more important than that of the woman. As the title of the film reminds us, it was Eve who was Adam's spare rib. Amanda may win the argument but it is Adam who finally wins the war.

Three

Strong Men, Twin-sets and Billowing Skirts in the Fifties

By the fifties, the post-war euphoria was well and truly over. Many people who had spent their childhood in the Depression, and then found that their adolescence and youth were dominated by war, wanted security more than they wanted change. '"Security", as in "risks", was in the headlines, as in atomic secrets, Communist espionage, the House Un-American Activities Committee, loyalty oaths and the beginning of the blacklists for writers,' Betty Friedan later wrote about the time.[1] In other words the cold war had begun. The invention and use of the H-bomb on Hiroshima and Nagasaki may have ended the war in the Pacific but the long-term psychological fall-out was world-wide. People were afraid again, and this fear was insidious, all-pervasive and invisible, like atomic radiation is invisible. In a cold war people are left with just that; the cold chill of the idea of war. In such a climate of insecurity it is perhaps not surprising that many people preferred to channel their energy into their home and their family; the area of life where they felt in control.

Owning a home in the suburbs suddenly moved to the top of many people's aspirations, along with material acquisitions such as a car, a television, a washing machine and a refrigerator. It is startling to note the speed and ease with which questions of equal rights and feminism were swept under the carpet, just three decades after the suffragettes had won the vote and just five years after so many women had discovered, through doing what had previously been considered man's work, a real sense of pride, satisfaction and fulfillment as rounded human beings.

Once again the home was assumed to be the woman's domain as housewife and mother, while their husbands were reinstated as the protectors and economic providers, along with the power those roles entailed. Of course the economic conditions for many families were such that huge numbers of women continued to go out to work, but theirs was 'women's work' – and as such neither a proper career nor well paid. The proof of success for an upwardly mobile working-class family was when the woman no longer needed to work and could at last enjoy the privilege of being a proper housewife.

In the early fifties two out of three women in higher education were dropping out before graduation either to marry or because they feared that too much education might spoil their marriage prospects. Most men were opposed to their wives working – it reflected badly on them as successful men. Many women expected to work between school or graduation and getting married, but then they would give it up for a life of motherhood and domesticity. 'Work experience is beneficial because it gives some insight into the husband's world,' is a quote from a typical fifties girl, illuminating how many girls expected to live through their husbands rather than have careers of their own.[2] Another contemporary study concluded that 'many Americans thought that single people were either sick or immoral, too selfish or too neurotic.'[3] In other words marriage and a home of your own were the pinnacle of achievement for both men and women and older single people were marginalized, although, of course, spinsters were also stigmatized for being sad and unfulfilled whereas bachelors were envied for their sexual freedom.

The attitudes of this generation were not only a reaction to the cold war. They were also formed by the 'baby boom' of the late forties and the obsession with Doctor Spock, celebrated for his child-rearing manual, and the increasingly fashionable Freudian school of psychiatry with its nineteenth-century ideas about gender differences. The psychiatrist Helen Deutsch advocated that the normal, feminine woman lived through her husband and her children – although it is unclear how she judged her own prominent career as a woman in this scheme of things.[4] Perhaps she just accepted that she had a 'masculinity complex', which was a popular psychoanalytic concept at the time. A 1947 best-seller, *The Modern Woman: The Lost Sex,* suggested that feminists were neurotically seeking revenge by claiming masculine power: 'Women should not seek to imitate men but to accept their femininity through subordination to their husbands and the joyful acceptance of motherhood.'[5]

In films the old and familiar split between the good and the bad feminine archetypes, the virgins and the whores, gradually became honed into two equally celebrated icons. Marilyn Monroe rose to stardom as the bad good-time girl, the self-absorbed and at the same time utterly self-effacing mistress offering the ultimate in sexual promise. Doris Day, who rose to stardom as a singer, was also one of the most popular female stars of the decade. She was famously known as 'the girl next door', the freckle-faced sensible virgin; warm, smiley, non-threatening, pure and wholesome. Although she exuded a vague air of flirtatious sexual promise, like all the best girls next door, she was far too sensible to deliver until after the marriage vows (when she also promised to become the ideal housewife for the ideal home). One of her producers is quoted as making the ironic jibe: 'I knew Doris Day *before* she was a virgin.'[6] This tells us how, like Marilyn Monroe, her image was consciously manufactured by the male studio bosses. There is even an eerie symmetry in their initials, DD and MM.

The dilemma for women was which of these two icons to aspire to? Men appeared to desire both. But women could hardly be both, or they didn't think they could. And neither icon added up to a whole, fulfilled person; they both involved cutting off, denying or hiding the parts of the self that didn't conform to the ideal – a dangerous short-term strategy in life and a recipe for crisis and disaster later.

Although men in most ways had considerably more power than women, they also faced a not too dissimilar dilemma between two conflicting icons of masculinity. John Wayne, the

Western hero, for many men represented the ideal father figure, admired as the biggest, strongest and bravest of men; a natural heroic leader and a good, honest, upright citizen; the ultimate protector and provider, even if, like many men, he was 'a loner' and largely absent from the family home. On the other hand, men also wanted the freedom to have a good time, to be bad, to enjoy the fun of the chase and of sexual conquest, a role which later became typified by the relaxed seductive charm of Rock Hudson, who only had to smile to be instantly forgiven his multitude of sins.

One of the key differences between men and women was that men could, apparently seamlessly, make the transition from one character type to the other; men could play the field before they settled down to get married, whereas few men wanted their wives to be 'soiled goods'. The ideal wife must save herself for her man. But a man wouldn't be a man if he didn't obey his natural biological urges before he settled down. And, given that biological urges don't necessarily go away with marriage, he could perhaps be forgiven if he slipped up in a minor way after the big day, so long as he was truly contrite. Feminism had questioned these double standards and the mythologies about 'natural sex differences' that imprisoned both men and women within their limitations. But feminism, at least in the fifties, appeared to be dead and buried.

The Quiet Man (1952)

Directed by John Ford; screenplay by Frank S. Nugent; based
on a story by Maurice Walsh; starring Maureen O'Hara and
John Wayne

> 'Hey is that real? She couldn't be!'

The Quiet Man was released in 1952, seven years after the end
of the war. The film captures the contemporary mood for
nostalgia and the desire to reaffirm the age-old idea that there
are supposedly basic drives underlying sex roles and relationships between men and women.

The film's hero, Sean Thornton (John Wayne), is a man
sickened by the brutal world of fighting – he killed a man in the
boxing ring – and wants nothing more than to return home to
find himself a hearth, a woman of his own and the warmth and
security of traditional community rituals and family values. The
theme, of a man trying to come to terms with the shock of having
killed in his past, also embraces a whole generation of 'quiet
men' attempting to put their past experiences in the war behind
them and to build a new future – often on an unstable founda-
tion that involves secrecy or denial of the emotional confusion.

John Ford's own creative journey shows a similar shift in
focus, for this film at least, away from his classic Westerns, such
as *Stagecoach*, *She Wore a Yellow Ribbon* and *Rio Grande*
where his mythic heroes, the pioneers of the new frontier, fought
and killed as a matter of course in their struggle for good against
bad, or for the rule of law against the ever-encroaching lawless-
ness or the feared wilderness and 'savagery' of the Indians. In
The Quiet Man, Ford returns to the grassroots. He goes to the
original 'home' in the 'old country', in this case Ireland, to
confront the hitherto secondary domestic themes that have
appeared with nostalgic affection in many of his Westerns:
courtship, marriage, family and cultural traditions. But instead

of allowing his style to be softened or diminished by domesticity he elevates the power of romance, and both the joyful and the dark forces that beset it, to his usual mythic proportions. He adds still more to this mythic dimension by setting the film in 'Innisfree', made so resonant of the archetypal desire to retreat to a lost simple life close to nature in the Yeats poem – 'I will arise now, and go to Innisfree . . . And I shall have some peace there, for peace comes dropping slow . . .'

Ford also brings to his subject many familiar faces from his Westerns and, as usual in his films, it is this supporting cast of stereotypical Irish cameo characters who provide much of the humour: hard-drinking men who love a good fight, a good sing-song and a woman – good or bad; prudish spinsters or widows who are shocked by the men but also secretly hold a torch for one or other of them; priests and vicars who continually succumb to minor temptations; and lovable old rogues who are as foolish as they are wise, drink too much and are available as cupid, should cupid be required.

When the film opens Sean Thornton (John Wayne), a smart American from Pittsburgh, alights from a train. He is taken by Michaeleen, who is a local taxi driver amongst other things, to the remote Irish village of Innisfree. The five-mile journey by horse and buggy marks a transition to a place still relatively untouched by the modern world. The buggy stops on a stone hump-backed bridge over a stream with a timeless landscape of lakes and mountains in the background. Harp music plays on the soundtrack. As Sean gazes at a small stone cottage nestling in a valley we hear his mother talking to him as a child, nostalgically reminiscing about his dead father and the roses he had planted for her around the front door of that very cottage. This is the reason Sean has come to Ireland; he's going to buy his dead mother's old cottage and he's going to build a new life for himself here in Innisfree.

Michaeleen, a childlike old man with a twinkle in his eye (typical of Ford's lovable old rogues), on learning that Sean was born in that cottage and that he knew him as a baby, asks curiously, 'How come you got so big? What do they feed you Irish men on in Pittsburgh?' This is the perfect question to draw our attention to the kind of man Sean Thornton is – the kind of man who was 'fed on steel and pig iron furnaces so hot a man forgets his fear of hell, and when you are hard enough, tough enough, other things . . .' He stops speaking and looks thoughtful – he's not going to tell us what other things make a man big, not yet anyway. Despite the fact that Sean Thornton is a single, childless man, as is so often the case with John Wayne's performances in Ford's films, he somehow epitomizes the ideal father, the kind of man who is so often absent doing what a man has to do that his image becomes embellished with our projected childish fantasies. We are entranced, like children listening to our mysterious, unknown father reminisce, and we are left in no doubt that he *is* big and strong, as all fathers should be. But, as his mother died when he was twelve and his father even earlier, he has been alone in the world fending for himself for a long time and so there is about him something remote, sad and needing of nurture. We are impressed, and curious about what he is *not* telling us, and thrilled with the kind of excitement generated when an absent father at last returns. 'And home I'm going to stay,' Sean assures Michaeleen with the certainty in his tone of a man who knows his own mind.

Of course a home needs a woman as well as a man and, almost as soon as we learn of Sean's mother's early death, a woman almost magically appears as if to offer herself as a possible replacement. In a lush green valley where dappled golden sun filters through the trees, Mary Kate Danaher (Maureen O'Hara), a tall, shapely, red-headed woman wearing a bright red skirt and blue blouse (the colours that typically depict the Virgin Mary in Renaissance paintings), and carrying a shepherd's crook, tends a flock of sheep. Sean stares at her as if mesmerized and she stares back; the attraction they feel for each other is palpable, before her modesty overcomes her and she runs away. 'Hey, is that real? She couldn't be!' Sean utters as if he's seen an apparition, or the woman of his dreams.

Mary Kate is only too real, as Michaeleen tells Sean, after he sees her again the following morning, this time in church kneeling before the altar. One of the reasons she has remained unmarried for the past fifteen years is that despite what Sean sees as her saintly beauty, there's no man who can handle her fiery temper. The character of Mary Kate, as her name suggests, embodies the mythological split in the nature of woman: on the one hand we have Mary the shepherdess – passive, accepting, the idealized virgin mother; and on the other hand we have Kate, who like her namesake in *The Taming of the Shrew* is wild, unpredictable, exciting, dangerous, uncontrollable and renowned for her temper. Also reminiscent of the Shakespeare play is Sean's role: like Petruchio he is a hard, tough man who has seen the world and is now looking for a woman in order to settle down and the implication is that it will take a big man like him to cope with a difficult woman like Mary Kate.

With his two larger than life characters in place, Ford prepares to bring them together for their first truly mythic encounter. In order to buy his mother's cottage Sean outbids Will Danaher, Mary Kate's big, burly elder brother, who wanted the land because it borders on his property. Furiously Will Danaher vows that Sean Thornton will 'regret this 'til his dying day, if ever he lives that long'. Sean is still too new to the community and its ways to realize the possible implications of falling out with Mary Kate's brother. In the pub when Will tries to pick a fight, Sean refuses to be goaded despite the risk of appearing to be a coward. Instead he takes his sleeping bag (which has been a cause of some amusement for the men in the bar as they have never heard of a man sleeping in a bag before) and heads for his cottage.

The trees are bent double in the howling wind and rain and in the dusk the cottage looks grim and forbidding, like a place of the dead. But when he opens the front door, although the inside is bare and empty, somebody has lit a fire in the hearth. He hears a sound and sees Mary Kate hiding in the shadows, like the ghost of his mother. Sean catches her and kisses her and the windows burst open with the full force of the wind, which snatches at her hair and her clothes and whistles around the derelict house. This image of their passion, unleashed and liberated by the ferocity of nature, is as mythically powerful as the rock formations in Monument Valley. Then Mary Kate suddenly struggles to free herself from his grasp and slaps him hard for taking liberties.

Sean has overstepped the mark. In Innisfree there is a rigid protocol for courtship, and marriages are arranged with property and money as the primary considerations. They also require the permission of the eldest male in the family – which means, as Mary Kate's father is dead, her future lies in the hands of her brother, Will Danaher, unless she rebels against him. As a newcomer from modern liberal America, Sean is prepared to go along with what he thinks are merely quaint local traditions. He employs Michaeleen as his matchmaker and the two men, dressed in their Sunday best and with a bunch of red roses for Mary Kate, go to the Danaher house to request permission from Will for the courtship to begin. Will flatly refuses. At first Sean doesn't understand Mary Kate's response. 'It's what *you* say, not him!' he pleads with her. But although, at an unconscious level, Mary Kate's temper tantrums may be her spirit railing against the injustice of her position as a woman (as were Kate's in *The Taming of the Shrew*), Mary 'the virgin' accepts unquestioningly that in Innisfree there is no issue of women's rights or men's rights. The rights of each sex have been clearly set out by patriarchal tradition: her brother's will must be obeyed. Sean angrily throws the roses in the gutter and walks away in the rain alone.

Tradition may be paramount but this is a comedy. It is also Ireland and true love is at stake. Michaeleen the matchmaker, the Catholic priest and the Protestant vicar and his wife conspire to rescue the situation. They know that Will wants to marry a wealthy village widow (presumably she is wealthy because she has inherited her husband's property). They convince Will that the widow will never marry him with his sister, Mary Kate, in his house. They add to this the ingredient of jealousy, when at the annual village horse race the men compete for the bonnets of the village women – another tradition in the game of courtship. Sean narrowly outrides Will, takes the widow's bonnet and receives her kiss as his prize – much to the fury of Mary Kate whose unwanted bonnet is left blowing in the wind. But nevertheless Will begrudgingly gives his permission for Sean to court and marry his sister.

At Sean and Mary Kate's wedding celebration the conspiracy becomes unravelled. Will proudly takes the opportunity to announce his engagement to the widow, assuming that Michaeleen, as matchmaker, has it all arranged. Michaeleen hasn't of course, and the widow walks out in a temper. Furious that he has been deceived, Will refuses to hand over Mary Kate's dowry and tries to force Sean to fight him. He knocks him down. The shock of the punch triggers Sean's memory: we see him in his old life as Trooper Thornton, a professional boxer, in the ring on the night when he knocked out a man who died – the reason he has taken a vow never to fight again and the reason he left America for a new life in Innisfree. Although there is no direct reference to Sean having fought in the war, his age would suggest that he did and his professional name, Trooper Thornton, implies that he was once a cavalry soldier.

We now know Sean's secret but Mary Kate doesn't. As his new wife, she can not understand why Sean refuses to fight for her dowry. Is he a coward? At home on their wedding night Mary Kate makes it clear that, as far as she is concerned, until she has her dowry, which is her right as handed down for hundreds of years through the women of her family, she is not properly married. She storms into the bedroom and slams the door. Sean storms in after her: 'There will be no locks or bolts between us Mary Kate, except in your mercenary little heart.' He kisses her masterfully and then tosses her on to the new bed. It breaks. He slams out of the room and goes to sleep alone in his sleeping bag.

For the coming days their situation remains deadlocked. Sean plants roses for Mary Kate, gives her a present of a horse and buggy of her own and the cottage is transformed into their ideal home, except for the bedroom, which remains out of bounds. When they go on a shopping expedition to the local town they see Will drinking with the men outside the bar. Kate demands that Sean confronts her brother for her dowry. Sean refuses. Why does she care more about a small sum of her brother's money than she does about her marriage to him? Mary Kate insists that the small sum is 'My money!' She furiously accuses him of being a coward and drives off, leaving him to walk the five miles back to Innisfree. It is interesting how even at the heart of this old-fashioned story, this small symbol of economic independence for women has such an important part to play. 'My money!' Mary Kate insists – she is not entirely owned by her husband, her self-respect depends on having something that is her own, and hers alone.

While Mary Kate confesses her unconsummated marriage to the village priest, Sean goes to see the Protestant vicar, the only man in Innisfree who knows his secret. The vicar is a keen boxing fan and has kept press cuttings of Trooper Thornton's last fight. He tries to explain to Sean why the dowry means more to Mary Kate than just money. It's a matter of tradition he explains. 'It's not worth fighting for,' Sean insists. 'Is your wife's love worth fighting for?' the vicar asks.

The next morning Sean wakes in his sleeping bag to find that Michaeleen has come with a message from Mary Kate. She has left him because 'she loves him too much to go on living with a man she's ashamed of'. At last Sean is spurred into action. He gallops valiantly on horseback to the station, masterfully pulls Mary Kate off the Dublin train and drags her the full five miles on foot back to Innisfree. Like the Pied Piper of Hamelin they are soon being followed by everyone they pass. Mary Kate falls, he drags her to her feet; she loses a shoe, he refuses to stop to let her pick it up; she raises her arm to strike him, he dodges her blow and kicks her when she falls again. One of the village women runs up to him with a stick, 'to beat the lovely lady with', she tells him. Sean takes it. When at last they arrive at Will

Danaher's farm the big fight begins. The dowry is handed over but, with Mary Kate's blessing, they throw it in the fire demonstrating that this was never a matter of the money but of self-respect and honour.

Despite the ignominy of having been dragged five miles by her husband in front of the whole village Mary Kate now proudly, even jauntily walks through the impressed crowd and makes her way home to cook her husband his supper while all the men in the village enjoy a good fight, with Michaeleen taking bets on who will win. Tradition has won the day and the marriage can now be consummated in the time-honoured fashion.

So, in *The Quiet Man*, the ideal woman is certainly not passive or submissive, she is in her own way powerful, but she also recognizes the traditional boundaries of her power and so knows its limitations. She acknowledges the superior power of her man, and in a sense as his wife she receives his reflected glory or glory by proxy. It is with this knowledge that Mary Kate walks away from her husband's fight with her brother, basking in the pride of being the woman fought over by the two strongest men in the community. This, according to John Ford's portrayal, makes up for all the humiliation she went through as she was dragged for the full five miles from the station back to her home.

Men may have come home from battle vowing that they will never fight again but in Ford's world fighting is an essential part of manhood and such displays of masculinity are as important to women as they are to a man's self-esteem. In common with many men of his generation Sean has come home wanting nothing more than the trauma of his past to remain secret and be forgotten. But he has learnt that in order to live a full life he must break his vow.

Although for this film Ford has turned his back on the Western and gone 'home', Mary Kate's character absolutely represents the female archetype of the frontier woman. She is the kind of woman who could survive wagon trains to the wild west; fight the Indians alongside her husband; bring up a large family in the most adverse conditions from the North American winters to the parched deserts of the south; support her husband in his endeavours rather than compete with him; and uphold family traditions, knowing that her domain is the home and never questioning her primary role as housewife and mother. Similarly Sean Thornton represents the male archetype of the protector and provider; the strongest of the male pack; tough enough to fight off all threats to the homestead whether they be Indians, bears, bad men, or in this case his wife's brother. The 'wild' other side of Mary Kate's nature, just like the supposedly savage or 'wild' otherness of native Americans, both attracts and fascinates the frontier man, but the uncontrollable also inspires fear and as such must be subdued or tamed in the interests of civilization, or at least in the interests of the supremacy of the white man.

The underlying message of *The Quiet Man* is that the road to happiness requires that both sexes respect the time-honoured roles of the male and the female. The man must prove himself in battle against other men in order to gain the woman's respect and the woman ultimately wants nothing more than to bow to her man's superior will. But just as in *The Taming of the Shrew,* when attempting to uphold the patriarchal tradition we veer dangerously close to the dark, violent and abusive side of the battle of the sexes. Unlike Shakespeare's play, where we are left puzzled and troubled by Kate's apparent about-turn and we are questioning Petruchio's 'taming' methods, *The Quiet Man* asserts its world view with such conviction that the complex undercurrents remain buried. The mythic dimensions of the film have such a powerful emotional sway over our psyches that we are tempted to dispense with an intellectual response. For the men of the fifties, who were attempting to build their peacetime lives on the shaky foundations of the trauma of war, the message is clear: trust the old ways and don't ask awkward questions or probe too deeply.

Roman Holiday (1953)

Directed by William Wyler; screenplay by Ian McLellan Hunter and John Dighton; starring Audrey Hepburn and Gregory Peck

'Life isn't always what one likes . . . is it?'

On first viewing *Roman Holiday* appears to be a mixture of a fairytale – it has been referred to as 'Cinderella in reverse'[7] – and a simple story about the frustrations of royalty. It can be no accident that the film was released in 1953, the year after the coronation of Queen Elizabeth II, which captured the public imagination by being televised and broadcast worldwide. With royalty as its subject it would appear that, like *The Quiet Man*, the film also reflects the contemporary mood of nostalgia for age-old rituals and continuity with the past. But *Roman Holiday* is a deceptively simple film: it is deceptive in that it is not about what it at first appears to be about, and the theme of the imperative for deception is embodied in its core.

Roman Holiday is about a short, secret love affair and, as with all secret or illicit love affairs, passion is fuelled by the necessity for lies and guilt, and by resisting the temptation to throw caution to the wind and grab hold of happiness while you can, before the dead weight of duty descends and snatches it away from you. The secret love seems to exist in a separate or parallel universe, outside of time. It is a peak experience, existentially perfect; time stops, everyday reality retreats, the meaning of your life feels as if it is encapsulated in the moment, which may be as simple as eating an ice cream together, or sitting side by side in a car staring out into the deserted night street. The world appears both magically beautiful and shrouded with a vague, sad awareness that this moment can not last, although at the same time it is, in itself, for ever.

On the surface *Roman Holiday* appears to be a fairytale – the film is about a runaway princess. But the power of the traditional fairy story, as we saw with Frank Capra's films in the thirties, is rooted in childhood conflicts and the awesome task of separation from our parents' love and finding our autonomous adult identity through a process of life tests or dragons that must be overcome. If the fairytale speaks to us through the child within, as we were before we began our passage to adulthood and adult love, *Roman Holiday* is the opposite of a fairytale. It speaks to the adult we have now become, of the perfect, innocent love we once desired but imagine we have lost. The spirit at the heart of the film is closer to that of the courtly love described by the troubadour poets as they wandered from castle to castle in twelfth-century Aquitaine. For these poets their actions were guided by a strict code of chivalry marking their respect for their beloved. Their love was pure and innocent and usually impossible to consummate because the women were queens, princesses or high-born ladies within the castle walls, beyond the reach of ordinary mortals and as such idealized to the point of abstraction. So long as the woman remains on a pedestal (even if the pedestal is of man's making), the love maintains its reason to exist, which is the numinous all-consuming experience of perfection. The greatest danger to such a love is the rough and tumble of real relationships and the all too real battle of the sexes.

In the opening of *Roman Holiday* we are presented with two distinctly different images of Princess Ann (Audrey Hepburn). We first see her public persona, which is the epitome of the universal fantasy of a princess. She is young, gracious and perfectly beautiful as she smiles and waves to the adoring crowds on her goodwill tour of Europe's capitals. It is only when she arrives at a sumptuous ball, thrown in her honour by her unnamed country's embassy in Rome, that we see how the strain of the tour is beginning to affect her. She is wearing the classic ballgown many girls would die for, but her escort is an elderly ambassador and while she is surrounded by admirers she is also isolated by her elevated position. As she graciously greets each guest with a formal smile, we notice an element of sadness in her huge deer-like eyes and when she surreptitiously slips off her tiny shoe, in order to exercise tired toes, the shoe falls and she can't reach it without losing her poise. The director William Wyler's intention is clear: all the men at the ball are old, there is not a Prince Charming in sight to rescue 'Cinderella's' lost slipper and save her from her lonely life.

Next we meet her private self. She is like a child standing on a huge bed in a grand palace bedroom, complaining petulantly about how she hates her old-fashioned nightdress and she hates all her underwear and she's *not* 200 years old. She wants to sleep in pyjamas, just the top half, or even better she wants to sleep with nothing on at all. The implication is that, like any adolescent, Ann is subject to burgeoning hormones, has sex on her mind and is deliberately trying to shock her mother, or in this case her mother substitute who is her lady-in-waiting. Ann's predicament is clear: outside her window a group of young revellers are partying in the garden below and inside her bedroom her lady-in-waiting is reminding her of tomorrow's endless round of duties. Ann screams hysterically and insists that she is dying. A doctor is fetched who gives her an injection to make her sleep.

Metaphorically Ann is dying. She is being suffocated by her royal position when she needs the freedom to explore, to experiment, to find out who she is. Which is precisely what she does. As soon as the doctor and the lady-in-waiting have gone she gets up, dresses in simple day clothes and escapes from the sleeping palace into the streets of Rome, which are bustling with nightlife. But soon the sleeping drug begins to take effect. She curls up on a wall and falls asleep.

Joe Bradley (Gregory Peck) is on his way home after losing a poker game with his fellow press-pack reporters. As he passes the wall, he hears Ann muttering her automaton mantra from her days of meeting foreign dignitaries, 'Thank you very much, delighted, no thank you, charmed.' Joe assumes that she is drunk but she looks so young and vulnerable, as a gentleman he feels obliged to look after her. She won't or can't tell him where she lives. She falls asleep again, this time with her head resting on his shoulder. He can hardly leave her alone in the streets so late at night, so he reluctantly takes her to his small bachelor apartment, although he pauses on his doorstep with a worried frown before taking her inside. He hands her a pair of his pyjamas, which she is delighted with. 'I have never been alone with a man before, even with my dress on. With my dress off it is most unusual. I don't seem to mind. Do you?' Her words could be interpreted as blatant flirtation if they weren't spoken with such enchanting, virginal innocence. Joe takes flight and leaves her to sleep with the excuse that he is going out for coffee.

His situation is clearly tricky. Ann is totally beautiful, utterly vulnerable and seems very young, with her long dark hair cascading down her back. He is tall, dark and unusually hand-some with sensitive features, but he also appears to be much older than Ann (at the time the film was made Peck was 37 and Hepburn was 24, although her character, Ann, is clearly still a teenager). Their age difference is never mentioned explicitly in the film. But at one level Joe appears like a father figure looking after a young girl and protecting her virtue; while at another the dynamic of an older mature man who is fascinated by the freshness and innocence of a young girl permeates the subtext with a sense of potentially dangerous illicit sexuality. Wyler works against this explosive combination by emphasizing the asexual innocence of their relationship and giving Joe a strong motive for his interest in Ann – he is a reporter working for an American news agency and she, as a runaway princess, is a big news story.

The next morning Joe learns of Ann's true identity. He sees her picture in the paper and hears news reports that she is ill and unable to attend her day's engagements – the palace's cover story to explain her disappearance. This is when Joe's deception begins in earnest. He does a deal with his boss for the princess's story without revealing that she is at that very moment asleep in his apartment. His idea is to spend the day with Ann, gathering exclusive information about her, without telling her who he really is. This reduces the element of dangerous sexuality from their relationship but replaces it with another dangerous element – deception for the purpose of financial exploitation. Now the reason for the casting of Gregory Peck becomes clear. His screen persona (as described by Ephraim Katz) emanates 'moral and physical strength, intelligence, virtue and sincerity'[8], hardly the kind of man who would ruthlessly exploit an innocent young girl for selfish profit. Our belief in Joe's ultimate moral virtue is also a crucial antidote to the dangerous temptation of illicit sexuality, particularly if we are finally to believe that his feelings for her are worthy of the high ideal of love.

Back at the apartment Ann at last wakes up. She tells Joe she dreamt that she met a young man in the street. 'He was tall and strong and he was so mean to me . . . he was wonderful.' She smiles radiantly. Ann's dream tells us how her unconscious has projected on to Joe an image of her ideal man, including her disturbing, if familiar, desire for a man who is mean, or punishing – which perhaps indicates her conflict between the need to be good and her secret desires to be bad, which may involve guilt and punishment in order to be good again. This idea that each of us has a dream or fantasy image of our ideal partner is further explored when Joe leaves Ann to take a bath and goes to his neighbour's where he can phone a friend in secret. The neighbour's sculpture studio is filled with bronzes of nude women in poses that express mature womanly sexuality, in contrast to Ann's innocent child/woman. We have a further contrast when we see Joe's friend, Irvine, a photographer who is busy taking pictures of a sexy young model in explicitly erotic poses.

Having hired a photographer to secretly take pictures, Joe and Ann spend the day wandering the streets of Rome, like two innocent tourists on holiday. At one point Ann becomes transfixed by a hairdressing salon window and finally, plucking up courage, she goes in and demands that her childlike long hair be cut off. This is clearly, at least in Wyler's eyes, an important transition; she went into the salon a child and emerges looking like a sophisticated young woman. The theme of lies and deception continues, although it is not entirely one-sided. Joe tells Ann that he is a businessman on holiday and that Irvine, whose camera is hidden in a cigarette lighter, is his friend. But Ann also lies, telling Joe that she is a schoolgirl who has run away from her oppressive school regime. She will eventually have to go back, but meanwhile she would like to spend the day doing whatever she wants: looking in shop windows, walking in the rain, just having fun. The difference between them is that Joe knows she is lying and why, whereas Ann trusts Joe implicitly. And although he redeems himself by acting as a kind father figure who can make her wishes come true, at the same time, behind her back, he is manipulating her for the best photo opportunities for his story.

As if Wyler wants to make the audience even more aware of the theme of deception, the couple visit an ancient Roman monument known as the 'Mouth of Truth'. The monument is a huge stone face of an old man. Joe tells Ann she must put her hand in the old man's mouth and, according to legend, if she is given to lying her hand will be bitten off. Ann gingerly puts her hand in the mouth and quickly withdraws it with a nervous giggle. 'Let's see you do it,' she challenges Joe. He pauses for a moment, perhaps contemplating his own guilt, and then, as a father might play with his child, he turns the situation into a joke by putting his hand into the mouth and pretending it has been bitten. Ann screams with fear and then throws herself into Joe's arms, helpless with laughter. As they walk away the scene ends on the impassive, uncompromising stone face of truth – inviting us to wonder what is the real dynamic underlying their relationship, what is their truth?

We soon find out. That night at an open-air dance some secret servicemen, charged with the mission to find Ann and return her to the palace, recognize her. Joe leaps to her rescue, valiantly fights the men and in order to escape he and Ann jump into the river Tiber and swim for safety. Soaking wet and shivering with cold on the riverbank downstream, he kisses her for the first time. We cut to the couple, now back in his apartment, when she emerges from the bathroom wearing his bathrobe. Whatever may have happened, if anything, between their first kiss on the riverbank and this moment, is left for each of us to imagine. Ann now wants to cook him a meal but he doesn't have a kitchen. 'Do you like that?' she asks. 'Life isn't always what one likes, is it?' he replies. As if in reply, she wistfully tells him she's a good cook, she can sew too and even clean the house. In other words she would *like* to be his perfect wife, but life is conspiring against them. He takes her into his arms. 'There's something I want to tell you,' he says. 'No please, nothing,' she insists. The moment of intimacy is sexually electric. They are now the universal illicit lovers. Even their dialogue is a kind of code where we have to read between the lines and fill in the gaps of what they dare not say to each other. They feel the imperative, as lovers, to confront the truth, but if they do it may destroy them. The truth is their enemy. Their love is built on deception and can survive, if only as an idea, if the deception is maintained. She is his secret, unobtainable love. She is the high-born woman who belongs in the castle, and he, like all troubadour poets, belongs outside of the walls. There is only one option left for them. He drives her through the deserted night streets to a place near the palace gates. They sit in the car together for a few precious moments. She tells him that she is going to walk away from him and he is not to watch her. Like the myth of Orpheus and Euredice, she must return to the underworld and he to the world of the living.

The next morning Ann tells her shocked attendants that 'Were I not completely aware of my duty to my family and my country I would not have come back, tonight or indeed ever again.' She has changed. She now looks and speaks like a mature, experienced woman. Joe has also changed; he now acts like the morally upright man we secretly knew he was all along. He refuses to sell Ann's story to the news agency. Instead he goes to the palace, which has called a press conference to celebrate the princess's recovery from her 'illness'. Ann graciously shows herself to the press pack to quell rumours about her mysterious disappearance. Irvine hands her, as a keepsake, an envelope containing the photographs he took of her day of freedom. Before she leaves the conference, Ann shakes Joe's hand, as if this is merely a part of her formal duty as a princess. But she also smiles at him, a smile that radiantly expresses the happiness of having found love and at the same time exudes the sadness of losing that love for ever – a love that will remain their secret and ours.

It is the allusion to purity that elevates the theme of *Roman Holiday*. There is no husband or wife to betray as neither Ann nor Joe are married. Ann's duty is to her country and Joe's past remains a mystery. In this sense their love is guiltless. We can inhabit Ann and Joe's story, and so experience the heightened feelings of illicit love without the danger of discovery and the weight of guilt and betrayal. In fact, at the end of the film, we can savour the purity of their perfect love and wish that they had betrayed their duty for their love. This would not be so easy if their duty had been to a husband or wife within the context of a failing marriage. That would have aroused all sorts of dangerous feelings both about our own temptations (acted-upon or un-acted-upon), and towards people who succumb to their temptations and betray. Because the potential wronged other is not a real person but a country, a state, which is an abstraction for most of us, *Roman Holiday* seems to exists on a higher, more noble plane.

Finally *Roman Holiday* is about how experience is fascinated by innocence and the imperative need to regain innocence, however temporarily. A man in his late thirties, approaching middle age, suddenly finds himself attracted to youth, innocence and purity; something that he has lost and now has the opportunity to regain. Men of that age usually have a wealth of relationship experience and mature women can be difficult, complicated, real. The innocent virgin has none of that reality. She enables the man to escape from his overwhelming sense of disappointment, both with his own experience of love and with the women he has loved. Through loving the unobtainable ideal he is able to love himself again. But in order to maintain love's perfection this must never be reality-tested, it must remain a secret, sealed from the real world. In this way the child/woman can remain on a pedestal, from where, like an ancient Greek statue, she forever ennobles love's ideal.

The Seven Year Itch (1955)

Directed by Billy Wilder; screenplay by Billy Wilder and George Axelrod; based on the stageplay by George Axelrod; starring Tom Ewell and Marilyn Monroe

'If I was your wife, I would be very jealous of you . . .'

The two most memorable things about *The Seven Year Itch* are: first, the title – many of us have wondered at some time or other if it's true, do people really get the urge to stray in the seventh year of marriage? And second, *that image* – Marilyn Monroe on a sultry summer's evening, standing in her high-heeled shoes with her long bare legs astride a subway air-vent as her white pleated skirt tantalizingly billows up to her waist like a sail adrift in the wind.

In the mid-fifties, when the film was released, happiness and success were assumed to be synonymous with the achievement of the bourgeois dream; a secure, well-ordered home with all the latest material appliances, a husband who goes out to work and a wife who does the housework and looks after the children. But what happens if we have achieved our dream and, instead of basking in contentment, our dangerous imaginations begin to dwell on forbidden fruit? How do we cope with the conflict between our desire for sexual novelty and adventure and our need for the love and security of a happy marriage? Is the price we have to pay for a happy family the repression of those parts of ourselves that don't fit into the idealized picture?

This is the conflict faced by the film's hero, Richard (Tom Ewell), when he, along with a multitude of other middle-class, middle-aged New York husbands, sends his wife and child to the countryside for the summer in order that they should escape from the stifling heat of the city. The men, of course, can not accompany their families because men have to work, heat or no heat, in order to pay the bills. So Richard returns to his silent apartment to contemplate the prospect of a summer on his own. He soon finds himself beset by fantasies of what he might do now that his wife is away and equally beset by the feelings of guilt and self-hatred induced by his fantasies. His imagination is caught, as if on a switchback machine, between experiencing the full force of his secret desires and the imperative that he must repress those 'bad' fantasies at all costs. In other words the film is about the conflict between the person we fear we really are and the person we think we ought to be; the battle is between our 'animal instincts' (as Richard refers to his forbidden desires) and our consciences.

Richard's fantasies take the form of an imaginary dialogue with his wife as he sits alone on his balcony having a quiet evening drink and proofreading (he works for a publisher) a book on '*The Repressed Urges in the Middle-Aged Male*'. In each of his fantasies he is the innocent victim of a woman's unrestrained passion: first his secretary tries to seduce him in his office, then a nurse accosts him while he lies helpless in a hospital bed, and finally on a seaside holiday his wife's best friend desperately confesses her desire to make love to him on the beach by the crashing waves. In each fantasy Richard passively succumbs while at the same time valiantly defending his honour as a married man. Finally, pleased with his imagined self-restraint, he fantasizes a scene where he tells his wife about the incidents. In this fantasy his primly dressed wife, Helen, is sitting in a homely wicker chair half-listening to him and half-concentrating on her knitting. 'It's a kind of animal thing I've got, it's really quite extraordinary,' he finishes. 'The only thing extraordinary about you is your imagination,' she replies, smiling with maternal indulgence as if he were her child inventing these adventures in order to spice up his account of his day.

Richard gets up to fetch ice and lemon for his drink when suddenly a tomato plant falls from the balcony of the apartment above. 'You want to kill me or something!' he shouts furiously before he realizes that he is talking to a girl (Marilyn Monroe) who is peering anxiously down from the balcony. She looks naked, although her breasts are concealed by the window-box. This startling impression is reinforced when, in a sudden rush of bravery, he invites her for a drink and she tells him she'll be down as soon as she's dressed – she keeps her underwear in the ice-box, she explains, when it's hot like this. She soon breathlessly wafts into his apartment, dressed in baby-pink skin-tight trousers and a matching loose shirt. While he fixes her request for a 'big, tall martini', she heads for his air-conditioning unit, where she lifts up her shirt and wafts the cool air around her naked midriff.

The girl is never named in the film (although towards the end Richard jokingly refers to her as Marilyn Monroe). Not knowing the name of someone we are fascinated by has the effect of preventing us from connecting with them fully; they remain somehow mysterious, or a blank screen on to which we project our fantasy notions of who they are, which often reflect our own desires and fears rather than informing us about the reality of the nameless person. This is why the name is usually the first thing we ask when we want to know someone; their name is the doorway to their individual separate identity. Although the girl is ostensibly real (and not a fantasy), not knowing her name maintains this element of doubt; she is both real and a projection of Richard's at the same time. (But it is disconcerting referring to her merely as the girl so I will call her Marilyn.)

The contrast between Richard's fantasy image of his wife and Marilyn is immediately apparent. His wife, Helen, with her motherly manner, appears sexless, somehow sapping his masculinity and reducing him to the dependency of a child. Whereas Marilyn epitomizes the ideal mistress, offering sexual promise with no strings. When she peers over the window-box, although we can't see her body, the idea of her nakedness is planted in our minds and she instantly becomes the object of desire. By breathlessly asking Richard for a 'big, tall martini' she re-endows him with the masculine power he has lost with his wife. And when she wafts the cool air from the air-conditioning unit around her bare midriff we again have tantalizing glimpses of her body and desire to see more. There is no let-up with the allusions to her potential as a bringer of sexual bliss. She tells Richard about her work as a model and a photograph that won an honourable mention in a photography journal, 'one of these artistic pictures . . . on the beach . . . It was called textures, you could see three different kinds of texture, the driftwood, the sand and me . . .' (We know from Richard's earlier fantasy that he finds the beach and the sea particularly erotic.) She even shows him a few of her best poses for the camera and her dazzling smile. She tells him that it was her birthday a few days ago and seizing the opportunity to celebrate, rushes back to her apartment to fetch a bottle of champagne and to change into a tight low-cut shoulderless evening dress which she asks him to zip up at the back. She then notices his wedding ring. He reluctantly confesses that he's married. 'Children?' she asks. 'No, no children,' he says, but then, struck with guilt for denying his own child's existence, he adds, 'Well, just one, but he's very tiny, hardly counts.' But rather than being put off she tells him that 'the wonderful part about being with a married man is he can't ask you to marry him because he's married already'.

It seems there is nothing that will put her off. She is utterly accommodating and at the same time totally egocentric. Her world consists entirely of her immediate physical concerns – her body, her clothes, her comfort, her desire to eat, drink or sleep. Her constant concern with her own body and appearance draws our attention to just that, her body and her appearance, and the result is to keep us continually aware of her sexuality. Her sexuality is her reason to exist – in this sense she conforms absolutely to a male erotic fantasy of an ideal woman who is there solely to excite him sexually. There is nothing about her that is threatening, other than the fear of all-engulfing sexuality itself. And, of course, the fact that her very existence represents sexual pleasure for its own sake, unencumbered by ties such as those of a real relationship or marriage.

After an abortive attempt to kiss her, which ends up with them both falling on the floor, not because she doesn't want to be kissed but because he is so nervous, Richard finally makes a supreme effort to conquer his temptation and asks her to leave. He then succumbs to an hysterical fit of abject self-hatred brought on by his guilt and he spends the next day at work wracked with anxiety and terrified that his wife will find out, even though so far he is only guilty of unfaithful thoughts. The turning point arrives when he phones his wife only to learn that she is out for the day with a writer friend of theirs. He immediately begins to imagine the writer seducing his wife and in retaliation – or as an excuse – he phones Marilyn to invite her out.

We next see the two of them leaving the cinema and Marilyn standing astride *that* air-vent in a heaven of sensuality. They are still talking about the heat when they get home and Marilyn twirls into his sitting room, throws herself on his armchair, kicks off her high-heeled shoes and props her long bare legs up on the air-conditioning unit. Richard wants to talk about psycho-analysis – a hobby of his, he tells her, as he likes to wander through the labyrinth of the human mind. But Marilyn is not interested. As Richard contemplates the notion that underneath our superficial veneer we are all savages, she worries about how she will manage to sleep in her apartment with no air-conditioning in this heat. It appears that the down-side of her character is that she is dumb. You may be in a kind of sensual heaven with a woman like her, but when it comes to discussing ideas you are essentially alone. But this hardly seems to matter, particularly when she suddenly suggests that in order to get a good night's sleep she would like to spend the night in his apartment, throwing Richard into agony as he battles with his desire for her and his fear of being a guilty husband. The brilliance of Monroe's performance here is that her suggestion appears innocent, without an ounce of calculation, and yet open to the possibility of sexual promise.

The next morning, when Richard wakes on the couch and

remembers that she is asleep in his bedroom, his terror reaches crisis point. He imagines his wife walking in and, assuming the worst, shooting him. Marilyn then wanders into the sitting room after taking a shower and finds him in such a state of fear that she's forced to ask what the matter is. At last they talk properly for the first time. He tells her about the nightmare of his wife shooting him and then, as if the act of admitting his fears frees him to at last face the truth, he tells her that in fact, if his wife really did walk in the door and catch them together she wouldn't think anything of it. His real problem is that his wife trusts him: 'How can anybody be jealous of somebody with a briefcase, who's getting a little pot belly and who's sleepy by nine-thirty? . . . Let's face it, no pretty girl wants me, she wants Gregory Peck.' Marilyn listens intently and reassures him by telling him that girls aren't dopes. They don't really fall for that 'I'm so-handsome-you-can't-resist-me look'. The kind of guy girls really want is the one in the corner, 'nervous and shy and perspiring a little. First you look past him but then you sort of sense that he's gentle and kind and worried and he'll be tender with you . . . that's what's really exciting. If I was your wife I would be very jealous of you.'

The doorbell rings and Marilyn hides in the kitchen while Richard answers it. It's his writer friend – Richard's wife has sent him to pick up his son's canoe paddle. The writer sniffs, he can smell fresh coffee brewing. Richard jokingly tells him that 'Marilyn Monroe is in the kitchen' and manages to get rid of his friend before the truth is revealed. But, as a result of his narrow escape, Richard finally realizes how much he values his marriage and with Marilyn's blessing he rushes out of the apartment to join his wife for a much-needed two-week holiday in the countryside.

Part of the eternal fascination with Marilyn Monroe is that, like Audrey Hepburn in *Roman Holiday*, she is also a child-woman. But whereas Hepburn's child was an innocent virgin with newly awakened sexual desires, Monroe's child is fully sexually aware but utterly guiltless. Like a pleasure-seeking sensual baby, her desire seems out of control because she knows of no need for restraint. Like a baby she acts spontaneously, in the moment, according to whim and self-indulgence. In this sense her very presence represents a lost part of ourselves, before we were aware of the self as separate from other people, and the feelings of guilt and hostility which arise with such awareness – particularly sexual guilt.

Of course, the character Marilyn appears to be on screen doesn't exist in reality. She has turned herself into a fantasy object in order to be loved. Her real self has been split off and hidden as being without value. In her final scene with Richard when she describes to him the kind of man girls really want, she is perhaps expressing for the first time what she really wants or needs for herself. Not a handsome hunk, a fantasy man, as he imagines, but a sweet, kind, gentle, loving person to take care of her. On the other hand, this might just be another example of her instinct to make a man feel good by telling him what he really wants to hear. Whatever the true nature of her insight, although it may be of some temporary help to Richard and his problem, she remains left alone, lost and adrift in her total identification with the shallow, nebulous image of herself which is little more than a male fantasy projection she imagines is the self she ought to be.

In this sense her problem is similar to his: she hates the self she really is and rejects that self for the person she thinks she ought to be in order to be loved. As John Berger expresses so well, in *Ways of Seeing*, a man's presence '. . . suggests what he is capable of doing to you or for you. By contrast a woman's presence expresses her own attitude to herself and defines what can and can not be done to her . . . in other words men act and women appear.'[9]

The two main female characters in *The Seven Year Itch* are the wife and the girl. The wife's attitude to herself, at least in Richard's fantasy, is that of a mother who has somehow ceased to need to be sexually enticing – she's already got her man. The girl's attitude to herself is that she is defined solely by her ability to entice sexually. But is there some kind of eternal feedback loop in operation here? While the man projects his image of his ideal fantasy woman on to the girl, she identifies with his projection and strives to become like his fantasy, believing this is the only way she will be loved. Somewhere along the line her real self has become devalued, rejected by both the man and the woman, and so must be repressed and kept hidden away.

Whatever happened to the bright, strong, feisty women of the thirties and forties films? Were they such a threat to the male ego that they had to be 'tamed' into pale reflections of their former selves, or even remade like Barbie dolls in order to transform them into the kind of women men imagine they want? Is this the price both men and women paid for erecting an idealized image of perfect marriage, restricting the wife's freedom to the boundaries of the home, giving the man the sole burden of economic responsibility and insisting on sexual fidelity? Finally Richard learns that he needs the security of his motherly wife more than he wants his sexual freedom. But does either option offer him the fulfilment he desires?

Pillow Talk (1959)

Directed by Michael Gordon; screenplay by Stanley Shapiro and Maurice Richlin; starring Doris Day and Rock Hudson

'I'd say five or six dates ought to do it.'

If a film could double as a coffee-table book, at the end of the fifties *Pillow Talk* would have been left lying casually in up-to-date sitting rooms, next to a tidy pile of magazines featuring fashion and beauty, the latest in furnishing and décor, perfect kitchens and the most streamlined cars. The film's theme tune, 'There must be a pillow talking boy for me', sung bouncily by Doris Day, would be playing softly on the record player in the background. The 'talking point' would be the film's innovative use of split screen.

The challenge for *Pillow Talk* was how to get together two apparently incompatible icons of femininity and masculinity: a sensible, honest, wholesome woman who would make a perfect accessory-wife skilfully presiding over dinner parties and enhancing her husband's promotion prospects, and a philandering, fun-loving, footloose, immoral bachelor. This somewhat odd dilemma also mirrors a challenge that was beginning to arise for many real people by the end of a decade that was forming such conflicting and in many ways incompatible ideas about what it meant to be a man and a woman. The man wants sex and the woman wants romance. The man wants adventure and the woman wants domesticity. The man is a sexual predator, the woman is a marriage predator. Marriage means a man loses his freedom to be the person he really wants to be, and a woman gains her power to be the person she really wants to be. Marriage is something men fear and women aspire to. Marriage is a trap constructed by women that all real men will inevitably, finally fall in to.

The film opens with Jan (Doris Day), a single woman who

lives alone in her own well-appointed and perfectly decorated apartment, getting up in the morning. She's wearing a baby-blue slip, her short blonde hair is already set in place like a helmet and her make-up is tasteful and immaculate. She primly ties the bow at the neck of her lacy bath-robe and picks up the phone to make a call. The screen splits three ways to show three separate apartments: Jan is impatiently listening in the centre to Brad (Rock Hudson), who is sitting at the piano in his bachelor apartment talking to one of his many girlfriends; this one is lying snugly in her big double bed telling him how much she loves him. Brad tells the girl that he has written a song just for her and sings 'You are my inspiration . . .' He pauses, trying to remember which girl he is singing to before he completes the line with her name. Jan is appalled.

We soon learn that the only problem in Jan's otherwise perfect life is that her telephone doesn't work properly – that is apart from the fact that she is still single and waiting for the right man to come along and sweep her off her feet. New York has a problem with the proliferation of people wanting phones and Jan has found herself in the awkward position of having to share her line with Brad, a complete stranger who appears to be wooing a different girl every time she wants to make a call. Finally Jan snaps and demands that Brad get off the line. He wants to know why she's so fascinated by his personal affairs. 'Not fascinated, revolted,' she retorts. He accuses her of being an eavesdropper, the kind of woman who lives alone and doesn't like it and suggests that if she's so interested in listening in on his calls she must have bedroom problems. 'I happen to like living alone,' she tells him frostily, 'I have no bedroom problems, there's nothing in my bedroom that bothers me.' 'Oh, that's too bad,' he replies implying that is precisely her problem. She furiously hangs up.

Jan has a successful career as a high-class interior decorator. From the moment she wakes up to the moment she goes to bed everything in her life is tidy, ordered and colour co-ordinated. She dresses smartly and fashionably; her neck-lines are never too low, her hem-lines are never too high and she never has a hair out of place. She knows how to make smalltalk, to say the right things to the right people. She is grown up and sensible. One can imagine that even as a child she was more interested in tidying her mother's dressing table than going out to play and getting her clothes dirty with the boys. She is the epitome of a good girl. Romance for her is being wined and dined in the best restaurants and afterwards being taken dancing to the best nightclubs. She never loses her cool or her poise. Her latest client, Jonathan, is a millionaire who also wants to marry her. But she makes it quite clear that she's not in love with him and she's not the type of girl to lead a man on. She's taking care of herself and keeping her emotions in check until the right man for her comes along. She's the kind of girl who never asks awkward questions about the nature of life and who takes it for granted that a girl's virginity should be saved for her marriage night. In other words she buys the bourgeois dream wholesale. She's honest and respectable and strongly disapproves of people who are not.

Brad (Rock Hudson) is a songwriter and bachelor. He is remarkably handsome: six feet six, chiselled features, thick dark hair, a stunning smile and an utterly charming manner. He's the kind of man who only has to walk into a room to make girls swoon. But he is also a philandering womanizer, the epitome of a man who is addicted to the chase. Seduction is his thing. He has no moral scruples, he lies and cheats and tells each girl anything she wants to hear to get her into bed. In fact his whole life appears to be designed around this one aim, including the décor of his apartment – he has a couple of switches within easy reach of his sofa: one locks the door, dims the lights and starts the soft romantic music playing on his record player; the other transforms the sofa into a large double bed (and this is 1959!). Marriage for Brad is a trap, to be avoided at all costs, as he explains to his best friend Jonathan (who happens to be the millionaire who is in love with Jan). 'Before a man gets married,' Brad tells Jonathan, 'he's like a tree in the forest . . . And then the tree gets chopped down . . . thrown in the river . . . taken to the mill and when it comes out it's no longer a tree, it's the vanity table, the breakfast nook, the baby crib and the newspaper that lines the family garbage can.'

In other words Jan represents just the kind of bourgeois woman Brad believes is out to ensnare him into a life he despises and Brad represents everything Jan loathes in a man. Brad's immoral character goes from bad to worse. When Jonathan tells him he wants to marry a girl called Jan, Brad gets interested, not out of concern for his friend's future but as a possible conquest for himself. He also realizes Jonathan is talking about the woman on his party line, although he doesn't tell Jonathan this. Instead he contrives to meet Jan 'accidentally' in a nightclub and decides that she is definitely attractive. Without giving his friendship with Jonathan a second thought, he cunningly thinks up a plan of seduction. Jan mustn't know he's the philanderer on her party line, so he pretends to be Rex Stetson, a good, wholesome, honest country boy with a strong Texan accent so she won't recognize his voice. He even refuses her offer of coffee when he takes her back to her apartment, saying it's long past his bedtime. As he walks back down the corridor to the lift, smiling with satisfaction at the progress of his plan of conquest, we hear his inner voice calculating: 'I'd say five or six dates ought to do it!' Meanwhile unsuspecting Jan innocently goes to bed thinking, 'It's so nice to meet a man you can trust. He obviously respected you, he didn't even try to kiss you.'

Brad's audacious plan is soon working so well that he even phones Jan, as Brad, pretending that he has just been eavesdropping on her phone conversations with Rex. He's called her to warn her, he tells her; Rex is obviously a phony, or even worse, as it appears that Rex hasn't yet made a pass at her. 'Well, there are some men who are very devoted to their mothers. You know the type who like to collect cooking recipes and exchange bits of gossip.' Jan is outraged by this veiled innuendo that Rex may be gay. Of course, as far as the story is concerned, this is all part of Brad's outrageous ploy to manipulate Jan so that she makes the first move sexually. But from today's perspective this ploy of Brad's hints insidiously at contemporary prejudicial attitudes to gay men. The tragic irony is that Rock Hudson the actor found it necessary, for the sake of his career, to hide his own gayness and, in order to play the part of Brad the manly womanizer, he had also to denigrate his own hidden sexuality.

Whatever we think of Brad's tactics, sadly Jan's honest trusting nature proves all too easy to manipulate as Brad wines her and dines her like a typical old-fashioned romantic man. In a nightclub they sit happily side by side on bar stools by the piano, which gives Jan the opportunity to show off her singing talent with a catchy little song, 'Ya Ya, Rolly Poley', while she and Rex/Brad move to the rhythm by coyly playing pattacake with each other's hands. After the song Jan plucks up the courage to ask him why he hasn't ever . . . She's too embarrassed to say what. Finally she takes the plunge and shyly tells him she appreciates him 'being the perfect gentleman and all, but well, it's not very flattering'. At last he has his invitation to kiss her. She's so overcome by his kiss she has to go to the powder room to fix her lipstick. The nightclub singer, a black woman who has been sitting at the piano knowingly watching Brad's cunning chat-up, begins to sing pointedly, 'You lies, you dog, and you'll be sorry/ You lies, you hound, and that's not fair.' Brad meets the singer's eyes and winks. She smiles secretly to herself; yes, she knows his game.

The implication here is that although Brad is a rogue, he is also loveable and fun and so beyond any real reproach. The fact that he has stolen his best friend's girl and has invented an entirely false persona to get Jan into bed is somehow condoned by the film as the kind of thing bad boys do before they settle down. And we love bad boys whatever they do. We love their nerve, their audacity, their charm and their sex appeal, and if we don't love them we are spoilsports – which is what Jan is in danger of becoming when she finds out the truth.

Jan does find out, of course. On a crisp winter's night Brad drives her in his open-top convertible for a weekend in the country. On the soundtrack we hear Doris Day singing 'Make love to me, my darling possess me', while Jan sits snugly in her white coat with a slight breeze ruffling her soft fur collar and her immaculate hair. We hear her inner voice worrying about how she feels guilty because she's been the one to make all the first moves; after all she practically invited him to kiss her and to take her away for the weekend. They arrive at a glamorous log cabin in Connecticut (owned by Jonathan who doesn't know they are together). Soon they are curled up together on the sofa in front of a roaring fire. But, while Brad is outside fetching more logs, Jan picks up his coat, just to bury her face in his manly smell and a sheet of music falls to the floor. She picks it up and recognizes the tune 'You are my inspiration . . .' Jonathan, having now discovered that Brad has taken Jan to his cabin, arrives in the nick of time to save her. Jan is devastated and cries miserably for the entire car journey back to New York.

Like all bad boys, Brad had to be found out and now he must have his comeuppance or punishment before he can be redeemed. And he has to be redeemed before he can be transformed from the philandering man to the ideal husband – and so meet the increasingly tenuous requirements for the ideal marriage. There is only one card left to play to make a happy ending credible: the idea that falling in love is as mysterious and magical as a bolt of lightning from a clear blue sky. Jan has fallen in love with nice, wholesome, gentlemanly Rex Stetson, despite the fact that he is really Brad the philanderer. And Brad, as he tells Jonathan when he gets back to New York, feels guilty for the first time in his life, which proves that he must have fallen in love with Jan despite the fact that she is the kind of bourgeois woman who wants to turn wild, independent forest trees into breakfast nooks, vanity tables and baby cribs.

In the final sequence, in order to get Jan to talk to him again, Brad hires her as an interior decorator to do up his apartment. To get her revenge Jan transforms his home into a tasteless, lurid brothel. Brad is so angry he marches into her apartment early in the morning, masterfully drags her out of bed, carries her, struggling and kicking, through the streets of New York and finally into his apartment. 'Now will you put me down?' she protests. 'Why? Isn't it customary for the groom to carry the bride across the threshold?' He tosses her down on to his bed and she gazes at him, starry-eyed – at last he has proposed to her, or sort of! Three months later Brad rushes excitedly to see Jonathan to tell him he is going to have a baby.

Do we detect echoes of Sean (John Wayne) masterfully dragging Mary Kate (Maureen O'Hara) screaming and kicking for the full five miles to her home in Innisfree at the end of *The Quiet Man*? Is this masterful behaviour part of Brad's transition from philandering bachelor to responsible husband and father? But with *The Quiet Man* it was easy to see why Sean and Mary Kate fell in love; their characters were full, rounded, complex and they were well suited to each other. It is not at all easy to understand why Jan and Brad fall in love unless we buy the myth that love is so mysterious and completely irrational that it has little to do with who we really are. The problem with the myth is that we are tempted to project on to our love object the idealized person we want them to be, rather than suffer the disappointment of discovering who they really are. And so we rush headlong into marriage, sealing our fate with our illusions intact.

The Seven Year Itch dared to focus on some dangerous cracks that were beginning to appear in the bourgeois dream of the perfect family and the ideal home. *Pillow Talk* blandly papered over those cracks. Yet the cracks remained, caused by the mass of contradictions between who we think we ought to be and who we fear we really are, what we ought to want and what we fear we really want. The cracks are like fault lines quietly grumbling beneath the neat rows of suburban houses and the newly renovated city apartment blocks where newlyweds set out on the adventure of their married lives.

Four

Bad Boys and Nice Girls Who Say Yes in the Sixties

As the children born in the post-war baby boom of the late forties became the new youth generation, they were confronted by two opposite and bewilderingly extreme visions of the future. In 1960 John F. Kennedy, who at the age of 43 became the youngest president in American history, announced that before the end of the decade man would walk on the moon. If we could build rockets to journey into space surely man's creativity knew no bounds? But just two years later the world was brought to the brink of a nuclear catastrophe by the Cuban missile crisis. Our capacity for destruction on a scale never conceived of before was equally awe-inspiring. Within a year Kennedy had been shot and in 1964 the cold war erupted into a hot war, although contained within the relatively small Asian country of Vietnam.

On the home front, although teenagers and young people were expected to have a good time – rock and pop music were in full swing – it was assumed that they would eventually 'settle down' and adopt their parents' bourgeois values with paramount importance placed on family, security and materialism. The problem was that when many young people looked at the role models set by their parents' generation they were beginning to question what they saw. Their parents' lives seemed to be governed by strict discipline, control, obeying society's rules, propriety, behaving and dressing properly, conformity and repression. There was a sense of the older generation living either in the past or the future but never in the present, and of an endless postponement of gratification. Fathers had too much power; mothers were treated as doormats. Sex was a taboo subject and sex before marriage was meant to be out of the question. The only alternative appeared to be the hypocrisy practised by those who pretended to conform but in order to enjoy themselves led a secret double life; which meant that many men appeared to be having it both ways with wives at home and girlfriends at the office, while women were getting hurt on both fronts. The moralists were repressed and the hypocrites were living a lie; both groups were living inauthentic lives. This was a generation that had lived through one world war and in some cases two, yet appeared never to have addressed the huge social and political questions raised by the wars. The idea that all that mattered was your home and family and that larger questions about life and society should be left to politicians was no longer acceptable – particularly if the politicians could bring us to the brink of nuclear catastrophe, and then go on to send yet another generation to war.

By the mid-sixties many young people were starting to reject their parents' world as a form of living death and to question every aspect of both personal and political life. The future may lie with man walking on the moon, but what was going on down here on earth? 'Make Love Not War' was the slogan for the new era with the emphasis on living in the present. Hedonism and protest became the twin pillars of sixties youth culture exemplified by the protest songs of Bob Dylan and Joan Baez, the bad boy pop groups such as the Rolling Stones and the Who, and the not-so-bad Beatles. Hedonism and protest were also reflected in the multitude of late-sixties rebellious and revolutionary movements: mods, rockers, hippies, flower children, student radicals, anti-war protestors, civil rights protestors, Black Panthers, International Socialists, Maoists and finally, by the end of the decade, feminists.

The media celebration of the unattached, hedonistic, philandering male icon (portrayed at the end of the fifties with such unquestioning panache in *Pillow Talk*), was to set the tone for men throughout the decade. Sixties men were seen to be, at heart, irrepressible, fun-loving, promiscuous free spirits. The threat to them came from women and respectable society who were out to trap them into domesticity, responsibility and marriage. This was the theme of many popular sixties 'bad boy' films such as *Billy Liar*, *Alfie*, and the bawdy historical sex comedy *Tom Jones*.

With the tone for men becoming increasingly libertarian, many women in the early sixties began to question their mother's assertion that they should save their virginity for marriage (which was the central issue facing Jane Fonda's character in *Sunday in New York*). Whether their mothers really had been so morally upright, given that many had met their husbands in the heady and often promiscuous climate of wartime, was a well kept secret. In *Sex and the Single Girl* published in 1962, Helen Gurley Brown asserted that 'As the young woman was expected for some time to be financially independent it followed that she should be sexually independent' and the magazine *Cosmopolitan* (which she edited in 1964) spread the word that 'Nice girls did it'.[1] By the late sixties the growing availability of the pill theoretically set women free and the sixties sexual revolution was in full swing. Out went the padded bras, going to bed in curlers, girdles and hourglass figures, and in came flower-children, kaftans, long flowing hair, mini skirts, white lipstick and the skinny Twiggy look. The paradox was that whilst the new look proclaimed women's sexual liberation, it also accentuated a waif-like, ultra-feminine, passive vulnerability. Consequently, towards the end of the decade some women, particularly those who were associated with the many radical and protest movements, were beginning to question the notion that sexual accessibility and their personal liberation were the same thing.

Men in the 'new left' may have paid lip-service to the idea that capitalism with its emphasis on property was the cause of sexism – 'the personal *is* political' was the popular slogan which led to the new morality of free love – but most did not practise what they preached. Men remained on top both sexually and politically, whether they were of the left or the right. Women were more accessible than ever before yet they remained subservient to men. The popular slogan 'Girls Say Yes to Guys Who Say No', which was meant to support the Vietnam war draft resistance in the new climate of sexual permissiveness, had somehow overlooked the problem of women who wanted to say 'yes' to sex but 'no' to sexism.

A symbolic turning point for women came in 1968 with the feminist protest against the Miss America contest in Atlantic City. 'Atlantic City is a town with class. They raise your morals and judge your ass!'[2] was chanted by the protestors who draped a live sheep with a banner outside the contest hall and crowned it Miss America (inspired by the Yippies, a radical protest group, who the week before had nominated a pig for president at the Democrat convention in Chicago). The women produced a large 'Freedom Trash Can' and into it threw girdles, false eyelashes, curlers, high-heeled shoes, *Playboy*, *Vogue*, *Cosmopolitan*, the *Ladies' Home Journal* and, of course, bras. The idea was to burn it and the image of feminists burning their bras was born, although in fact the city barred them from doing so because of the fire risk.

Although during the sixties many young people of both sexes had realized that if they were to find happiness they had no alternative but to turn their back on their parents' example, like babes in the wood, it is far easier to get lost than it is to find yourself again. It is far easier to throw out what you don't want than to formulate what to put in its place. But by the end of the decade 'what to put in its place' had risen to the top of the agenda as people became increasingly interested in experimenting with new ways of living and loving. *Bob & Carol & Ted & Alice* tackles just such an experiment in the quest to find an alternative to the eternal conflict between monogamy and betrayal.

Finally President Kennedy was right: before the decade was out man did walk on the moon, but the question of whether a woman would ever walk on the moon, and if not why not – a question that would have delighted Katharine Hepburn's character of Amanda in *Adam's Rib* two decades earlier – had yet to be asked.

The Apartment (1960)

Directed by Billy Wilder; screenplay by Billy Wilder and I. A. L.
Diamond; starring Shirley MacLaine and Jack Lemmon

> 'Why can't I ever fall in love with someone nice,
> like you?'

Although in many ways *The Apartment* looks and feels like a
fifties film, the driving force behind the story is anger and disgust
at a society that is driven by hypocrisy, lies and exploitation –
which was very much the mood that was to become increasingly
prevalent in the sixties.

Beneath the harsh, realist surface of *The Apartment* one can
just detect the shadow of a familiar fairytale – the story of the
unlikely hero, the unnoticed boy who must prove himself by
living by his wits and goodness until eventually he saves his
damsel in distress from the clutches of the bad father figure. But
it is the moral dimension, not the fairy story, that most concerns
the director, Billy Wilder. He's not interested in romantic or
fantasy characters or great heroic deeds. Quite the reverse! He
wants us to perceive the plight of the *good* against what appears
to be the overwhelming odds in favour of the *bad*, in the most
simple, real, everyday and even banal aspects of our lives. The
comedy lies in the extremes: on the one hand, Wilder delights in
exposing the dark ironies that lie behind his story, but on the
other he delights in celebrating the absurd and surreal details in
the small everyday aspects of life, such as the sense of achievement his hero feels when he is awarded the key to the executive
washroom or tries on his first bowler hat. Just as Wilder chose
to shoot the film in black and white, so the comedy is equally
black and white.

As with *The Seven Year Itch*, Wilder tackles the subject of
married men and their desire for illicit affairs, but in *The
Apartment* he tells a very different, much darker and much

sadder story. In *The Seven Year Itch* he only touched on one side of the story, the man's. Perhaps he even felt guilty; after all Monroe may have been the kind of fantasy mistress most men wished they had, but even the real Monroe couldn't live up to her screen persona. Instead, behind the scenes she remained a tragically exploited woman convinced that she was only loved for her highly sexualized performance, and couldn't possibly be loved for her whole self. In *The Apartment* Wilder sets out to tell us the untold story, the true tale behind the fantasy office affair, what it is really like to be a mistress tucked away in a small corner of a married man's life.

The film opens by panning across the grey New York City skyline. We then focus on just one of the many skyscrapers as if we are a very small person craning our necks back in order to stare up at the impressive, alien tower with its hundreds of geometric unseeing windows. This icon of anonymous power, this 'kingdom', houses the offices of one of America's largest insurance companies. Our 'unlikely hero' is Bud Baxter (Jack Lemmon), a bachelor who works on the nineteenth floor. To emphasize just how insignificant a cog he is in this gigantic corporate machine, we see him sitting in a vast open-plan office packed with busy employees seated in regimented rows attending to their work. Bud's desk is number 861. He is average height, average weight, average looking; he certainly wouldn't turn women's heads if he walked into a party.

He also has a major problem: about a year ago he lent his apartment to one of his office superiors, a married man who needed a place to take his girlfriend. Word got around the office hierarchy and more of Bud's superiors, also married men, decided they wanted to use Bud's apartment for their illicit liaisons. In exchange they offer to put in a good word for Bud on the promotion ladder. But meanwhile he is forced to spend his evenings walking the freezing city streets waiting for his own apartment to be vacated so he can go home, tidy away the debris of bottles and snacks, eat his TV dinner and go to bed. Bud has such a problem asserting himself and saying 'no', that he even finds himself spending the night on a park bench while one of his superiors uses his apartment to entertain a Marilyn Monroe manqué he picked up in a bar. Here Wilder is ironically contrasting *The Apartment* with *The Seven Year Itch*. The men using Bud's apartment only want a good time and sex; they are insensitive, they have no moral qualms about betraying their wives and no feelings for the women they bring there. The women may try to act like Monroe, but without her glamour they come across as sad, pathetic imitations of their icon – their aspiration to be like Monroe only makes it easier for the men to use them and dump them.

In contrast to these men, when it comes to attitudes to women, Bud is quite different. This point is made most clearly when we learn that Bud is secretly nurturing hopes for a relationship with Fran Kubilick (Shirley MacLaine), the elevator girl. Whereas most of the men in the office treat her like a sex object, just another dumb broad to make passes at, Bud treats her with sensitivity and courtesy. And Fran appreciates this. In fact Bud likes Fran so much that when he gets called upstairs to meet Mr Shelldrake, the big boss of the corporation, he makes sure he takes her elevator and excitedly confides to her that he thinks he's going to be promoted. She's touchingly pleased for him and tells him he's the nicest guy around, he's the only one who takes his hat off in the elevator, which for her is the sign of a gentleman. Just as Bud is different from the other men, so Fran is different from the other women – she doesn't put on a hard, worldly act or try to be sexy or provocative. She is bright-eyed, simple, honest, straightforward, unpretentious. But she also has an air of sadness about her – something in her life is very wrong.

We soon learn what Fran's problem is. Like all the other married men in the corporation, the boss, Mr Shelldrake (Fred MacMurray), is only interested in Bud because he wants the key to his apartment and he mercilessly uses his power – Bud has the choice of promotion or the sack – in order to get it. Unknown to Bud, the woman Shelldrake wants to take to his apartment is no less than Fran Kubilick. Shelldrake's affair with Fran began in the summer when his wife and children, like so many New York families, left the city to get away from the heat (again this is reminiscent of *The Seven Year Itch*). In the autumn, when Shelldrake's family returned, he dumped Fran, but now it's approaching Christmas he wants to begin their affair again. Fran's problem is that she's in love with Mr Shelldrake. It's easy to see why she fell for him; it must have been overwhelmingly flattering for a lowly elevator girl to find herself desired by the big boss, the father figure of the corporation, with his fatal combination of power, good looks and sophisticated charm. But he has already hurt her once, very badly, and now it looks like he's going to hurt her again.

When he takes her to the Chinese restaurant (which we later learn is where he takes all the girls he wants to seduce), she tries her best to stay cool and adopt an attitude of cynicism, but she's so emotionally confused when he tells her he's going to get a divorce, and all because of her, that she grasps hold of this ray of hope and agrees to go out with him again. Triumphant that he has won her over, Shelldrake immediately hails a cab and takes her to Bud's apartment. Fran is of course unaware that the apartment belongs to Bud, just as Bud is unaware that Shelldrake's girl is the nice Miss Kubilick.

So within the towering walls of the skyscraper – itself a phallic icon of male power – from the big boss at the top of the corporation down through the male dominated hierarchy, Wilder paints a portrait of a whole network of men who are playing power games to consolidate their sense of superiority over those men further down the corporate ladder, and rewarding themselves for their achievements with sexual peccadilloes. Power in the workplace also means sexual power: each step you take up the ladder means you have something to boast about, you become more attractive to women and of course your spending power is expressed when you take women out. Exploitation is the name of the game. Married men are exploiting single women because they have the power to do just that. But the men are also exploiting each other for selfish gain. The idea that the work environment is the place where hard-working, self-sacrificing, honourable men go each day to earn money to support their trusting wives and children at home is exposed as a sham. The myth is simply a cover; work is where married men go to escape their boredom with their wives and the dull confines of domesticity, to play power games with the boys and to play sex games with the available women, and all without their wives knowing. In other words the insurance corporation, whose stated aim is family security, is in fact a microcosm for a society fuelled from the top down by hypocrisy, lies and betrayal, the very things that threaten the security of families.

The only two characters who don't fit into this tarnished world are Bud, because he still nurtures dreams of an old-fashioned, honest romance and Fran, because although she isn't technically innocent, her straightforward, trusting nature gives her an air of vulnerability. In fairytale terms she's clearly a damsel in distress, in the thrall of the most powerful man in 'the kingdom', the bad father figure, who is using her for his own selfish ends. Like Rapunzel, psychologically at least, Fran is imprisoned, if not at the top of the tower, then in the even more limited confines of the elevator shaft. Ironically, one of the first things Bud notices about her when he meets her in the elevator is that she has recently had her hair cut short, so she doesn't even have Rapunzel's lifeline to save her from the bad king.

The crisis comes on Christmas Eve at the office party. When Bud sees Fran standing alone by her elevator he has no idea why she is so sad. To cheer her up he takes her to see his new office and tries to amuse her by showing her his brand new bowler hat, 'the junior executive model'. But while he fetches Fran a glass of champagne, Shelldrake's tipsy secretary takes the opportunity to tell Fran a few home truths about their boss; he's a serial adulterer who is busy working his way through all his attractive female employees. He once had an affair with the secretary herself, she tells Fran – he dumped her a few years ago and she clearly still hasn't forgiven him. Fran is left to stare at the corporation Christmas card on Bud's desk – it's a photograph of

Shelldrake and his wife and children smiling happily for the camera – the model of an ideal happy family.

Later that evening Fran, still shocked by what she has learnt, goes with Shelldrake to Bud's apartment. There Shelldrake dismisses what his secretary has told her as a pack of lies and makes matters worse by giving Fran a $100 note for Christmas – he hasn't had time to buy her a present. He then picks up a pile of gaily wrapped parcels he has bought for his wife and children and hurries home for Christmas. As she stares at the money the reality of what it means to be the mistress of a man like Shelldrake finally hits Fran: in his eyes she's little more than a prostitute. She goes to Bud's bathroom to wash away her tears and there, in the medicine cupboard, she sees a bottle of sleeping pills. Bud arrives home for his own lonely Christmas to find Fran half-dead in his bed. Luckily his next-door neighbour is a doctor who agrees to treat Fran, despite disapproving of what he believes is Bud's wild womanizing lifestyle, given all the noise he regularly hears through the wall.

Just as nothing in life is ever quite what it appears to be, so out of tragedy comes opportunity. Fran is too ill to go home, so instead of spending Christmas alone, as he expected, Bud now has Fran to look after, which, because he's sensitive, caring and quite domesticated, he's very good at. He even manages to make her laugh, particularly when she sees the novel way he strains spaghetti though a tennis racket. 'Why do people have to love people anyway?' she wants to know. And while he tries to cheer her up with a game of cards, she asks, 'I just have this talent for falling in love with the wrong guy in the wrong place at the wrong time. Why can't I ever fall in love with somebody nice? Like you?' 'That's the way it crumbles, cookie-wise,' Bud tells her, instinctively knowing that it is too soon to declare his feelings. But his hopes are rising by the minute. A few days later Fran is happily tidying Bud's apartment and washing his socks while he prepares a candlelit supper for two.

But there is one final twist to the story. After Christmas when they return to work, Shelldrake's domestic circumstances have changed. His vengeful secretary has blown the whistle; now his wife knows about his adulterous affairs. Consequently he has been thrown out of the marital home, at least for the time being. Just as Bud is plucking up courage to tell Fran that he loves her, Shelldrake summons Bud to his office to demand the key to his apartment; he wants to take Fran there again. Bud is devastated. He's convinced that in Fran's eyes a little guy like him has no chance against a powerful man like Shelldrake. But nevertheless, despite Shelldrake's threat to fire him, he refuses to hand over the key to his apartment. 'I've decided to become a mensch,' Bud tells him, 'You know what that means? A human being!' Bud recklessly walks out on his boss, and on his way gives his precious new bowler hat to the cleaner in the hall.

At last Bud has learnt to stand up for himself and say no. He has also literally saved the life of his damsel in distress, although he believes he has now lost her. But at least he has proved himself as a man by confronting the 'bad father', the most powerful man in the corporate equivalent of the kingdom.

On New Year's Eve, while Bud is alone in his apartment packing all his belongings into boxes, Fran is sitting miserably by Shelldrake's side at a party, listening to him complain about how Bud threw his promotion in his face and resigned rather than give him the key to his apartment. She suddenly perks up: 'I guess that's the way it crumbles, cookie-wise,' and she smiles, recalling Bud's words to her in the apartment. It's midnight, the lights go out and, while the party revellers sing 'Auld Lang Syne', Fran slips away and runs to join Bud, the man who really loves her and whom, as she now realizes, she really loves in return.

Just as Bud has learnt that love is more important than promotion, so Fran too has changed. Despite the irony of the tragic circumstances that threw them together, through sharing the simple things in life like playing cards, cooking and cleaning, they discovered they were happy. Shelldrake selfishly exploited her but never really cared. For him she was just another dame on his long list of office affairs. Bud looked after her. He also looked after her reputation: he didn't care how he appeared in the eyes of others – the doctor, his colleagues at work, even the most important person in the corporation, Mr Shelldrake. He never betrayed her affair with Shelldrake or her suicide attempt. In this sense his caring for her was selfless. He gave up his job for love and in his own small way fought for her honour and his own. In the small-minded world of the corporation this was heroic. When Fran realized this, when she was finally able to distinguish Bud's real love from her boss's phony love, she too was able to change. It was Bud who rescued Rapunzel from the volatile emotional life of a neglected mistress – imprisoned in her elevator in the king's corporate tower, up one minute and down the next, suspended by endless hoping but never grounded in a real life.

In *The Apartment* love is not about being struck by a bolt of lightening with the first kiss, as it was in *Pillow Talk*; it is about the pleasure to be gained from honesty, intimacy and companionship. By exposing the ubiquitous hypocrisy behind the oversimplified myths of love and the happy family, the film represents the beginning of the quest for new and more honest ways of living and loving.

Sunday In New York (1963)

Directed by Peter Tewksbury; screenplay by Norman Krasner;
based on the stageplay by Norman Krasner; starring Jane
Fonda and Rod Taylor

'Men marry decent girls, that's the way it is.'

The Apartment attacked the edifice of the fifties happy family
and the hypocrisy many people resorted to in order to find some
relief from the strict moral codes that appeared to rule their lives.
It also exposed the painful emotional fall-out suffered particularly by women. But finally, although the film is amusing, its
portrait of life's lot is also bleak. Too bleak for a new generation
who want to perceive themselves as the inventors of a brand new
world order, bright, vital and modern, not as victims of dreary
old ways. Although 1963's *Sunday in New York* is also about
hypocrisy and double standards, from its opening frame,
accompanied by a lively upbeat jazz theme, the whole look and
tone of the film is colourful, modern and filled with a new
vitality for a new era.

In 1963, although what was later to become known as 'the
sexual revolution' had barely begun, girls were increasingly
beginning to question whether to keep their virginity for
marriage or not. Of course this has been a problem facing girls
through the ages, but in the sixties they started talking openly
about it. For many men, in principle, the answer was simple: nice
girls keep their virginity, bad girls don't. The confusion for nice
girls arose when nice boyfriends tried to persuade them to lose
their virginity. The principle that 'nice girls don't' remained in
place, but exceptions could be made, particularly if, as a couple,
they were 'in love'. What was a nice girl to make of this
proposition, having learnt from the grapevine of girl's chatter
and from their mothers that men 'only want one thing'? If they
give in they risk no longer being seen as a nice girl. And what if

afterwards they are dumped? On the other hand, what if the man who is trying to persuade her to lose her virginity really means it when he says he loves her and she's the only girl for him? How can he believe that she loves him in return unless she proves it by trusting him? Nice girls must be virgins, but they must also cater to their man's ego by reassuring him that he is the most wonderful man in the world. If she says 'no' she risks hurting him and spoiling the magic of their relationship. But shouldn't she be saving her virginity for marriage? And is he really such a nice man if he wants to make love with her before their wedding night? And what if he loves her and leaves her? So she's damned if she does and damned if she doesn't. Either way he has all the cards and she has none. For girls once their virginity is gone it's gone. If they get it wrong they have cast themselves, for eternity, into the bad girl category. There is no turning back.

This is the dilemma confronting Eileen (Jane Fonda) when she arrives in New York and turns up unexpectedly at her brother, Adam's, modern, open-plan bachelor apartment. 'Is a girl that's been going around with a fellow for a reasonable length of time supposed to go to bed with him or not?' she demands angrily of her brother. Adam, an airline pilot who, although he's on flight-call, is at that very moment expecting his girlfriend to arrive with bagels for breakfast, tries to evade her question. But Eileen's in no mood for evasion. 'As a living, breathing member of the enemy sex would you mind betraying your kind just enough to tell me what the right procedure is,' she insists. 'Eileen, men marry decent girls, that's the way it is,' he replies uncomfortably. But she's still not satisfied. She demands to know if he has slept with any of the girls he goes with. He answers 'no', but still can't look her in the eye. 'Sacred honour?' she asks, eyebrow raised, evoking the all-important code of trust between elder brother and younger sister. 'Sacred honour,' he concedes unhappily. 'Well,' she announces, sardonically, 'we're the only two left in the world.'

Eileen's problem is that her boyfriend, who she was

practically engaged to, has just issued her an ultimatum: if she won't make love to him their relationship is off. Although she thinks she loves him, rather than give in and lose her virginity before marriage, she has left home and come to New York to get over him. She's upset, angry and utterly confused. Her bewildered brother watches as she takes an old blue bathrobe belonging to their mother out of her bag and drapes it over a chair. Mother made her swear on the bible to put it there, she informs her brother, so if she has any 'gentlemen callers' they will think she lives with her mother. The doorbell rings: it's Adam's girlfriend, Mona, arriving for bagels in bed. Adam quickly ushers Mona out of the apartment on the pretext that they have made plans to spend the day together ice-skating.

Eileen isn't a prude. To look at her, dutifully rushing to catch a bus to the ice-rink (the airline has phoned wanting her brother urgently), you would never know she was struggling with the burden of her virginity. In her knee-length skirt and a neat little bolero top, she's the epitome of a very attractive, smart, modern, twenty-two-year-old girl. (The issue of at what age 'a girl' should be called 'a woman' was still dormant in 1963.) But as fate would have it, no sooner has she boarded an overcrowded bus than she gets hooked up with a man, literally – her broach buttonhole gets hooked to his jacket and the only way to disentangle them is for him to rip off his jacket pocket, which Mike (Rod Taylor) gallantly proceeds to do. They are still discussing how she can repay him – for Mike it's not an issue but Eileen insists – when they arrive at the ice-rink where, of course, there is no sign of her brother. Adam and Mona are in a telephone kiosk on a fruitless search for a bed for the day.

Eileen is far too nice a girl to be easily picked up on the street and she and Mike soon part company, only to be thrown together in a similar situation on another bus. Mike again comes to her rescue; this time by ripping off the pocket of another man's jacket. Two such coincidences and such gallantry on a sunny Sunday in New York deserve at least a boat ride on the lake, which is also the perfect opportunity for them to discover how much they have in common. He is a writer and music critic and she also works for a newspaper, occasionally writing music criticisms. The heavens are on their side too: it is soon pouring with rain and they are forced to run to Eileen's brother's apartment in order to dry off. This is when things get tricky: being alone with a strange man in the street, or even on a boating lake, is one thing; being alone with him in an apartment is quite another.

Confronted by the blue bathrobe, draped threateningly on the chair, Eileen boldly calls out her mother's name, as if she might be somewhere in the apartment, or at least due to arrive home at any minute. She then decides to sew on Mike's jacket pocket, both to settle herself that there is, or could be, a proper reason for him being there, and as a way of calming her nerves. Particularly as their conversation keeps uncannily veering towards sex in the guise of the differences between men and women, how unpredictable women are and how men, according to Mike, have to stay alert in their presence. The hunt for her brother's sewing kit takes her to a locked cupboard. Inside she is confronted by the sight of an array of women's provocatively transparent lingerie. When Mike innocently suggests that maybe they belong to her mother, she glares at him as if he is mad. 'You have just witnessed one of the big disappointments of my life,' she announces, 'involving sacred honour and brothers.'

To his amazement, she suddenly throws down the jacket she is mending in disgust and marches upstairs to the bedroom. Seconds later she reappears a changed woman – or at least trying her best to be a changed woman. She seductively descends the staircase, grabs her mother's bathrobe and hurls it into the cupboard (her mother won't be coming after all). She demands a stiff drink and lies down provocatively on the sofa. 'If I were you I would kiss me,' she tells him, somewhat disarmingly.

Meanwhile, just as fate appears to be conspiring to throw Eileen and Mike together, it is also conspiring to keep Adam and Mona apart. Adam has phoned his airline, only to receive his flight call. So, instead of finding a bed he and Mona are forced to race to the airport where they get into an incredible mix-up with a missing pilot. Mona is now on a flight to Denver (where Adam has assured her they will find a bed), believing Adam is flying the plane. In fact he is still stranded in New York airport.

Back in Adam's apartment things aren't going too well for Eileen either. She is now sitting furiously in her mother's bathrobe while Mike, wearing her brother's bathrobe, is fixing himself a stiff drink. Eileen's valiant attempt to rid herself of the shackle of her virginity has gone disastrously wrong. She made the mistake of telling him she was a virgin and he refused to go through with it. 'In a situation like this a girl is not supposed to be a beginner,' Mike insists. Eileen is not impressed. What if she called him next week, having meanwhile made it with other men, would it then be all right? He reluctantly concedes that it probably would be. So he's just another hypocrite, like her brother! He tries to explain that on this subject he too would lie to his sister. She looks at him with contempt; having finally decided to do what a girl has to do in this world, if for no better reason than to meet the competition, she has to find herself with a man like him! She's tired, she says, of being in the wrong group (the good group); she wants to be in the other group (the bad group) and she has to start somewhere. Mike gently suggests that she really should wait until she's in love. She *is* in love, she insists in exasperation, with her boyfriend at home and she said no to him because . . . it didn't seem right.

It's easy to see here how, in men's eyes, women can appear to be bewilderingly inconsistent and unpredictable. But it's also possible to interpret Eileen's apparently irrational behaviour as little more than women's confusion in their attempt to respond to the inconsistency of the male position. Men's problem with trying to work out what women want appears to be little more than a distorted reflection of women's problem trying to work out the contradictory messages they are receiving about what men want. Particularly as, except for the dictum 'no sex before marriage', many women have been brought up to believe that their role is to give men what they want.

Eileen's confusion is exacerbated, quite suddenly, when her boyfriend throws open the apartment door, sweeps her off her feet and asks her to marry him. It seems that her refusal to give him what he wants has made him want her even more – which he has decided (projecting his own manipulative disposition on to her) was probably her plan all along. It is instantly apparent that Eileen's boyfriend is brash, callow and egotistical, which contrasts strikingly with Mike's sensitivity and maturity. The fact that Eileen and Mike are wearing nothing but bathrobes doesn't deter him. Just as he assumes that Eileen wants nothing more than to marry him, he also assumes that Mike is Eileen's brother – a convenient misapprehension that lets Mike and Eileen off the hook. The situation becomes even more confused when Adam arrives shortly afterwards. Mike leaps to the rescue and quickly introduces Adam to Eileen's boyfriend as his old friend Mike.

This is a classic farcical situation. Adam and Mike must conspire to keep Eileen's boyfriend from knowing the truth. On the other hand, Adam's protective brotherly instincts are aroused. He is deeply suspicious of Mike's intentions, although he agrees to go along with the pretence for the sake of his sister's forthcoming marriage. While the men's natural instincts seem to be to resort to lies in order to get out of a tricky situation, from the outset of the film Eileen has been in pursuit of the truth and she's not about to change now.

Adam goes back to the airport to see if Mona's flight from Denver has arrived. Mike departs for his home, supposedly never to see Eileen again. And Eileen tells her boyfriend the truth, the whole truth, including her failed attempt to seduce Mike in order to lose her virginity. Her boyfriend is appalled by her extraordinary behaviour. How could she refuse to lose her virginity with him, her steady boyfriend, and then go and offer herself to a complete stranger? He needs to be alone to review the situation. Outside in the street he passes Mike, punches him in the nose and leaves him lying in a puddle in the gutter. Mike then arrives, soaking wet, on Eileen's doorstep. He tells her he was worried that she and her boyfriend might be up arguing all night so he decided to come back to see if he could help her explain.

Mike's excuse for his return may seem a little lame, but Eileen is happy with it. Also it gives Mike the opportunity to prove himself as an honourable suitor. Eileen is concerned that he has been hurt and may catch a cold. She insists that it's too late for him to go home and makes him a bed on the sofa. She laughs off his protests, after all she, of all women, can 'testify that he can be trusted'. Of course neither of them can sleep. In the middle of the night, not realizing that Eileen has come down to the kitchen, Mike suddenly goes up to her bedroom, locks the door from the outside and dramatically tosses the key out of the window. Now that he has demonstrated so graphically that his intention is not to take advantage of her, he declares, through the closed door, that he loves her and wants to marry her. As for the key, he says that in the morning on his way out he will ask the caretaker to unlock the bedroom door and let her out. Then he will phone her later to see if she will accept his proposal. Satisfied that all the details of his plan to convince Eileen of his sincerity are in place, he goes back to the sofa. Eileen suddenly appears from the kitchen and throws herself into his arms just as Adam walks into the apartment. Seeing them kissing, he tactfully leaves them alone.

As the film ends we hear Adam telling us that Eileen and Mike were married and had three lovely daughters who grew up and were lectured by their father and uncle about the nice things that can happen to a girl if she remains virtuous (and saves her virginity for the man she loves) even on a rainy Sunday in New York. Significantly we are told nothing about what happened to Adam's marriage to Mona, to whom he rashly proposed, when she eventually arrived back from her pointless trip to Denver, in order to soften her fury and alleviate his guilt.

The message of the film is clear. Eileen has learnt that she was right to say no – good men like Mike prefer decent girls like her. And the reward for saving your virginity until your wedding night is a long and happy marriage. In contrast, the silence about Adam's future life with Mona implies that, if he went through with the marriage, given its tenuous basis, it probably didn't last. This is what happens if you give a girl the kind of runaround Adam has given Mona, and then ask her to marry you simply to alleviate your guilt. And, of course, this is what happens to bad girls like Mona who arrive bearing bagels for breakfast in bed. Finally the film is clearly upholding the double standard. Nice girls should save their virginity for their wedding night but good men needn't. Men can have it both ways, girls can't.

The Graduate (1967)

Directed by Mike Nichols; screenplay by Calder Willingham
and Buck Henry; based on the novel by Charles Webb; starring
Dustin Hoffman, Katharine Ross and Anne Bancroft

'Benjamin, I'm not trying to seduce you.'

The Graduate, released in 1967, is often hailed as the quin-
tessential sixties film. There are few explicit references to the
burgeoning protest and revolutionary movements forming on
many university campuses at the time, inspired by the civil rights
campaign and anti-Vietnam war protests, but the film's simmering
anger with the older generation brilliantly reflects the mood of
the late sixties. The overpowering feeling generated by Nichols
is to make the viewer want to shout out to the older generation
to get their hands off the young, stop trying to spoil them, to turn
them into images of themselves, particularly as they have made
such a mess of their own lives.

In the film the young are young and beautiful while the
middle-aged are not, although they wish they were. Instead,
despite their material success, they are brash, loud, exaggerated
and repressed distortions of their former selves. In contrast the
young, although often confused, are like a breath of fresh air:
unspoiled, still believing in their potential and not yet disappointed with themselves or with life, unlike their parents who
are continually trying to live through, and control, their children
as a way of justifying their own life choices and not facing their
own problems.

Another reason for the film's enduring reputation is its
association with the sixties 'sexual revolution'. Themes such as
the issue of virginity portrayed in *Sunday in New York* or young
women being seduced by middle-aged married men in *The
Apartment* already seemed dated. The sexual climate was now,
at least amongst the young, permissive and experimental.

Shocking was no longer to be hidden away in a closet. Shocking, as exemplified by the many contemporary avant-garde art movements, was interesting and exciting. And the theme of a young man being seduced by a married woman twice his age, particularly a bitter, vindictive woman who only wants sex for its own sake, was shocking.

When the film opens Benjamin (Dustin Hoffman), a diminutive, awkward, youth, returns home from college to suffer an acute embarrassment – his proud parents insist on showing him off at a party thrown for all their friends to celebrate his graduation. Poor Benjamin retreats to an upstairs room to commune with the goldfish, only to find that Mrs Robinson (Anne Bancroft) has followed him and is behaving rather oddly. She walks into his room, uninvited, and instructs him to drive her home. Issuing instructions comes naturally to the sophisticated Mrs Robinson. When they arrive at her house she instructs him to come in with her, saying that she doesn't feel safe until the lights are on, and once inside she demands that he stay with her because she doesn't like to be alone in the house. Mrs Robinson's depiction of herself as a weak and vulnerable woman is in stark contrast to her confident and controlling demeanour. But it is not until she announces that her husband won't be back from the party until 'quite late' that it occurs to Benjamin that seduction is on her mind.

Much to her amusement, he panics. As if to emphasize that there is nothing further from her mind, she suggests Benjamin might like to see the new portrait of her twenty-year-old daughter Elaine. Now the subject appears to be on the safer terrain of his own generation, Benjamin willingly accompanies her to Elaine's bedroom to admire her daughter's beauty. 'Benjamin, I'm not trying to seduce you,' Mrs Robinson informs him innocently, when he turns from the portrait to see her standing in front of him quite naked. 'Would you like to seduce me, is that what you are trying to tell me?' she then asks, charmingly crediting him with her own initiative. Benjamin stares at her, confused and terrified. Outside a car screeches to a

halt. He runs. Downstairs he attempts to gather his senses as he
greets the unsuspecting Mr Robinson, who insists on giving the
young graduate a few words of fatherly advice: 'Sow a few
wild oats, take things as they come and have a good time with
the girls.'

Nichols' uncompromising portrayal of the generation gap
becomes even more explicit in the next scene. Benjamin is again
inveigled by his father, this time to show off his twenty-first
birthday present, a wetsuit and aqualung, in the family
swimming pool. From Benjamin's point of view through the
snorkel mask, his parents and their friends all appear like
grotesque distortions of human beings and he like a remote,
alien creature trapped in their goldfish bowl. His only escape is
to lie submerged in his own thoughts in the deep blue peace and
tranquility at the bottom of the pool. It is from here that
we learn, in flashbacks, about the beginning of his affair with
Mrs Robinson.

Her proposition proves too much for a young man to resist.
He arranges to meet her in a hotel, itself the epitome of
bourgeois sophistication, as he makes his way, consumed by
nervousness, down the long empty carpeted corridors and into
an anonymous room with its bewildering array of Venetian
blinds and louvred doors. 'Why? Do you find me undesirable?'
Mrs Robinson asks when he suddenly wants to leave. 'No,' he
stammers, 'I think you are the most attractive of all my parents'
friends.' So, she demands, is it his first time, or maybe he is
inadequate? This challenge to his masculinity has the required
effect. Back in the family swimming pool Benjamin is now
floating on a Li-lo surrounded by refractions of golden light
waving on the surface of the turquoise water; cool, relaxed, post-
coital.

The portrait of Benjamin as a relatively innocent victim of an
archetypal bad woman is finally clinched when we next see them
in bed together. It has been months now since their affair began
and he's still calling her Mrs Robinson and she still won't talk.
He suggests they could discuss college experiences, she turns up

her nose. He suggests art, she's bored. He asks about her husband, don't they sleep together? She's on the defensive, although she reluctantly concedes that they don't, they have separate bedrooms. He asks why she married him: she got pregnant in a car, a Ford. He's amazed: 'So Elaine got started in a Ford?' For the first time she shows some emotion and that emotion is anger. She grabs him by his hair and forces him to promise never to talk about Elaine and never, ever to take her daughter out.

Mrs Robinson is the evil witch, the Medusa, the siren who beckons to men at sea causing them to smash their vulnerable vessels on to the rocks. Although she is outwardly beautiful, her eyes remain strikingly dead, her lips turn down at the corners and she smiles sardonically on occasion but never laughs. It is as if her spirit is dead, her inner light has gone out. She wants Benjamin like an alcoholic wants a fix; he's a bodily need, nothing more. She certainly doesn't want a relationship. She's not interested in getting to know him and she doesn't want him knowing her. She talks to him about herself only in response to his persistent questions, not because she wants to share any of her feelings about the person she has become. Feelings are something she is adamantly not interested in. Mrs Robinson may want sex but her kind of sex is the opposite of a life-force and her deadly nature threatens to suck you into her world and annihilate you. But the most stinging attack on Mrs Robinson, reserved for her as a bad mother, is yet to come.

Benjamin reels from her hotel bed back to his childhood home only to find his parents insisting that, as Elaine is home from college on her semester break, he must behave like a normal young person and take her out. If he doesn't they threaten to invite the entire Robinson family over to dinner, which is something Benjamin definitely could not handle. For Benjamin the forced date is a kind of torture. When he arrives to pick up Elaine he promises Mrs Robinson, in a brief moment of privacy, that he will never take her daughter out again. But her anger is cold, ugly and unremitting. In contrast Elaine (Katharine Ross) is sweet-natured and radiant with youthful beauty. But Benjamin is determined to keep his word to her mother. In order to make sure Elaine has a miserable time he takes her to a sleazy strip club and ignores her completely. This is the kind of joint their fathers' disillusioned generation might visit to sublimate their repressed sexuality. Elaine deliberately sits with her back to the strippers' lazy undulating bodies but soon tears of embarrassment and humiliation slide down her burning cheeks until she can't stand to be there any longer and runs. Benjamin chases after her desperately trying to explain that he's only acting like this because his parents forced him to take her out. He catches her up in the street outside, and kisses her to stop her crying. Their date now begins properly.

They go to the kind of places young people go and they have fun and talk, like young people in a relationship talk. Finally Elaine guesses that he is having an affair. She asks if the woman is married and if it's over now? He looks at her sincerely and with obvious relief says 'Yes'. Now he is with her it is as if his whole life so far has been 'just nothing'. Benjamin's relationship with Mrs Robinson and her self-obsessed and lonely world of alienated sex is here starkly contrasted with the young people's world where relationships are about getting to know each other, caring and exploring feelings together as well as sex. Mrs Robinson has stolen Benjamin's youth, Elaine is offering to give it back.

Mrs Robinson strikes with a viper's venom when Benjamin next arrives to take Elaine on a date. He pulls up in his car outside the house, but it's Mrs Robinson, not her daughter, who climbs into the passenger seat out of the torrential rain. She tells him that if he ever sees Elaine again she will personally tell her daughter everything. Benjamin suddenly races into the house and up to Elaine's room to confess to her himself. 'That woman, wasn't just some woman,' he manages to utter breathlessly. But Elaine can see over his shoulder. Her mother is staring at them both with deadly eyes, looking like a drowned Medusa. Elaine guesses the rest and screams at Benjamin to get out. The knowledge that her rival is her own mother is just too incestuous and too much to bear.

When Benjamin announces to his bewildered parents that he is going to marry Elaine despite the fact that he hasn't yet asked her and she won't even speak to him, his position appears to be agonizingly impossible. Mrs Robinson has inveigled him into her miserable, hypocritical world and now he will have to somehow purge himself in order to win her daughter. And of course, if he is to win her, Elaine will have to overcome her own horror of taking her mother's lover. His situation appears even worse when he eventually tracks Elaine down on her university campus at Berkeley. She is the personification of carefree, youthful beauty with her long flowing hair, fashionable PVC mac, trousers tucked into brown boots, bundle of books tucked under her arm, surrounded by relaxed fellow students. She is also accompanied by her tall, blond, if somewhat conservative looking, boyfriend. This environment is idyllically free from her mother's tarnished world. The only hint of the student unrest and Vietnam war protests at Berkeley at that time is when the landlord of the room Benjamin rents suddenly demands to know if he is one of those 'outside agitators'. But Mike Nichols, the director, is determined to keep our attention focused on the family battleground – this is the all-important microcosm that will illuminate the conflicts underlying the climate of youth unrest.

Elaine's need to know the truth finally overcomes her determination to ignore him. 'How could you do that Benjamin? Do you just hate everything? How could you possibly rape my mother?' she demands when she visits him in his lonely rented room. Rape? So that was her mother's excuse. Benjamin tries to explain his side of the story but Elaine has an hysterical screaming fit. The landlord hears, assumes the worst and orders Benjamin out of the house. As Elaine watches Benjamin dejectedly pack his bags she's overcome by an almost maternal concern for him. She wants to know where he's going to go? What is he going to do? He really shouldn't go anywhere until he has a definite plan. (Elaine's concern for his future is in stark contrast to her mother's earlier indifference.) At last they are talking again and Benjamin soon has the opportunity to propose to her. Elaine is confused. She *might* marry him, she says, but she doesn't know yet. Benjamin grasps this straw of hope and proceeds to woo her in earnest, in the university corridors, the library, the tutorial rooms, anywhere he can find her. But she still can not stop vacillating. She doesn't see how they can marry after all that's happened between him and her mother, and anyway she's already told her boyfriend she *might* marry him.

The crisis comes when Benjamin arrives in his lodgings, having just bought a huge bunch of flowers and an engagement ring. Mr Robinson is sitting waiting for him in his room. The man who earlier claimed to think of him as a son now turns on him with vituperative loathing, accusing him of being filth and scum and threatening to prosecute if Benjamin doesn't stay away from his daughter. Mr Robinson is a vengeful older man determinedly projecting his self-hatred on to Benjamin. He blames Benjamin for all his family's ills as a way of avoiding facing his own culpability as a father and a husband and denying how his own problems and sexual hang-ups have contributed to the situation. This reflects the attitude of many older people towards the young at the time and is almost as shocking as the film's portrait of Mr Robinson's embittered wife.

Parents wield enormous psychological power over their children, and the Robinsons proceed to use their power over Elaine with devastating effect. Elaine disappears leaving Benjamin a note telling him she loves him but 'it would never work out'. Benjamin frantically rushes to find Mrs Robinson and demands to know where Elaine is. While calmly phoning the police to have him thrown out of her house, she tells him with fake charm: 'Sorry we won't be able to invite you to the wedding, Benjamin, but the arrangements have been so rushed.'

If Benjamin has been bad, and as far as conventional morality is concerned he was very bad when he succumbed to Mrs Robinson's initial temptation, he has also been well and truly punished. He must now prove his gallantry by finding the location of the church and getting there in time to save Elaine from the fate her parents have in store for her. After a frantic drive through the night he arrives at the suburban church only to find himself locked out. He runs upstairs to the visitors' gallery, hurls himself against the glass screen and screams Elaine's name just as the wedding ceremony draws to a close. Elaine looks up, along with all the guests, and sees him with his arms splayed out against the glass as if he has been crucified – which, as her parents' scapegoat, is precisely what they have done to him.

Elaine tries to run to him and pandemonium breaks out in the church. Benjamin fights off Mr Robinson and pushes her boyfriend (now her husband) away in order to get to Elaine. He picks up a huge cross, wields it as a weapon against the whole congregation, grabs Elaine, and once outside, significantly, uses the cross to bolt them all into the church. As Elaine and Benjamin run across the church lawns to freedom, we see the Robinsons, along with their guests, who represent their entire generation, depicted as grotesque ape-like caricatures imprisoned in their church cage – signifying the role religious repression has played in their lives.

Unlike the runaway bride scene at the end of *It Happened One Night*, the ending of *The Graduate* is curiously ambiguous about Benjamin and Elaine's prospects for the future. They jump on a passing bus and sit side by side, much to the curiosity of all the passengers as Elaine is still in her wedding dress. But instead of hugging or kissing or even looking into each other's eyes, Benjamin stares fixedly at the road ahead while Elaine glances timidly at him a few times, but getting no response also stares fixedly ahead. Although the film makes it quite clear that the parents are a lost generation, this uncertain ending suggests that their children may have discovered how to rebel and escape the clutches of the older generation but, given such inauspicious beginnings and the damage their parents have caused, who knows what their future has in store.

As we have seen, the splitting of women into good and bad

archetypes has been a theme running through romantic comedies since Shakespeare's *The Taming of the Shrew* and probably earlier. But what do *The Graduate*'s two icons of womanhood, Mrs Robinson and her daughter, tell us about the sixties sexual revolution? Mrs Robinson is portrayed as a gorgon. Although we understand that she is angry with her marriage, sexually frustrated and disappointed with her life as a woman whose potential was never realized, we are never invited to sympathize with her plight or to consider how the very restricted roles for women of her generation may have affected her self-esteem. But her daughter, although young and beautiful, is like a character in a mist.

Unlike the feisty portrayals of young women we have seen in earlier decades, or even the stridently cross Eileen, played so wittily by Jane Fonda in *Sunday in New York* just a few years earlier, Elaine Robinson is sweet but she is also a strangely vacuous, vacillating cipher. Which leads one to wonder what the 'sexual revolution' has done for her and for other young women in the late sixties? As the women's liberation movement, which was just beginning to re-emerge after lying dormant for decades, was later to point out, the greater sexual availability of women is not synonymous with personal liberation. The daughters of late forties and fifties mothers still had a long way to go to sort out their confusion and find out who they really were.

Far from *The Graduate* being a flagship for an all-inclusive sexual revolution, the message, for envious members of the older generation, was clear – free love is a prerogative of the young and beautiful. The hope for the future lies with Benjamin. He is the one who, having confronted his parents and Elaine's head on, has learnt that he doesn't want a life like theirs. He has also fought for and won the woman he loves. What he will now do with his future and how he will treat his love, is perhaps what he is thinking about as he stares at that long road ahead.

Bob & Carol & Ted & Alice (1969)

Directed by Paul Mazursky; screenplay by Paul Mazursky and
Larry Tucker; starring Natalie Wood, Robert Culp, Elliot Gould
and Dyan Cannon

> 'I hope we will always be open and honest with
> each other.'

What are the alternatives facing married couples? To restrict our
sexual lives to a single life-long monogamous relationship, or
serial monogamous relationships that fail if the rules are broken,
or to lead a double life maintaining the surface veneer of our
happy marriage while having affairs in secret? What if we
discover that life-long monogamy doesn't work for us and rule
out leading a hypocritical life? What if we try to explore the
complexity of our sexual feelings openly and honestly? How
might this affect our conflicting desire for a lasting relationship?
Is it possible to have a secure marriage and the freedom to
explore the full range of our sexual desires? Or do we all have to
choose – it's one or the other?

Bob & Carol & Ted & Alice, directed by Paul Mazursky and
released in 1969, was the first film to address head on the
possible implications of the sexual revolution on marriage. In the
film Mazursky starts with the premise of honesty: what would
happen if we began to explore all of our feelings openly and
truthfully? This soon leads to the question of what would
happen if we were honest about our affairs? How would we deal
with our feelings of jealousy? And what about the double
standard – if free love is acceptable for the man, how would he
feel if the woman tries it? The subject soon dovetails back into
the difficult underlying problems of sex within marriage and, of
course, guilt. And finally, in an attempt to find out if and where
the boundaries lie, at least for his four protagonists, he follows
their attempts to maintain their love through their journey of

sexual experimentation to its logical conclusion.

The film opens with the panoramic scenery of the Californian hinterland surrounding a place called The Institute (what might now be described as a New Age retreat). We see people of all ages: some swimming in the pool and sunning themselves in the nude, others learning t'ai chi; others sitting in pairs amongst the trees exploring each other's faces with their fingertips, and some being taught how to scream out their repressed feelings to the surrounding mountains. Bob (Robert Culp), a documentary film-maker in his mid-thirties, and his wife Carol (Natalie Wood), a housewife and mother in her late twenties, arrive in a sports car. They are obviously a successful young couple, dressed to appear fashionably casual, he with longish hair (he thinks it's long anyway) and beads around his neck, she in a suede waistcoat and tight check trousers. They have come for a 'marathon' encounter group, which means they are spending the weekend, day and night, in a room with ten strangers. The group leader introduces the session by explaining how the idea of the group is to look at each other, to see, to try to make contact, to show each other what you feel and who you really are. 'We talk a lot about love,' he tells them, 'but we don't feel it a lot, so perhaps this group will open up some doors.'

Mazursky shows us key moments from the ensuing weekend, beginning with the participants' first embarrassed and tentative attempts to look into each other's eyes. They learn to express their anger by beating cushions, they scream, cry, laugh, hug each other and sit in a circle on the floor talking quietly about what they are experiencing and feeling. As the weekend progresses so does their physical and emotional exhaustion. Finally Bob and Carol are sitting together by the wall, both in tears. Bob tells Carol that he feels she doesn't share her feelings. He wants her to look at him. Carol is too upset to look at him, she tells him he's pushing her again, trying to make her do something. Bob starts crying again. 'What are you feeling now?' the therapist asks. 'I feel guilty and confused,' Bob says, 'I want Carol to open to me more but that I close her up, I force her to open. I hide my feelings and then I accuse her of hiding hers.' 'I do hide my feelings,' Carol bursts out, 'I'm afraid of you.' The therapist moves over to sit by Bob: 'Tell her what you feel right now.' Bob tells Carol he loves her and he wants her to help him: 'As long as I've known you I've always been afraid to ask for your help.' On hearing this the other participants crowd round Bob and Carol hugging them and each other.

It's easy to laugh at encounter groups, not least because encouraging people to express and discuss intimate feelings in a group disturbs and embarrasses many people, especially those who have never experienced it. But although Mazursky's film is a comedy, he is not inviting us to laugh at or mock his characters. On the contrary, the documentary style brilliantly conveys the emotional power of the group and Bob and Carol's intimate experience as they struggle with their separateness and difference as man and woman and with the difficulty of their overlapping feelings as a couple. We can see Bob's struggle with his tendency to dominate and its effect on his marriage and Carol's struggle with her tendency to withdraw or passively submit and how at a deep level they both feel trapped and restricted by their gender roles. Bob, as a man, has been too afraid of weakness to ask for help and Carol, as a woman, has hidden the full range of her feelings because she is afraid of his dominance. In the film Mazursky is inviting us to question, along with his characters, some of the familiar myths about our gender roles and relationships, and to see if we can find some alternative ways of being together as couples.

Bob and Carol are in a Los Angeles restaurant with their best friends, Ted (Elliot Gould) and Alice (Dyan Cannon), talking enthusiastically about their encounter group experience. Ted and Alice glance at each other in embarrassment as their friends rhapsodize about how they love each other as friends but how they are never really honest with each other. 'The truth is beautiful,' Carol breathes as if she has just discovered the holy grail. She takes hold of Ted and Alice's hands, declaring how 'moved' she feels. Nearby restaurant guests glance at the friend's table with a mixture of fascination and condescending amusement. 'I hope everything was satisfactory,' the waiter says stiffly. 'Do you really?' Carol demands, 'Do you really hope, I mean *feel*, that you wish the meal was satisfactory?' The waiter looks abashed. Alice mutters to Carol under her breath, 'What do you expect the poor man to do? He doesn't know your life changed over the weekend.' Ted suddenly announces that he *feels* something. They all look at him in surprise and wait eagerly for his confession. Finally he says with mock intensity, 'I *feel* that you have to pay the check.'

Humour, thank god, to get them and us off the embarrassment hook. We can now satisfy our curiosity about what effect the encounter group will have on Bob and Carol's marriage by identifying with what appears to be the safer perspective of Alice and Ted's instinctive desire to diffuse the whiff of phony emotional intensity with humour. In this way Mazursky skilfully offers us the distance we may require in order to engage with the subject of the film.

It doesn't take long for openness and truth to topple Bob and Carol into the tricky terrain of infidelity. Bob arrives home from a business trip to San Francisco and confesses anxiously to Carol that he has had an affair, well not really an affair: sex with another woman. But what would normally precipitate a major problem of jealousy and guilt is turned on its head. 'Darling, I don't see how I can feel jealous about a purely physical thing you had with some dumb blonde,' Carol insists. 'Not dumb, she got her master's at Berkeley,' Bob says crossly, convinced that if Carol doesn't feel jealous it means she doesn't care about him. But as far as Carol is concerned, the fact that he told her means that he hasn't done anything wrong. She is so proud of their new credo of sexual experimentation and how it will enrich rather than threaten their relationship, that when Ted and Alice come to dinner she excitedly announces that she has 'something really beautiful to share with them' and proceeds to tell the appalled couple that Bob has had an affair, well not really an affair, 'it was just sex'.

Ted and Alice's different reactions when they get home now become the focus of our attention. Ted, as the man, is utterly perplexed, not by the fact of Bob's infidelity, but why he told his wife. 'The point is *not* that he told her but that he did it. He cheated on his wife!' Alice insists furiously as Ted digs himself into an even deeper hole. By the time they get to bed she's so upset that she refuses to let Ted, who wants to make love, touch her, which soon becomes a problem for Ted because he can't sleep. 'Do you want to do it with no feeling on my part?' she demands. 'Yes,' he pleads. She stiffly lies back down on the bed making it quite clear that if he makes love to her she has no intention of enjoying it. 'Go ahead, do what you want,' she challenges him. He tentatively reminds her that she hasn't taken the pill. After a frantic search though her drawers she realizes that she has forgotten to re-order them. That does the trick – making love is now out of the question.

In other words, the reason Alice is so upset by her friends' 'sexual experiment' is because it confronts her with some real and pre-existing problems in her own marriage and sex life which hitherto she has been too afraid to face. As she angrily tells the male psychotherapist she visits, 'I don't feel like doing it, that's all. I just don't want to be touched.' The documentary naturalism of the therapy session gives us time to wonder, along with her therapist, about how what she is not saying is as significant as what she is saying. And when she accidentally refers to Ted as Bob, and realizing her mistake descends into uncontrollable giggles, we begin to wonder, if she was brave enough to face the truth of her own feelings, might she admit that she finds Bob attractive? But such an admission would simply be too hot to handle. 'Sex is very important to a man, you know that,' she says, neatly evading the question of what sex means to her as a woman.

Meanwhile Ted is also growing increasingly mixed up by their friends' 'sexual experiment' and is intensely curious about Bob's affair. At a poolside barbecue he attempts to seize the moral high ground: 'I'm not going to do anything I don't want my wife to do . . .' he tells Bob. He then confronts him with what he suspects is a double standard: 'I don't believe you could handle it if Carol had an affair.' Bob complacently insists that he could handle it and insists that affairs are a part of life, you have to 'seize the moment' and 'live to the full'. Ted finally confesses to having been sorely tempted, but how do you handle the problem of guilt? 'You've got the guilt anyway, don't waste it,' Bob challenges him, leaving poor Ted even more disturbed and confused.

While Ted is on a business flight to Miami battling with temptation, guilt and Bob's advice 'to seize the moment', Bob arrives home unexpectedly early to be confronted by the double standard head on. Carol greets him nervously at the door and insists that he mustn't go into the bedroom: 'There's a man in there.' At first Bob doesn't understand: 'Doing what? What do you mean there is a man in there?' The truth suddenly hits him and he reacts: 'I'll kill him, the son of a bitch! He's not in my pyjamas is he?' Carol manages to restrain him and fetches him a drink to calm him down, although the sight of the man's Maserati in the street outside, and the information that he is a professional tennis player, almost sets him off again. He can't understand why Carol didn't phone to ask him if she could have an affair. Carol points out that he didn't phone her first to ask her permission – that hardly fits in with the philosophy of spontaneity and seizing the moment. Reassured that it is a 'purely physical thing, no love', Bob manages to control his jealousy and together they go into the bedroom to tell the terrified tennis player, who complains plaintively that he feels 'very uncomfortable sitting here in your bedroom', that every-thing is fine. In other words, when it comes to our instinctive feelings it's not good to repress our sexual urges but it is good, even necessary, to repress our feelings of jealousy.

In the climactic scene the four friends go to Las Vegas for the weekend. They take a suite of rooms in a hotel and while they are having drinks together, before the concert, we notice that Alice is acting strangely. She announces tipsily that she has learnt in therapy that she must not impose her values on the world and demands to know whether Bob has been getting 'any action' in San Francisco recently. Ted is embarrassed by Alice's question, but Bob tells him not to be, he likes Alice being more up front, 'going for the nitty-gritty. It's good, it's marvellous. I hope we will always be honest and open with each other.' He then goes on to tell them, much to Ted's discomfort, that Carol has had an affair.

Ted suddenly blurts out that he too has had an affair, in Miami, 'I did it. It was fantastic.' Hearing this Alice stands, unsteadily, and much to her friends' amazement strips to her underwear. 'I'm being honest. I'm doing what we came up here to do. To have an orgy,' she announces almost hysterically. Carol, Ted and Bob are shocked. They don't want an orgy, they insist. They don't want to sleep with each other, that would be altogether too incestuous. But Alice is not having it. When they hotly deny that they find each other attractive she accuses them all of lying and copping out. Bob tentatively admits that maybe he does find her attractive, 'but only intellectually', and Ted agrees that he does find Carol attractive, but 'like a sister'. But Carol then changes sides; she's had an insight, Alice is right, they are copping out. Slowly Carol begins to take her clothes off: 'I'm beginning to feel excited,' she says, 'Now do you want me to deny that?'

The four go to bed, where they sit carefully under the sheet in an awkward, embarrassed row. What to do next? Who will make the first move? How do people make love in a foursome? Ted and Bob begin discussing a share deal on the stock market – anything to avoid what's really going on. The women wait. Bob then tries kissing Alice and Carol kisses Ted. They kiss for a while, but then stop. It is as if, without saying anything, each of them know that this is just not going to work. Slowly, and in silence, they get out of bed, get dressed and leave for the concert.

In the final sequence, accompanied by the song 'What the world needs is love, sweet love' we see the two couples leaving the concert hall holding hands along with a procession of other couples of all ages and ethnic groups, also holding hands. Gradually the couple groupings begin to break down as they mix and mingle freely with each other, looking into each other's eyes and smiling, reminiscent of the encounter group in the opening scenes.

In many ways *Bob & Carol & Ted & Alice* is the most radical film we have explored so far both in style and content. Mazursky has used improvisation techniques with his actors in order to achieve an extraordinary complexity in his characters' performances and to reveal some of the underlying truths of the dilemmas they confront. He has also dared to enter the hitherto unexplored terrain of the almost anarchic range of our sexual feelings, once they are freed from the constraining myths of romantic love, happy marriage and how each of us ought to behave and feel. The film's outcome will remain controversial but its message is clear. Conforming to social conventions does not necessarily lead to happiness. It is therefore up to each of us to decide where to position ourselves on the spectrum of possibilities from monogamy to free love and how to confront the difficult questions of truth, lies, jealousy and guilt in a relationship. Openness and trust is just the beginning.

There is no hint of the splitting of women into good and bad archetypes – Carol and Alice are complex, whole people. But neither is there any hint of the burgeoning feminist movement and of the impact this will have on women's sense of themselves, on men, on relationships and on the establishment in general. It is easy to see, from the films made earlier in the decade, how the mood of rebellion and the questioning of hypocrisy and traditional values has naturally lead to the premise for *Bob & Carol & Ted & Alice*. But California was, and is, at the forefront of lifestyle experimentation and is in many ways a world apart, not least because of the wealth of its population. The encounter group movement and its many offshoots was just beginning in 1969 as a part of the wider 'personal growth movement' (as opposed to the more traditional use of group therapy in psychiatry). As with so many of the personal and political revolutionary movements in the sixties, it was difficult at the time to foresee which would have a lasting effect.

Five
Starting Over with Women Who Say No in the Seventies

By the early seventies, even though the war in Vietnam wasn't to end until 1975, many of the revolutionary and protest movements were themselves in crisis, particularly following the failure of the rash of student uprisings in 1968. Many of the students who had now left university and joined the workforce realized that they didn't actually want old-fashioned revolution in the Marxist sense, which simply replaced one corrupt power hierarchy with another. But neither did they want the kind of bourgeois lives advocated by their parents' generation. What they wanted was to exploit the freedom made possible in a modern democracy for radical experiment; the freedom to find new ways of doing things and new ways of living.

The personal growth movement, which had begun in the sixties, as we saw in *Bob & Carol & Ted & Alice,* was now taking off, even in conservative heartlands. Encounter groups flourished, as did all forms of group and individual therapy. Some people began to experiment with communal living, open marriage and, even in the conservative suburbs, wife-swapping parties. Western religions were eschewed by many as rule-bound and moribund and Eastern philosophies such as Buddhism, and practices such as t'ai chi and meditation, became popular in the quest for new spiritual meaning. The Stonewall riots of 1969 launched the gay liberation movement with its gay pride marches and belief in the therapeutic importance of 'coming out'.

This desire for experimentation by both men and women provided a fertile bed for grass-roots feminism, which suddenly began to flourish on a scale never seen before. In the sixties a woman's lot – whether she had been a housewife, a barefoot freedom-loving flower-child or a mini-skirted revolutionary – had usually been to look beautiful while she made the tea and supported the men, whose job it was to debate important issues such as the future of the world. Women were expected to compete with each other, not with men; divide and rule was the name of the game in male-dominated hierarchies, whether at work, in politics or in the family. But all that was about to change. 'Don't Iron While the Strike Is Hot' read a banner in a US national women's strike marking the fiftieth anniversary of the suffragettes obtaining the vote for women. Many young feminists were, of course, aware of the suffragettes and their struggle but were also under the impression that after their grandmothers had won the vote they had simply downed tools and gone home. The struggle for women's rights in the thirties and the battle of the sexes in the forties appeared to have been largely forgotten. As far as many young women were concerned, feminism was their battle and it was new.

One of the reasons for the phenomenal growth of feminism was the way it adopted some of the tenets of the personal growth movement, in particular the small leaderless group. Women's groups proliferated like mushrooms appearing silently in the night: support groups, consciousness-raising groups, self-help groups, self-defence groups, single mothers' groups, battered wives' groups, gay women's groups, black women's groups, women's studies groups, professional women's groups, the list seemed endless. Men hardly knew what had hit them as the women they lived with, or were hoping to live with, or were hoping to get away with not living with, were changing and demanding that men changed too.

Every aspect of male and female behaviour was under scrutiny, from the intimacy of sexuality to the pursuit of success in the workplace and in politics. The first popular feminist magazines were launched – *Spare Rib* in Britain and *Ms* in America – and even the traditionally staid women's magazines were forced by the competition to enter the feminist debate. Simone de Beauvoir's *The Second Sex* (first published in France in 1949), Kate Millet's *Sexual Politics* and Germaine Greer's *The Female Eunuch* became the seminal intellectual texts underpinning the women's liberation movement. Their intention was to demystify every aspect of women's lives, from love, romance and marriage to the roots of oppression, misogyny and male power. Arguments raged about the distinctions between what was innately masculine or feminine and what was culturally conditioned. Women began to talk openly about their sexuality: if they faked orgasms and why, whether they experienced orgasms in the clitoris or the vagina, and if the vaginal orgasm was a myth. Abortion was also high on the agenda. In America the Roe vs Wade Supreme Court case became a celebrated test case for the legalization of abortion, and in France prominent women such as Simone de Beauvoir, Catherine Deneuve, Marguérite Duras and Jeanne Moreau supported the cause by publicly announcing that they had all had abortions.

Male and female icons from the past, such as John Wayne and Marilyn Monroe, were now seen as mythic encapsulations of outmoded assumptions about gender differences. Feminists pointed to how the myths themselves were a form of gender enslavement upholding the universal power of men. Men retaliated by pointing out how in their experience many women were immensely powerful. The feminist rejoinder was to suggest that this was just another myth which defined the nature of women's power according to men's experience of women, rather than women's experience of themselves. The women's project was to find out who they were, independent of men – which was, of course, for liberal, heterosexual feminists who were determined to make their way in the mixed sex world, immensely complicated and confusing. Liberal feminists also had the additional problem of finding themselves under attack from their own sex. On the one side were the conservative women who didn't believe in feminism at all, and on the other side were the radical feminists who believed that all men were oppressors because all men benefited from the exploitation of women, therefore the only logical stance was to refuse to wear make-up or clothes designed to attract men and to pursue the path of total separatism.

Despite the often vitriolic rows between the various factions, over the decade grass-roots feminism changed the lives of vast numbers of women, irrespective of their age or social background. The effect on romantic comedy was inevitable: while nothing could destroy the desire for both romance and comedy, in the prevailing climate the battle of the sexes was a deadly serious business. This perhaps explains the paucity of traditional romantic comedies in the seventies, particularly ones with happy endings. Women's problems, such as those explored in *Diary of a Mad Housewife* released in 1970 and *An Unmarried Woman* released in 1977, were no longer seen as being solved by men and marriage; rather men and marriage were the problem. But it is also interesting to see, when examining the portrayal of the female protagonists in these two films, just how much seven years of feminism had changed the outlook for women.

But just as women were encouraging each other to be creative, expressive, assertive and fulfilled, not to put up with playing second fiddle to men but to claim their rights as equals in the home as well as in the workplace, so men were beginning to feel beleaguered, attacked, put down, insecure and reproachful, and marriages and live-in relationships were breaking down in larger numbers than ever before. Feminism wasn't just a woman's issue, as we see in *Starting Over*, released at the end of the decade: the impact on men and their understanding of themselves and their relationships, was equally seismic. Romance and the fun of sexual relationships had to change just like everything else.

Diary of a Mad Housewife (1970)

Directed by Frank Perry; screenplay by Eleanor Perry; based on the novel by Sue Kaufman; starring Carrie Snodgress, Richard Benjamin and Frank Langella

'You are a mean cool bastard and you manage to spoil just about everything.'

My decision to include *Diary of a Mad Housewife* may seem perverse. The film is certainly about relationships between men and woman and it is a comedy, although the humour is somewhat dark. But can it properly be described as 'romantic'? The dictionary defines romantic as ' . . . evoking or given to thoughts and feelings of love', but the overwhelming feeling evoked by this film is the absence of love, rather than love itself. The film could perhaps better be called an anti-romantic comedy in that it is a cry from the empty space vacated by romance.

I suspect it is no accident that, although *Diary of a Mad Housewife* is, as usual, directed by a man (Frank Perry), it is the first film in this book to be written entirely by women. Eleanor Perry has sole screenplay credit and the story is adapted from the novel by Sue Kaufman. Released in 1970, it also marks the beginning of a decade when feminism would become firmly implanted in the popular consciousness, and creative women behind the scenes were at last beginning to find their voice in film. The theme is again the battle of the sexes but, unlike the battleground of the forties when women were fighting for their position alongside men in a man's world, the new feminism had set about deconstructing and demystifying the underlying foundations of masculine dominance and the tone was altogether more serious, more angry and less fun – at least for men.

The comedy constantly draws our attention to the incongruity between what is expected and what actually is, particularly in the details that illuminate the truth of what is really happening between people. The film eschews sentimentality, but it is also suspicious of the way cynicism can be used to ward off the truth. Although the truth about what is really going on in human relationships is, of course, always subjective and so a battle-ground of opposing views. But in the seventies the truth concerning love for many women, and consequently for men, was fraught with difficulty.

The 'mad housewife' of the title is Tina Balser (Carrie Snodgress) who, although only in her late twenties, has almost forgotten that before marriage she was an attractive woman. The film opens with Tina reluctantly waking up in the morning only to find herself forced to listen to her husband, Jonathan (Richard Benjamin), who has already begun his endless stream of criticism: 'What's the matter with you these days? How could you be exhausted the moment you get up in the morning? You're too thin . . . and that godawful hair of yours, just hanging down. Maybe you don't care about what you look like in front of me and the girls but what about the rest of the world? You are Mrs Jonathan Balser, my wife, a reflection of me. I'm only telling you this because I am deeply concerned about you, Tina.' The expression on Tina's face, as she listens in silence, is stoical – she's heard it all before. At breakfast Jonathan complains about the eggs not being cooked perfectly, he issues instructions about the housekeeping, he lists all the items of clothing she must pack for him for his coming business trip and finally, when he and his two obnoxiously rude daughters (they obviously prefer their father, not their mother, as a role model) leave for work and school, she is left alone for a day filled with frantic, never-ending housework. Tina is a woman in a trap, the trap of her marriage to a man like Jonathan.

Jonathan Balser, a lawyer in his early thirties, lacks charm and sex appeal, not because of his appearance – he is quite good-looking in a conservative way, tallish, dark and slim – but because, as we discover very quickly, he is arrogant, complacent and self-obsessed. For a person to be truly attractive they need to have at least a modicum of self-doubt, a smidgen of vulnerability and preferably a sense of humour. Jonathan has none of these attributes. He is obsessed with being 'a player' in a world that values only success and celebrity. But rather than admit the truth, that he is insecure and frightened of not making the grade, which would at least make him a little endearing, his way of dealing with self-doubt is to project it on to Tina – he blames her for everything that may appear wrong in his life. He compensates for his insecurity in the competition for success, which he can't control, by assuming total control on the home front. As the man and economic provider he takes charge of every aspect of family life, taking for granted that Tina's job, as the woman, is to be everything from his cleaner and his valet, to his mother and his accessory wife and, of course, to always do as he says. The comedy lies in the brilliance of Richard Benjamin's performance as he captures and slightly exaggerates Jonathan's many familiar character traits, and the result is both devastatingly awful and awfully funny.

Jonathan is a man in denial; he denies everything that does not reflect his inflated self-image. If Tina once shared his illusions about himself, marriage to him has dealt a heavy blow. Her problem now is the ever-widening gap between her perception of reality and his. This becomes clear when Jonathan first has the idea of throwing a big party to show off how well he's doing on the ladder to success. At the time the two of them are alone together in a restaurant because, although Tina was instructed to find some friends to go out with them, she couldn't find any – which doesn't bode too well for his party plans. 'About a hundred people and a cocktail buffet,' Jonathan persists, 'None of those crummy little dinners we used to have. We are way beyond that now.' He intends to get Beaumont's, the caterers, to do the party. 'Beaumont's are pretentious,' Tina comments bluntly. 'What's that?' Jonathan demands – the word 'pretentious' has been deleted from his personal vocabulary. He turns to the problem of Beaumont's being booked until Christmas, three months away. 'Think you will be able to get the silverware ready by Christmas, Tine?' He calls her 'Tine' when he wants to humiliate her. Silently she begins to cry. Jonathan looks anxiously around at the other diners: 'For God's sakes get a hold of yourself, people are staring at you.' As it happens they are not, but his priorities are clear: he is more concerned about appearances than he is about Tina. The Italian waiter leans down and whispers sympathetically into Tina's ear, '*Coraggio*.'

'Courage' is what many in the audience may also be mentally whispering. Tina needs help. She needs someone to throw her a lifeline, to show her an escape route, or at least to give her some love to nurture her battered self-esteem.

At a party the following night, Jonathan, unconscious of how out of place he looks in his three-piece suit, has left Tina alone while he 'circulates', which means fighting his way through the throng of long-haired, exotically dressed people dancing wildly to the Alice Cooper Band's pulsating rock music, searching for successful people to get to know. Tina is hovering nervously by the door when George Praeger approaches her to ask if she has seen a friend of his pass by. In contrast to Jonathan, George definitely has sex appeal. He wears the top buttons of his tight chest-clinging shirt undone and he has a way of standing – casually resting his hands on the belt of his slim-fitting hipster trousers. He is also beautiful – large playful eyes, a perfect nose, sensual flirtatious lips and thick locks of dark hair framing his face and giving him an air of feminine vulnerability. Talking of hair, he stares at Tina's with breathtakingly blatant amusement. Following Jonathan's instructions Tina has been to the hair-dressers and it is now piled up on top of her head in a bush of back-combed bird's nests interlaced with waves of beads. 'Is there anyone else here with an aborigine hairdo?' George asks with feigned innocence. Tina is too appalled to reply but a woman passing by does the job for her: 'What a terrible thing to say to a lady. I'm going to report you to women's lib.' At home, while Jonathan is in bed carefully pasting a wine bottle label into his scrapbook of wine bottle labels, Tina comes in from the bathroom furiously rubbing her hair with a towel. 'What did you do to your hair?' Jonathan asks. 'Held it underwater until it drowned,' she replies, clearly wishing that she had drowned with it.

If George hasn't yet excelled himself in chat-up lines he tries again at their next chance encounter, this time at a gallery private view. The centre-pieces of the exhibition are fetishistic images of women, such as Allen Jones' celebrated coffee-table sculpture made up of a sheet of glass balanced on the back of a semi-naked woman kneeling on all fours. George approaches Tina, who has again escaped to a quiet spot. He leans against the wall, looks down at her and says, 'Tell me, does screwing appeal to you?' Tina suddenly bursts out laughing. George is intrigued: 'What's wrong?' 'Just mad,' she says, 'or loony, as you would say.' She tries to move away from him but he pulls her back. 'You're exciting the hell out of me and I excite you too, don't I? Oh my goodness, this hasn't happened to me in years. Not since I was a horny teenager.' He tries to move her hand down to his crotch. 'You are the most disgusting man I have ever met!' Tina announces, and rushes away to find her husband – although her expression tells us she is amused and even stimulated by the encounter. Jonathan can barely contain his excitement when she joins him – she has actually been talking to a celebrated writer. 'What were you talking about?' he asks. 'Sex,' she replies abruptly. 'Well, if you can talk about sex with someone like George Praeger,' he proudly places his arm around her, 'You are not as insecure as I thought.'

Luckily, in this instance, Jonathan shows no understanding whatsoever of Tina or her capacity for irony. His ability to see her as an autonomous human being is so limited that even when she speaks the truth, if he listens at all, he either rejects it out of hand if he doesn't like it or, if he can see a way to make it fit, he adds it as yet another feather to his own cap. As he said himself in the opening scene of the film, her role in life is to be a reflection of him, or to be more precise, to reflect back to him his delusion of his own importance. In contrast George, who we now know is a celebrated writer, prides himself both personally and professionally, on having no illusions about himself or anyone else. In George's world the truth is fun, and the more shocking or dangerous it is, the more he enjoys the game. Although when he phones Tina and, dispensing with the usual preliminaries, invites her round for sex, she is too nonplussed to respond.

Then Jonathan goes down with the flu. 'Tina! Tina!' he yells constantly from his sick-bed, causing her to run back and forth whenever the smallest idea or whim crosses his mind. He wants ginger ale with lots of ice, cracked not cubed; he wants Carr's water biscuits; he wants homemade lemonade with fresh sliced lemons and a dash of grenadine; he wants her to find a new gourmet recipe for Thanksgiving dinner rather than the boring meals she usually serves; he wants her to write out the party invitations, all one hundred of them, and to post them immediately, despite the fact that it is below freezing outside. Tina finally snaps.

Soon after entering George's dockside bachelor apartment with its stylish leather sofas and walls adorned with black and white abstract expressionist paintings, she wants to go home. 'You're just scared to death,' George tells her, but he adds endearingly, 'Goddamn it, so am I.' His fleeting, although probably manipulative, confession of vulnerability does the trick. But after they have made love George begins to get worried. He knows her type; with females like her, 'for sex, particularly great sex, there's got to be love.' And if there's one thing George is definitely not interested in it's love. He suggests that they meet in a week's time, which will give her a chance to decide whether she can take a 'straight sex thing' and give him a chance to think about whether he can cope with all her emotional tantrums, because 'You're going to be crazy about me . . . and then throw fits and get all upset and possessive and make demands.'

The problem for Tina is that although she wants to believe she can take this 'straight sex thing', there is a large element of truth in George's taunt – although not because she's that 'type of female', but because he's the kind of male to induce such behaviour in almost any woman capable of genuine feeling.

She's never been unfaithful before, as she tells him when they next go to bed together, and she's always believed in all those ' . . . square virtues; fidelity, loyalty. Nothing,' she tells him, 'you'd understand.' If it wasn't for the fact that Jonathan is literally driving her mad, she would still believe in them.

Things in the Balser household are going from bad to worse. At the family Thanksgiving dinner, which Tina has spent all day preparing, her daughters refuse to eat because they hate the gourmet turkey stuffing Jonathan insisted she made, and Jonathan decides to leave in the middle of the meal for a finance meeting, which he makes quite clear is none of Tina's business. Left alone in the kitchen, Tina at last expresses all the pent-up anger she feels and hurls the untouched pie at the wall.

The sex may be good with George but she can no more talk to him about her feelings than she can to Jonathan. George is more interested in who taught her how to be so good in bed – he's convinced that for a woman to be good sexually a man must have taught her. Tina insists that with some women sex is just instinctive: 'Remember what Proust wrote about Albertine? "She instinctively knew what would give the male body pleasure."' George roars with laughter and tells her that Proust was a homosexual and Albertine was a 'goddamned boy'. Tina is mortified, her attempt at a literary discussion, or any intelligent conversation, which she craves, has been thrown back in her face. 'Sweetheart, cookie, you really are a smart dame but sometimes you got marbles for a brain,' he tells her, in a lame attempt to repair the damage. But she's not impressed: 'You are a mean cool bastard and you manage to spoil just about everything.'

At least George recognizes that she is smart, but in reality George is just as narcissistic and self-absorbed as Jonathan, and certainly no more interested in who she really is. At home, as the date for their big party draws near, Jonathan becomes increasingly insufferable. He demands regular updates on the party arrangements, hands her lists and instructions as if she is his personal secretary, and then suddenly announces that just as he is about to realize 'his creative potential', she is doing everything to hold him back. Tina retaliates: 'This whole kick you are on, throwing big parties for so-called celebrities, running after them. I think it is idiotic and demeaning. They don't care about you. They just want to use you.'

Tina is proved horribly right – the party is a disaster. The guests don't care about her or Jonathan. Beaumont's, the caterers, look down on Tina and Jonathan as if they are representatives of a despised inferior species and by mid-evening even the few guests who had nowhere more interesting to go have left. 'On the whole I think everything went quite well,' Jonathan insists – at least his capacity for self-delusion remains intact.

Tina's affair with George also ends in disaster. She finally stops pretending to herself that she can be the kind of woman he wants her to be and faces the truth – she *is* jealous of his other women. 'Poor little housewife,' he taunts her, 'You can't take it straight, can you. You want it all tied up with hearts and flowers and lyrics by Hammerstein. There will always be other broads and broads and broads. What the hell has it got to do with you, Mrs America?' He's right again, she can't take it straight. But she doesn't want sentimentality either, what she wants is what he is incapable of giving – to be seen and accepted as the person she really is. But she can no more break into the closed system of George's ego-projections than she can that of her husband.

At home Tina finds Jonathan in the kitchen making hot milk and honey – just like his mother used to give him when he was a kid. He talks pathetically about the night they first met when he was young and hopeful and idealistic. Tina remembers; he was also 'witty and charming and very sexy' she tells him. For a fleeting moment it looks as if the love that had first brought them together may be rekindled. But, encouraged by her words, Jonathan finally confesses the truth: he's lost all their money on foolish investments, he's in trouble at his law firm, and he's been having an affair. Tina listens in shocked silence, which he interprets as her support. He tells her how wonderful she is, 'so patient and understanding. Do you think we could maybe pick up the pieces and work out a better marriage than maybe we ever had?' When he deluded himself that he was successful he expected her to passively reflect his glory and to be a receptacle for the anxiety and fears he refused to own himself; now he admits that he has failed he expects her to reflect his need for a wonderful, patient, nurturing mother. Tina is still unreal in his eyes. He is incapable of seeing her as a whole, separate, autonomous person with needs of her own – the chief need of which is to be recognized and loved for who she really is. Tina's mouth is open, she is about to tell him about her affair with George. But she thinks better of it and says nothing.

The resolution scene is a shock and clinches the idea that *Diary of a Mad Housewife* is indeed an anti-romantic comedy – or an ironic cry from the vacuum that was formerly occupied by romance. Tina is in a therapy group finishing telling the story of the dissolution of her marriage (the story of the film). The group members, men and women, all suddenly begin to argue. One man attacks her for not telling Jonathan about her affair with George: 'you leave the poor slob dragging his tail in guilt and you are just as guilty as he is'. This incenses the woman next to him who demands to know why Tina should lift a finger to 'make that silly bastard feel better!' Another woman can't understand what Tina is complaining about – she had a husband, a lover, a large apartment, what more could she want? The film ends with Tina listening to their argument stoically, just as she had listened to Jonathan's criticisms of her in the opening of the film.

No doubt some women in the audience at the time of the film's release will have been screaming out for Tina to join a women's consciousness-raising group. And no doubt some men will have complained about how the portrayals of both Jonathan and George were unfair, stereotypical and obviously invented by 'man-hating feminists', despite the fact that capturing familiar stereotypes is, of course, the essence of many comedies. The final scene of *Diary of a Mad Housewife* may be a shock, but it is a very clever shock. It not only tells us how, by daring to portray to the group her husband and her lover as she truly sees them, Tina has taken the lid off a powder keg of explosive feelings and opened herself to criticism from both sexes; it also tells us that the film's authors are well aware that Tina's story, told so uncompromisingly from her point of view, is likely to have a similar effect on the much larger group in the cinema, who as they leave will no doubt all be rowing about what Tina should or should not have done and who was unfair to whom. Which just about sums up the nature of the battle of the sexes in the seventies.

Finally, Tina may have found the courage to confront both the men in her life, but she is far from living happily ever after. She is still quite alone. But there is hope. She, like many women of her generation, has begun the struggle to understand herself and her relationships with men.

An Unmarried Woman (1977)

Directed by Paul Mazursky; screenplay by Paul Mazursky;
starring Jill Clayburgh and Alan Bates

> 'I just want to see how it feels to make love with
> someone I'm not in love with.'

By the mid-seventies both feminism and the pursuit of more
freedom, openness and experimentation in relationships were
sending shockwaves through many people's lives. Marriage was
becoming a risky business for both men and women, but more so
for women, particularly those who were housewives and mothers
and had always assumed that their husband's career was more
important than their own. They were not only emotionally
devastated when their marriage broke up, but also left wondering
why they had never attended to their own careers, their ticket to
economic independence. What happens when a woman's husband suddenly announces that he has fallen in love with another
woman and walks out? How does she cope? What does she do
next? What are the repercussions for her and her future relationships with men? These are the questions posed by director Paul
Mazursky in *An Unmarried Woman*, released in 1977.

When the film opens Erica (Jill Clayburgh) appears to be the
model of a happily married woman. She's lively, attractive, in
her mid-thirties and lives with her husband, Martin, and their
precocious fifteen-year-old daughter, Patti, in a spacious, high-
rise, New York apartment, which overlooks the river. She works
as an assistant in an art gallery, which, as an art history
graduate, she enjoys although the job has no real career
prospects and her income is a fraction of that of her husband
who is a Wall Street banker. In the morning she and Martin go
jogging together and they make love before breakfast. In the
evening she attends one of her regular meetings in a sophisticated restaurant with three attractive women of a similar age –

Elaine and Jeanette, who are both divorced, and Sue. They jokingly refer to their meetings as a 'club' where they spend more time complaining than consciousness raising – they talk a lot about sex and they complain a lot about men. (A forerunner to the American TV comedy series *Sex and the City*.)

At home Martin and Erica argue a little about trivial matters and he accuses her of becoming more like his mother every day. But he also assures her that he's not tired of her, he loves her, his tetchiness is due to his dissatisfaction with his work and a feeling that he would like to change his life, although he's not sure how. Patti diagnoses her father's irritability as middle-age crisis and announces that she's never getting married because everyone they know is either miserable or divorced. She challenges her mother to name three couples who are happily married – Erica can't. But Patti's challenge appears to be academic rather than personal, and certainly doesn't prepare either mother or daughter for the bombshell Martin is about to drop on them.

Martin calls Erica at the gallery and suggests they have lunch together. After lunch Erica is happily making plans for their summer holiday while they are walking together down a busy street, when Martin suddenly stops by a pile of yellow refuse sacks and bursts into tears. He's going with someone else, he splutters, he has been for over a year. The woman is twenty-six, he met her in Bloomingdale's when she was buying a shirt for her father and she wanted to know what he thought. He's fallen in love with her and wants to live with her but he doesn't want to hurt Erica or Patti. He becomes convulsed by another fit of pitiful sobbing and looks at Erica as if he were a child appealing for her to comfort him – if only Erica would say that she understands and of course he must leave her and be happy with this other woman, then everything would be all right. But Erica is staring at him in stunned silence. 'Is she a good lay?' she manages to ask eventually, but she doesn't wait for a reply. Instead she turns and walks away. She crosses at the lights and reaches the end of the next block before it hits her. She staggers, grabs hold of a lamp-post for support and throws up.

The extent of Erica's shock is palpable. She had no idea; she had trusted her husband absolutely. This is a bolt from the blue and she doesn't know how to begin to understand what is happening to her. In the evening she meets the 'club' in a bar. They argue about what she should do. Elaine and Jeanette, speaking from their own bitter experience of divorce, insist that she should get a good lawyer, move fast, don't let it drag on and on or it hurts more. Sue says wait, he might come back, it's probably just an affair – her husband has lots of affairs and she turns a blind eye. Her advice is for Erica to keep busy to take her mind off it. Elaine disagrees, she hopes 'Martin gets a permanent case of the clap and his pecker falls off'. Erica listens to them in a daze. A women's support group may be helpful in many circumstances but in her present state she's in no mood for support. 'I'm sad, I'm lonely, I'm depressed, what more can I say?' she announces and picks up her bag and leaves. At home she looks at herself in the mirror, as if wondering who the stranger staring back at her might be. She laughs bitterly: 'Balls said the queen, if I had 'em I'd be king.'

There are no quick-fix solutions to Erica's situation – separation, like bereavement, is a process that takes its own time. While you are going through the process you become, hopefully temporarily, crazy and extremely angry with the opposite sex. As Paul Mazursky so acutely observes, the comedy lies in the craziness and the sometimes sad, sometimes tender and often bitter humour that has such an important role to play when coping with disillusion, disorientation and pain.

Erica's anger builds like a distant but approaching storm. She visits her doctor because she is tired all the time. He diagnoses divorce as the problem and prescribes a date with himself as a possible solution. She is singularly unimpressed. How come he never asked her out when she was married? 'It's a pass Arthur, a definite fucking pass,' she accuses him, witheringly. Obviously, just like the rest of his flawed species, he can only relate to women by making passes at them. At home in a sudden frenzy she gathers all Martin's things: aftershave, golf clubs, photos, clothes, and hurls them into the rubbish. As a grand finale she bites off her wedding ring and tosses it in with the rest. She resists Elaine's suggestion that she see a Hindu Swami for spiritual guidance, but reluctantly agrees to a blind lunch date although she warns Elaine that, 'If he tries to touch me I'll break his arms.' He does try to touch her, in the taxi after lunch. She shrieks at the taxi driver to 'pull the fuck over' and demands that the man gets out. 'I didn't do anything. This is ridiculous,' he protests as the taxi pulls away leaving him bewildered and stranded on the busy freeway.

By the time Erica gets home the sight of Patti and her boyfriend innocently kissing in the bedroom is the last straw. Erica grabs hold of the hapless youth, ejects him from the apartment and proceeds to have a monumental row with her now equally furious daughter. 'How was your date?' Patti asks when her mother has finally exhausted herself. 'I was almost raped,' Erica replies bluntly. 'You mean he made a pass? I don't see what's wrong with that,' Patti tells her in exasperation. She may be only fifteen but when it comes to the art of dating she's clearly got the edge on her mother. 'You're beginning to sound like my date,' Erica says ruefully and the two of them burst out laughing.

For Erica the support of her daughter, her 'club' of female friends and regular sessions with a woman therapist soon become crucial as she oscillates wildly between fury, tears and laughter in her attempts to make sense of her shattered life. 'The club' meets in Erica's bedroom and, like four teenage girls, they sit drinking together on the bed discussing their problems with self-esteem and the perplexing question of where all the strong women role models like Bette Davis, Joan Crawford and Katharine Hepburn have disappeared to. Patti joins them on the bed and informs them seriously that, 'We are getting to an age when the dominant cult figure is bisexual or unisexual.' The older women look at the teenager blankly. Elaine begins crying: 'I could write a book about self-esteem and the American woman,' she says bitterly through her tears, 'divorced, sleeping around, drinking too much, pretending to have a lot of self and really having next to none.' Is this what life now has in store for Erica?

Therapy sessions had an important part to play in Mazursky's earlier film, *Bob & Carol & Ted & Alice*, but then the therapist was male and the feminist agenda hadn't begun to impinge on the content of the sessions, which remained traditionally Freudian and formal in their approach. Just seven years later Mazursky's depiction of the therapy sessions are noticeably different. The therapist is female, which, given Erica's anger with men, is understandable. She is tall, plain, has strikingly kind eyes and both she and Erica sit on cushions on the floor, dispensing with the usual formal distance between doctor and patient. She also breaks the Freudian rule of anonymity by mentioning that she herself has been through a divorce just three years ago, which brings to the session a sense of solidarity between women. On the other hand, she listens carefully as Erica goes through the stages of embarrassment, anger, tears and then gradually, as time passes, she begins to come to terms with what she's going through. She talks about how she sees couples everywhere she goes and feels jealous of them. She's worried about what will happen to her in a few years when Patti leaves home. She's afraid of loneliness. She feels as if she no longer has a future, only a past. And she misses sex. Eventually her therapist tentatively suggests that she might be ready to try risking it with some new men: 'They are people you know.' 'Yuk,' Erica responds, as if in disgust, but then she laughs at herself for saying it.

Erica does try 'risking it'. She goes to a bar and we can see how her whole attitude has changed. She's still nervous but now she's on the lookout for men. She spots Charlie, a painter who habitually flirts with her at the gallery, and picks him up with the immortal line, 'Take me to your loft, hon'.' Hardly able to believe his luck, he does. He then launches into his set speech about how he's a short-term guy, he doesn't fall in love and the only thing women can count on with him is sex. Erica is not in the least put out. She's only there for one thing. And after the sex, much to his consternation as he's now decided he wants to see her again, she ignores his protests, gets dressed and leaves.

She's still in casual pick-up mode when she meets Saul (Alan Bates), an English abstract expressionist painter with long dark hair, a beard and Heathcliff's smouldering eyes. They have sex in Saul's light and airy loft which is also his studio. Afterwards Saul is surprised when she instantly dresses and prepares to leave. She's experimenting, she explains. She knows that sounds a little cold, but that's the way it is these days, 'I just want to see how it feels to make love to someone I'm not in love with.' 'How does it feel?' he asks. 'Sort of empty,' she replies casually. He suggests that she sounds a little hostile but she refutes that. She likes him, she says, but that is as far as it goes.

Whether Erica is defending her vulnerability or whether she now genuinely believes that all men are untrustworthy bastards, it takes a major incident to jolt her out of her new-found modus operandi. The incident takes place at a sophisticated private view. There she bumps into Saul and Charlie almost simultaneously. Charlie, whose ego is still bruised by the fact that she didn't want to sleep with him again, begins to embarrass and insult her. Saul leaps to defend her honour and soon the two men are engaged in a full-scale fist-fight and have to be dragged apart by an assortment of private view guests.

Could it be that, despite this being the decade of feminism and sexual experiment, this demonstration of old-fashioned male gallantry – the knight in shining armour defending the honour of his damsel in distress, the man who is prepared to fight for the heart of the woman he loves – is still the key to breaking through Erica's defences? Or is it that Saul's good looks, spontaneity, wild charm and humour make him simply irresistible? Whatever it is they leave the private view together and outside in the wet, deserted street Erica begins to soften. Saul talks entertainingly about himself, his likes, his dislikes, his divorce, his working-class London childhood and the time when his mother threw a pickled herring at his father and it missed and hit the wall: 'I took one look at that pickled herring and that's when I decided to become an abstract expressionist.' He kisses her passionately and she responds, until she pulls back and looks at him seriously: 'Your work does remind me of pickled herrings.'

Although Saul talks a lot about himself, he also wants to know everything about her. He wants to take her to Vermont, when he goes there to paint for the summer, he wants to meet her daughter, he wants her to meet his children. When Erica points out that he seems to have her life all worked out for her, he doesn't disagree. They make love; they are in love. Saul pours cans of brilliantly coloured paints on to his huge canvas. Erica breaks equally bright egg yolks into a pan in his studio kitchen. She brings him the omelette, which they eat together out of the pan, and she tells him she feels so happy she doesn't know what's going on, this is craziness. She's filled with a new optimism for the future. There are so many things she wants to do in life. She could open a little restaurant, sing, travel the world, go back to school, leave the gallery. She needs a real challenge in her work. He suggests she live with him; that would be a real challenge. She looks at him steadily and repeats, 'I could use a real challenge in *my work*.'

However happy and in love she is, Erica has changed. Feminism, her woman's 'club', her therapy, her separation and recent divorce: they have all changed her. She no longer wants to be dependent on a man. She is more interested in how she might become independent of men.

Martin turns up on her doorstep to tell her that he and his girlfriend have separated – the fun stopped as soon as they moved in together. He wants to come home, he says. Couldn't she just think of him 'as this guy who was sick for a long time and then recovered'? Erica looks at him sympathetically but shakes her head: 'It doesn't work that way.' It doesn't work that way with Saul either. She's happy to live with him in New York, but the problem is that he wants her to go with him to Vermont for the summer, which would mean her giving up her job and then what would she do? Watch him paint? She tries to explain

that she's 'been on vacation for sixteen years already'. Saul
patiently concedes that he approves of her wanting to do her
own thing, but she doesn't need to work, he has enough money
for both of them. 'What do you mean *you approve*?' Erica
demands – she's not doing this for his approval. How does he
know what she needs to do for herself? They have reached an
impasse and they both refuse to shift their positions. 'Men!'
Erica finally exclaims in exasperation.

Later she goes to his studio and finds him sitting despondently
on the floor. She sits by him and gives him a peace offering, a jar
of pickled herrings. She'll come to Vermont for the holidays, she
offers as a concession. He hurls the pickled herring jar at the wall
in frustration: 'Come with me for Christ sakes!' She insists she
can't. 'Independent?' he asks. 'Trying to be,' she says. He
concedes defeat and bends down to kiss her knee. 'Woman!' he
mutters. She smiles and tenderly strokes the top of his head.

The film ends as the two of them are in the street lowering one
of Saul's large canvases on ropes down from his studio to the
street. Saul asks Erica to hold on to the painting, which resembles
a rainbow and is taller than her, while he walks to his waiting car,
packed ready for his summer in Vermont. 'Bye,' he says to Erica,
who looks at him in surprise. 'What about this?' she asks. 'Oh,
that's for you,' he smiles and climbs into his car. 'How the hell
am I going to get it home?' she calls to him in exasperation. He
grins broadly and drives away – that's her problem.

The painting is far too big for a taxi. It's so big it is almost
impossible for Erica to carry, but she does. She struggles through
the streets, swirling under its weight, almost falling over,
steadying herself with a little help from a few passers-by, hardly
able to see where she is going. She wanted her independence and
now she has got it. Or has she? Does lugging Saul's painting
through the streets represent her independence? Or is his canvas
a representation of him; a beautiful, valuable but cumbersome
thing which will take all her strength to cope with? On the other
hand, she has learnt that independence isn't just about
economics, it's a way of thinking about yourself, it's about

confidence, self-esteem, finding your own place in the world rather than living through your man – freedom is not something you can be given, it's something you must claim as your right. But she needs a relationship in order to be fulfilled and as a heterosexual woman she needs a man, even if the man, like his painting, is as much of a problem as a solution.

Annie Hall (1977)

Directed by Woody Allen; screenplay by Woody Allen and
Marshall Brickman; starring Woody Allen and Diane Keaton

'She's making progress and I'm getting screwed.'

As the writer, director and lead actor in *Annie Hall*, it would be
easy to assume that the film is about Woody Allen, rather than
Annie Hall. The film is about Allen, of course, in the guise of
Alvy Singer, and a more appropriate title for the film may have
been 'Alvy and Annie' as the film is about their relationship,
although told from Alvy's point of view. But the brilliance of
Annie Hall is that while Allen certainly explores his problems as
the man in the relationship with remarkable candour as well as
his usual wit, the film also reveals a deep understanding of
Annie, and what it was like for her to be in a relationship with a
man like Alvy. This insight into both sides of the story is one of
the reasons why *Annie Hall* continues to be one of the best loved
of all romantic comedies.

Another reason for the film's enduring success is that it
manages to be a celebration of a relationship while also
embracing the many complications and confusions resulting
from feminism, which in 1977 when the film was released were
undoubtedly affecting many people's intimate lives. At each
stage Allen gives us fresh insights into what makes Annie and
Alvy so good together and the conflicts that are driving them
apart as they attempt to understand themselves, each other,
what they want and don't want, what they feel and don't feel,
what makes them happy, what upsets them, what they are afraid
of and the ever-present and increasingly tricky problem of what
they each feel about sex.

The film opens with Alvy, a small forty-year-old with intense
eyes that peer through large horn-rimmed glasses, introducing
himself to us, the audience. He's Jewish, a professional comedian,

has lived all his life in New York and has been divorced twice. His problem is that, even though it's a year now since he broke up with Annie, he still can't get his mind around it: 'I keep sifting through the pieces of the relationship . . . examining my life and trying to figure out where did I screw up?'

Alvy first meets Annie (Diane Keaton) after a game of tennis. He is fixing his shoelace when she walks by. She's about thirty, taller than he is, and her appearance, in beige baggy trousers, white shirt, tie, black waistcoat and black floppy hat, is as eccentric and self-conscious as her attempts at conversation. When Alvy tells her she plays well, she positively lights up: 'Oh Yeah? So do you. Oh God, what a dumb thing to say, right? You say you play well, and I have to say, you play well . . . Oh God Annie . . . Oh well . . . La-di-dah.' She laughs at her own nervous confusion and offers to drive Alvy back into town. In the car she tells him she's an actress; well, she's taken acting classes. On the pavement outside her apartment he tells her he's been in analysis for fifteen years. 'Fifteen years? No, really?' She does a double take while she tries to work out if he's serious or joking. Their getting-to-know each other conversation continues over a drink in her chaotic apartment. He picks up her copy of Sylvia Plath poems: 'An interesting poetess whose tragic suicide was mis-interpreted as romantic by the college girl mentality,' he informs her with learned assurance. 'Well, I don't know,' Annie looks abashed, 'yeah, well some of her poems seem neat.' She's even more abashed when he tells her the word 'neat' went out at the turn of the century.

By the end of their first encounter, despite the fact that he's asked her out on a date, Annie is already feeling worried that she's not smart enough for him. This is a problem for Annie, which, as we soon learn, is to underpin their entire relationship. It's as if she is on a mental switchback machine. As soon as she says something she criticizes herself for what she has said. She's intelligent, witty and bright but at the same time she's constantly observing herself and criticizing the fruits of her own spontaneity. She has a go, yet immediately has to mock herself and laugh at what she thinks is her own ineptitude. While they both play with the idea of their insecurity, deep down Annie is genuinely insecure, while Alvy knows he's smart. Alvy's jokes are his strength. Annie's jokes constantly hint at her deep-seated lack of confidence.

At first things between them go swimmingly well. Annie takes Alvy to a club where she's performing as a singer. Afterwards she's mortified: 'I was awful, I'm so ashamed, I can't sing,' But Alvy's not having it; she has a great voice and he's not going to let her quit – it looks as if Annie has found the perfect man to help her with her confidence problem. Alvy is a little put out when they first make love because Annie insists that she needs marijuana to relax her, but he accepts it. He even seems to take her intellectual education in hand; while they are browsing in a bookshop he buys her a copy of *The Denial of Death* and when he takes her to the cinema his choice of film is *The Sorrow and the Pity*, a harrowing documentary about the Second World War in France. Eventually, when they are strolling by the river at night, they admit, in a roundabout and embarrassed kind of a way, that they are in love.

Then their problems start. Annie decides to move in with him and Alvy panics. Not, he insists, because she's moving in – they are practically living together anyway – but because Annie wants to give up her apartment. That means they will only have one place, his, and that feels just too much like marriage. If she keeps her apartment, she doesn't have to go to it, but the fact that it is there will be symbolic, 'like a free-floating life raft'. Annie is mortified. She's convinced that the real issue for Alvy is not her apartment: there is something wrong with her, she's not smart enough for him, that's why he's always encouraging her to take these college courses, 'Like I am dumb or something.' Alvy tells her not to be ridiculous, but it looks as if his self-appointed role as her mentor could backfire.

The next problem they run up against is sex. Alvy decides to put his foot down about Annie smoking marijuana when they make love. He takes the joint from her and insists they try making love without it. But Annie's not happy: we see a double image of her, as if she has split into two, with half of her sitting on a chair by the bed coolly watching her other half trying to have sex with him. He senses that something is wrong. At first she says nothing, but then she admits it, she wants grass. He says it ruins it for him if she has grass. They have hit another impasse.

Their solution to the impasse is that Annie goes into therapy. She arrives home from her first session bubbling with excitement and eagerly tells Alvy how it went while they unpack the groceries. She's been talking to her analyst about her family, her feelings about men, her relationship with her brother, penis envy, guilt, a dream she had – she even cried. Alvy, who's just finished washing-up, is impressed – she's covered more ground in one session sitting on a chair than he has in fifteen years lying on a couch! But just as Alvy's hopes, that Annie's therapy might be the answer to all their relationship problems, are rising, she tells him her dream. In the dream Frank Sinatra was trying to suffocate her with a pillow. Alvy immediately launches into his own analytic interpretation: Sinatra is a singer and she is a singer, so she's obviously trying to suffocate herself. 'It makes perfect sense,' he finishes, pleased with this demonstration of his analytic abilities. But Annie's not having it. She and her analyst have already worked on the dream and *his* name is Singer, Alvy Singer. So he is trying to suffocate her! Also in her dream she was trying to break his glasses and she did 'this terrible thing to him, so when he sang he sang in this really high-pitched voice.' She looks at him defiantly and adds, 'And then I told her how I didn't think you'd ever take me seriously because you don't think I'm smart enough.' She finishes unpacking the groceries and walks out of the kitchen.

In Annie's dream she attempts to break his glasses, which is yet another manifestation of her anger at his assumed intellectual superiority, and she makes him sing in a high-pitched voice, which obviously implies castration. Her dream is clearly showing how she is so angry with his masculine power that she wants to cut him down to size, or to feminize him, to turn him into a woman and so redress the power imbalance. (Of course there is always the possibility that, as the film was written and directed by Allen, his portrayal of Annie's dream reveals his own projected fear of feminism as manifested in this image of Annie as a castrating woman.) Whatever our conclusion, the issue that has been with Annie and Alvy since the very beginning of their relationship has again reared its head. Annie is upset about being intellectually inferior, or because she thinks he thinks she is intellectually inferior; either way she's angry, she wants equality and she doesn't feel like she's got it. It's beginning to look as if, rather than therapy being the solution, it could just add to their relationship problems.

Soon they are having full-scale rows in the street. Alvy is jealous of her adult education class professor. He's convinced Annie is having an affair with him, which is doubly frustrating as he encouraged her to go to adult education classes in the first place. In her defence Annie points out that he is the one who set the terms for their relationship: 'You wanted to keep the relationship flexible. It's your phrase.' In other words she's either calling his bluff and finding out just how 'flexible' he wants it, or she's just responding naturally to his lack of real commitment. Either way she's fighting back and Alvy doesn't like it, particularly as the thought of her having an affair with her professor robs him of his exclusive role as her mentor.

Annie moves back into her own apartment and Alvy tries taking out another woman. But he's bored, his new girlfriend is no fun, not like Annie. In the middle of the night the phone rings: Annie demands that he come round right away, it's an emergency, there's a spider in her bath. Alvy rushes to her place, kills the spider with her tennis racket, and then finds Annie sitting on her lonely single bed crying. 'Alvy let's never split up again,' she manages to utter as she dries her tears. Now their traditional gender roles are re-established: Alvy as the gallant spider-killing man, Annie as the damsel in distress – they are happy again, for a while at least. Annie moves back into Alvy's apartment. They take a nostalgic trip to Brooklyn to see where Alvy grew up, which gives him the opportunity to indulge in one of his favourite occupations – telling funny stories about his childhood. Annie resumes her budding career as a nightclub singer. But, as we soon realize, she has changed; her singing has become more mature and assured. One night she gets noticed by a record producer from California. She is torn between her own career opportunity and Alvy, who takes an instant dislike to the smooth, assured producer, who is even smaller than he is.

The screen splits enabling us to see both Annie and Alvy in their separate analysis sessions at the same time. Annie is sitting on a chair telling her analyst how she's been moody and dissatisfied lately. Alvy is lying on a couch complaining to his analyst about how he and Annie never laugh together any more. Both analysts ask about their sex life. 'Hardly ever, about three times a week,' Alvy says dejectedly. 'Constantly, about three times a week,' Annie announces crossly. Although there is no direct mention in the film of the contemporary feminist discourse, the polarity of the male and the female position is becoming increasingly acute. While Annie tells her female analyst that since her sessions began she's started to feel that she has a right to her own feelings and she's really begun to assert herself, Alvy is somehow being left behind to bemoan his lot. As he says to his male analyst, 'I'm paying for her analysis, she's making progress and I'm getting screwed.' Seen from Alvy's point of view, by encouraging her to 'improve herself' and to go into therapy, he's had a hand in creating her, making her what she is, and his reward, as he sees it, should be that he benefits from her improvement. Annie should be happy to inhabit his world and do the things he likes to do. The problem is, as Annie grows increasingly independent, she has other ideas, in particular pursuing her own career.

Alvy reluctantly accompanies her to California to a meeting with the record producer, but from the moment their plane lands at Los Angeles airport he begins acting up like a recalcitrant child. He hates everything about Los Angeles, the heat, the health food, the beautiful people. We suspect that what he hates most is that he is being forced to do what Annie wants to do; he is losing control of her. Soon he retreats to his hotel bed suffering from a mysterious, undiagnosable illness and Annie finds herself having to spend her time by his bedside nursing him. But she finally manages to get him to go with her to her record producer's glamorous mansion. Alvy tries to stay cool while the record producer invites Annie to come out to 'the coast' for six weeks to cut an album.

It's Christmas in Alvy's New York apartment. The tree is gaily dressed and the fire burns brightly in the hearth. But despite this idyllically happy setting they both agree that by ending their relationship they are 'doing the mature thing'. Annie enthusiastically packs up her things while Alvy fusses over who owns *Catcher in the Rye*. 'All the books on death and dying are yours, all the poetry books are mine,' Annie says. Alvy hands her *The Denial of Death* reminding her that he gave it to her as a present soon after they met. She glances at the book distastefully and hands it back: 'I feel like that is a great weight off my back.' He's hurt. She briskly tries to repair the damage by telling him how her analyst thinks this move is really key for her. 'Yeah,' Alvy agrees uncertainly, 'and I trust her, after all my analyst recommended her.' They finally congratulate themselves; not many couples could handle what they are doing, breaking up but at the same time remaining friends.

Alvy can't handle it either. At great risk to his mental and physical health he flies to California where Annie is now living with the record producer. They meet in a Sunset Boulevard pavement café and Alvy takes the plunge: he asks Annie to marry him. But Annie is adamant, she doesn't want to get married. 'Alvy,' she says, 'you're incapable of enjoying life, you know that. You are like New York City . . . you're like this island unto yourself.' Alvy returns to New York alone.

Finally the only way Allen can give the film a happy ending is to manufacture one through art. Back in New York we see Alvy attending the rehearsal of a play he has written about his relationship with Annie. In the scene the young actor and actress are speaking the same lines that he and Annie spoke in the pavement café on Sunset Boulevard. But instead of the relationship ending when the actor playing Alvy stands to leave, the young actress playing Annie rushes to stop him: 'Wait, I'm going to go with you, I love you.'

As Alvy points out (speaking to camera as he did in the opening frames of the film), whereas you can 'get things to come out perfect in art, it's real difficult in life'. However, as he goes on to tell us, he did run into Annie again on a visit to the cinema. Ironically she was taking the man she was now living with to see *The Sorrow and the Pity* – so Alvy did manage to influence her intellectually. He also tells us that he and Annie went out for a meal together to 'kick around old times'. We see Annie laughing with him in a restaurant and a nostalgic montage of the high points of Alvy and Annie's relationship. The film finishes with Annie and Alvy, viewed from the distance of the now empty restaurant across the street, as two anonymous people, hugging briefly and then going their separate ways. Time moves on, the romantic moments have become great memories, and as such perhaps even more vivid and romantic than they ever were in reality.

But whoever said that love has to last forever? Relationships are one long negotiation or, as Alvy puts it when he and Annie are breaking up yet again, 'A relationship is like a shark, it has to constantly move forward or it dies. And you know what I think we've got on our hands is a dead shark.' Although the image of a dead shark is sad, as is the reality of a dead relationship, particularly while we are still mourning its demise, the fact that it didn't last forever doesn't necessarily invalidate the excitement, beauty and pleasure the relationship gave us when it was alive. Life goes on, people learn and change in relationships and then go on to learn and change some more with other people. And in the seventies understanding the detail of how people learn and change was the challenge, not questing after the mythic fairytale romance.

Starting Over (1979)

Directed by Alan J. Pakula; screenplay by James L. Brooks;
based on the novel by Dan Wakefield; starring Burt Reynolds,
Jill Clayburgh and Candice Bergen

> 'Excuse us gentlemen, the divorced men's group
> meets from nine 'til ten.'

To judge by the behaviour of the characters in *Starting Over*, by
1979 a catastrophe has taken place between the sexes and men,
as well as women, are reeling from the shock. After a decade of
women finding their voice in consciousness-raising groups,
assertiveness training courses, self-defence classes, women's
studies classes and a multitude of other feminist activities, men
have been left behind feeling confused, beleaguered, attacked,
insecure and reproachful. Relationships are breaking down.
After all the talk about gender roles, nothing between the sexes
is straightforward any more. Both sexes view the other with deep
suspicion and need help learning to trust each other if they are
to risk living together again. Every little detail of how the sexes
approach each other and behave in a relationship must be
attended to in this new climate of heightened sensitivity. One
wrong step by either sex may result in the other retreating into
their defensive shell, and it will take a hell of a lot of work to get
them out again. The need for love is as strong as ever, but how
to find it in such a climate of confusion, hostility and
misunderstanding? This, as the title suggests, is what *Starting
Over*, directed by Alan J. Pakula, is about.

When the film opens Phil Potter (Burt Reynolds), a forty-year-
old freelance writer, tall, dark and comfortably good-looking, is
utterly bewildered. 'I swear to God we are getting a divorce
when all we need is separate vacations,' he tells his wife Jessica
in a last desperate attempt to repair their marriage. 'When I walk
out of that door what are you going to do? Just stand here and

start crying?' But Jessica (Candice Bergen), a statuesque woman whose classical beauty is quite breathtaking, just smiles at him calmly. Nothing will change her mind and she has no intention of crying. When he leaves she will probably work on her song, which she assures him is not like her painting or her photography; with singing and songwriting she is at last really finding her true self. As Phil reluctantly closes the door to their luxurious New York apartment behind him for the last time, Jessica begins to sing: 'It's gonna be easy for you, it's gonna be harder for me, but this woman's got a right to be more than a shadow of a man . . .' He winces. Whatever one might think of the words or the tune, Jessica's voice is the diametric opposite of her physical appearance – it is harsh, discordant and mind-numbingly flat. If Jessica is Pakula's idea of the liberated woman finding her voice, maybe it is best to do as she wants and leave her alone for a while as she goes about finding it.

Phil arrives, with his two suitcases, on the doorstep of a cottage in a sleepily peaceful village on the outskirts of Boston. Mickey, his portly elder brother, and Martha, his brother's wife, welcome him into their cozy home for tea and cakes by the fire. They know about his marriage break-up and are concerned. Martha, an intense, caring, homely woman, wants him to look at the whole thing positively; just think of the possibilities for growth and self-awareness. Mickey, a psychiatry lecturer, says he has already set him up in a weekly divorced men's workshop. Phil is appalled by the prospect, but he is too emotionally and physically exhausted to argue, all he wants to do is to go to bed.

He moves into a gloomy apartment in town. He buys a couple of chairs, a mattress and a lamp but the place still feels cold and miserable. In desperation he phones his brother from the communal phone in the hall and Mickey, who was asleep in bed, suggests he come to dinner the next night. Phil's bus draws to a halt in a deserted village street. He gets off, and so does a woman, and they both walk down the street, which is badly lit and silent but for their footsteps. The woman, who is wearing a shapeless quilted coat, a woolly hat and a long scarf, keeps glancing suspiciously at Phil. He takes a big step to avoid a patch of old snow and the woman suddenly reacts, jumping backwards screeching, 'Get the fuck away from me. I've got a knife. I'll cut your fucking balls off, so help me.' Before Phil has a chance to respond she runs away.

A few minutes later he arrives at his brother's house only to find his brother on the verge of calling the police because on her way here Marilyn, their other dinner guest, was almost attacked by a pervert. Phil goes into the sitting room to find the woman, Marilyn (Jill Clayburgh), ensconced in a blanket by the sitting room fire with Martha comforting her. Marilyn takes one look at Phil and retreats under the blanket in embarrassment. 'I'm really not this kind of a person,' she calls out. When she finally plucks up the courage to poke her head out, she tries to explain that on her self-defence course she learnt that if someone attacks you in the street you scare the hell out of them. 'You must have got very high marks in your course,' Phil grins at her amiably.

Despite the calamity of their first meeting, the dinner, which is obviously a matchmaking set-up, is fun. Marilyn, a nursery school teacher in her mid-thirties, is no stunning and sophisticated beauty like Jessica, but she's intelligent and funny and quirkily attractive. After the meal Martha accosts Phil in the hall. 'Marilyn is a terrific person,' she whispers to him urgently, 'she's got herself together after her divorce and I don't want to see her hurt.' Phil is surprised and insists that he wasn't even planning to ask her out. 'Why not?' Martha demands in a bewildering about-face, 'Because she doesn't have large enough breasts?'

Poor Phil, it seems, can't act or not act without being accused of something or other in the present climate where women fiercely support each other and they have the advantage of all these groups where they learn to assert and defend themselves. He's even more confused when a little later, while they are waiting at the bus stop together, he asks Marilyn out, only to have her turn him down flat. It's too soon after his separation from his wife, she informs him with the benefit of her own experience. This is too intense a time for him, and she really doesn't want to have to nurse him through his break-up. He should call her in a few months.

The divorced men's group is held in a spartan room in the basement of a church hall. There are eight men in the group with ages ranging from thirty to seventy. Phil listens, bemused, as a small man in a cardigan talks about how he keeps marrying the same woman; he knows it always gets balled up but he can't stay away from her. The man takes off his glasses and cries. A young man in a black polo-neck accuses him of being a masochist. The seventy-year-old tells the group how his wife left him on their forty-third wedding anniversary because 'there were no surprises left'. As the group sinks into a depressed silence there is a loud knocking on the door above. A shrill woman's voice calls out, 'Excuse us gentlemen, the divorced women's workshop meets from nine to ten.' The men make their way up the stairs as the women clatter noisily past them down to the meeting room. The atmosphere between the two groups is distinctly hostile as they studiously ignore each other.

At home in his empty apartment Phil's loneliness is getting to him. He phones Marilyn and promises, 'No romance, I just want to have dinner with somebody, anybody. I'm not going to touch you. I may not even talk to you.' 'Sounds perfect,' Marilyn grins. Dinner goes well and afterwards Marilyn invites him up to her single person's one-room apartment. He's a little surprised by the number of locks and bolts on her front door, but the modest room is cozy in an ethnic way, with red cushions on the floor, wall rugs and a bed in the corner. After nervously kissing, Marilyn tentatively steers him towards the bed. But Phil pulls back, he can't do it right now, he thinks he had better go. At first Marilyn nods understandingly; of course, it's too soon. But then she gets worried. What if the problem is her: 'You don't like me enough? Or you like me too much? Or you're frightened? Or you're guilty? Or you can't get it up, or out, or in or what?'

In the group the men also try offering Phil explanations for why he's avoiding going to bed with Marilyn. One suggests that this is what happens after a divorce, you become afraid to open up, to care, and you end up questioning your own ability to love someone. Another says Phil's problem is that he still feels married. Another suggests that maybe Marilyn is too special? After the group Phil arrives unannounced on Marilyn's doorstep, interrupting her candle-lit dinner for one, and bluntly declares that he wants to have sex with her. He's sorry, he didn't put that very well, but he's trying to avoid the whole romantic thing. She suggests that he could try personalizing it a little, something like, 'I want to have sex with you, Marilyn.' And then she can reply, 'I want to have sex with you, Potter.' That does it. They sleep together.

The sex is good, they enjoy each other's company and they make each other laugh. On the other hand, with every tentative step forward they take in their relationship they also seem to take two steps back. The terrain is littered with the ghosts of their painful past relationships and, particularly Marilyn's, fears that the mean, predatory and exploitative nature of the opposite sex is about to be confirmed yet again. At first she's convinced that she's going to wake up and find he's run out on her. Then, just as she's beginning to trust him, Jessica phones during their Thanksgiving dinner. Phil takes the call and pretends to Jessica that Marilyn is nothing more than a friend. Marilyn is mortified. This just proves what she has suspected all along, that he is the 'hung-up on the ex-wife type' and she should 'save her ass'. With that said, she refuses to have anything more to do with him.

Phil soon finds his opportunity to win her back. At her school fête Marilyn is presiding over a stall called 'Dunk the Teacher'. The object of the stall is for Marilyn, who is wearing a light summer dress although it is mid-winter, to sit on a seat that has been fitted to the edge of a paddling pool and connected to a target. The children throw balls at the target and if they hit it their teacher will be tipped into the water. Marilyn, however, appears to be quite safe so long as the children are not strong enough to hit the target. But when Phil arrives it is another matter. He hurls the balls at the target with relish. 'Will you talk to me now?' he demands, when Marilyn surfaces in the freezing water and drags herself to the edge of the pool. He launches straight into what he wants to say: he thinks the reason why she went berserk when Jessica called was because she didn't know where she stands, so in order to remedy this he's asking her to move in with him. 'What do you think?' he finishes hopefully. Marilyn, her teeth chattering with cold and looking like a drowned rat, can barely think at all, but despite this she nods and attempts to smile.

The subtext of this bizarre scene couldn't be more packed with conflicting messages. 'Dunk the Teacher' is strongly reminiscent of the medieval custom of strapping shrewish women on to ducking stools and dunking them in a river to force them to curb their tongue and mend their shrewish ways. While Phil clearly relishes the opportunity to use his manly strength to duck her in the water, at the same time he is also striving to prove to her that he really is a 'new man' – considerate, thoughtful and sensitive to her point of view. We know that Marilyn is not really submitting to force; she does want to move in with him, although previously she couldn't trust him or herself enough to admit it. But the more powerful message emanating from the scene is the old *The Taming of the Shrew* story – the woman who is finally brought to her senses by the man's masterful behaviour.

Pakula's ambivalence to the feminist message and its effect upon men emerges even more disturbingly in the next sequence. On the very day when Marilyn moves in with Phil, Jessica decides to pay an unexpected visit. She's wearing a stunningly seductive transparent blouse, which, as Marilyn whispers to Phil, shows off her 'very nice tits'. Despite being a little put out that Phil isn't 'sprawled out on a couch suffering from malnutrition and muttering her name', Jessica is supremely confident of her seductive charm and doesn't even consider that little Marilyn, in her sensible dungarees, may be serious competition. She couldn't be clearer about her intentions when Phil takes her back to her motel room. She hangs the 'do not disturb' sign on the door, orders ice for the champagne bucket and gazes lovingly into his eyes. But just as Phil begins to succumb to her charms, she switches on a tape of the music to her latest song and sings: 'Better than ever, I'm better than ever, I needed some time 'til I found myself . . .' Phil stares in horror as Jessica sings and dances in front of him – her movements horribly exaggerated, her voice mind-numbingly flat and rasping, her stunning beauty suddenly revealed as a monstrous caricature. Is this what the women's liberation movement has done? Has it made women like Jessica completely deluded about their own talent? The chances are that women like Jessica would be deluded about something or other whatever decade they happened to live in, but as far as *Starting Over* is concerned, the association Pakula is making, between Jessica's striving to find her voice and the feminist movement as a whole, is inescapable. 'Have you lost your marbles?' Phil asks when the song is over and, appearing to come to his senses just in time, retreats to find Marilyn.

But this is not the end of the story. In his next session at the men's group he tells them about Jessica's visit. At the end of his dispassionate, factual account, he finally admits, 'I never wanted a woman so much in my life.' Despite her dreadful singing, the power of Jessica's extraordinary beauty is stronger than he can cope with. In Bloomingdale's, where Phil goes to meet Marilyn to buy a sofa for their apartment, he suddenly finds that he can't breathe. A small crowd gather round and watch as he curls up on a bed hyperventilating like a helpless child. He's having a full-scale panic attack and the sight of Marilyn's concerned face makes it worse. He only calms down when his brother Mickey arrives to look after him. Clearly, as Phil tries to explain to Marilyn, he has some unfinished business with Jessica. Marilyn is devastated. She moves back into her own apartment and makes him swear on his brother's life (she's now seen how important his elder brother is to him) never to call her again.

Back in New York it doesn't take long for Phil to realize that his fantasy of wanting Jessica is just that, a fantasy. In reality their relationship has died. He rushes back to Boston and arrives at the men's group just as they finish comparing their worst Christmases. The women's group upstairs is already knocking on the door. As if to symbolize that change is in the air, the men's group invites the women's group to join them for a little Christmas party. After some urgent whispering upstairs, the women's group slowly descend the stairs and the two groups survey each other suspiciously. But the ice is broken and the introductions begin. Meanwhile Phil goes to find Marilyn and proposes to her. She's so shocked she bursts into tears. He says he's sorry, if she wants they can go slower. 'What do you want?' she asks. He wants to live together, to get married, to have kids, to watch them grow up, to put their teeth in the same glass at night and to be buried in a family plot with the same headstone. 'What do you want?' he finishes. 'I want a separate glass for my teeth,' she says, beaming with happiness.

At the outset of the seventies the feminist agenda had barely begun to impact on the popular consciousness. In *Diary of a Mad Housewife* neither Jonathan nor George questioned how their behaviour and attitudes as men affected women, other than in the traditional sense. And Tina remained isolated and alone with her feelings. Now, at the end of the decade, we see in *Starting Over* the impact the feminist movement has had on the lives of both women and men. Marilyn has learnt to stand up for herself and to live alone and finally she also learns to trust her feelings and to allow herself to love again. Phil is unashamedly confused; he struggles to open up and talk honestly about intimate things with other men, just as he strives, sometimes against his own nature, to be more sensitive and understanding with women.

On the other hand, the bizarre scene with the dunking stool and the portrayal of Jessica's self-obsessed determination to find 'her voice' hints at many unresolved issues of anger and resentment on both sides of the gender divide. We have also discovered that of all the counter-culture, lifestyle and protest movements started in the late sixties, the two that survived and went on to have the greatest impact on society and relationships in the seventies were feminism and the rapid expansion in individual therapy and small therapy groups, which provided people with a forum for exploring and understanding what was happening to them.

But despite *Starting Over*'s attempt to embrace feminist values, beneath the surface the feeling is of an undercurrent tugging backwards, a desire to get back to normality and the kind of fairytale love that will last happily ever after. After all, feminism or no feminism, Phil and Marilyn finally have the same dream as their parents and grandparents. Or could it be that just as the feminist agenda has gained respectability the male backlash is also beginning to take hold?

Six

Power and Power Dressing in the Eighties

The eighties saw two of the most powerful countries in the western world presided over by an Iron Lady and a cowboy. This was how Margaret Thatcher, the first woman prime minister of Britain and Ronald Reagan, President of the USA and former Hollywood movie star, appeared in the popular imagination. Perhaps more surprisingly, these two figureheads, each representative of their nation and their gender, actually liked each other. Thatcher was even rumoured to be a little bit in love with Reagan although, of course, in the nicest possible way, and rumours abounded about how the men in her all-male Cabinet were lusting after her – her dominatrix manner rekindling their long-buried secret desires for their boarding school matrons. But while an Iron Lady and an archetypal wild-west hero may have formed an unlikely alliance at the top, what did this mean for the rest of man and womankind?

Thatcher and Reagan were both right-wing conservatives dedicated to the supremacy of free-market economics and a return to old-fashioned 'family values'. A simplistic interpretation of Darwin's theory of evolution was presented as the justification for an economic model where, according to the God-given natural order of things, the fittest survive and the weakest fall along the wayside. In a devastating attack on the values of mutual solidarity and community, Thatcher famously said, 'There is no such thing as society.' The new work ethic dictated that just getting through a normal working day was not enough; 'voluntary overtime' was the name of the game if you were to outpace your competitors and succeed. Ruthless managerial concepts such as 'restructuring' and 'downsizing' were the new mantras which threatened the lives of millions of workers. But unlike in the thirties when redundancy had been seen as a social evil, mass unemployment was now seen as a necessary result of the purging of the old order, the inevitable by-product of market forces in the competitive reality of the corporate jungle.

Along with jungle economics came a revived interest in jungle psychology. A New Age 'new masculinist' movement was spearheaded by the poet Robert Bly (who later wrote *Iron John*). In the seventies Bly had conducted 'Great Mother Conferences' where he had advocated the importance for both men and women of embracing their 'feminine principle'. Now in the new climate of the eighties his concern turned to his 'missing masculine side'; missing, he is reported as saying, as a result of overexposure to feminism and strong women generally, including his mother.[1] To redress this imbalance, which he assumed to be a problem for most men, he began running all-male weekend wilderness retreats with the aim of reintroducing men to the 'wild man within'. On these retreats men would wear tribal masks, dress up in wild animal costumes and with the powerful accompaniment of drum music, evoking the spirits of their distant ancestors, rediscover the long-repressed need for masculine ritual in their unnatural urban lives. 'Men, Sex and Power' weekends taught the emasculated how to become 'real men' once again. Despite accusations by feminists that the New Age masculinist movement was merely another example of 'the male backlash', Bly insisted that this was unintended. As he explained, just as women's consciousness-raising groups excluded men, so men also felt that they could 'be more honest when women weren't around'.[2]

Reagan himself, as president, father figure and fictional wild west hero, appeared to embody the archetypal conflict between the seduction of the wild frontier and the restraining influence of civilization. The film *Greystoke* revived the mythic hero of

Tarzan, the boy-child nurtured by apes. With the help of Sigourney Weaver, *Gorillas in the Mist* combined this jungle fascination with that other myth of the decade – the tough-minded, courageous superwoman. And the romantic comedy *Crocodile Dundee*, as we shall see, attempted a somewhat unsettling match between the noble savage and superwoman.

The eighties 'back to nature' movement may have been just another manifestation of the desire to escape from the alienation of the unnatural modern world. But it may also have reflected the new imperative, experienced by many young men, to relearn or get back in touch with primitive survival skills such as remaining alert at all times, watching every move, seizing opportunities and meeting aggression with aggression.[3] This archetypal masculine mindset was thought to be just as applicable in the ruthless competition of the corporate jungle as it was in the wilderness. But as men, such as Harrison Ford's character in *Working Girl*, discovered, the excitement of being a player constantly chasing deals was not without its downside – the lurking fear of failure and sky-high stress levels.

Women's consciousness-raising groups rapidly became a thing of the past. Feminism was superseded by post-feminism, which for some meant 'backlash' and for others was a natural progression – time to forget the sisterhood and join the ruthless battle for achievement alongside men, and may the best man, or woman, win. The post-feminists pointed to Margaret Thatcher: if she, as a woman, had been elected prime minister, this surely demonstrated that the feminist struggle was over. Just as Thatcher remained the sole woman in her Cabinet, so it became standard practice for businesses, managerial teams, committees and interviewing panels to appoint a token woman as proof, if proof were needed, that now any woman of merit could make it to the top if they were bright enough and tough enough. Whatever the reasons, there were more high-achieving women than ever before breaking through the 'glass ceiling', including that of the film industry. *Crossing Delancey*, released in 1988, is an example of a romantic comedy that was both written and directed by women in an industry that had formerly seen relatively few women writers and even fewer women directors – a scarcity that is reflected in the films chosen for this book.

But the very fact that feminism was showing results was in itself becoming a problem. Many men pointed to Thatcher as an example of how, if feminism wasn't dead, it ought to be. Hadn't the whole subject of women's rights become deeply boring? Feminists were whingeing women, while post-feminists were real women who got on with the job, preferably 'power dressed' in forties-style high heels and smart business suits with padded shoulders. In other words if women wanted equality in a man's world they had to play the game the man's way. Or, as a lawyer observed at the time, 'unless somebody acts like a man, she is not perceived as managerial material'.[4]

Conversely, if a woman acts like a man she is not perceived as wife material. Just as in the romantic comedies of the forties, women were once again having to walk the difficult tightrope between appearing masculine enough to succeed at work and feminine enough to find a relationship or husband. The problem was highlighted by films such as *Working Girl* and the glut of magazine articles in the popular press with headlines such as 'Loveless, Manless: the high cost of independence', 'Are You Turning Men Off?' and 'The Single Woman's Lament'.[5] In 1986 *Newsweek* published an article claiming that, 'Many women who seem to have it all – good looks, good jobs, advanced degrees, high salaries – will never have a mate.' The Harvard and Yale statistics used to underpin these stories suggested that 'a college educated, unmarried woman at the age of thirty had a 20 per cent likelihood of marriage, at thirty-five a 5 per cent chance and at forty no more than a 1.3 per cent chance.'[6] But, as Susan Faludi argues so compellingly in her book, *Backlash*, these often quoted statistics, fallen on with such relish by the popular press, were later demonstrated, by the US Census Bureau, to be fallacious.

The press were more interested in the myths than the truth. In 1986 *Newsweek* printed a story suggesting that single women over forty 'are more likely to be killed by a terrorist' than marry.

Again this was taken up by women's magazines, talk shows and advice columns, although it later emerged that the basis of this story was a trainee journalist's joke rather than serious reporting. Meanwhile many single women over thirty, including the heroines of *Crossing Delancey* and *When Harry Met Sally*, had begun to panic about the relentless ticking of their 'biological clock' and what had become known as 'the man shortage'.

To make matters worse, in 1984 *Time* magazine declared that the sexual revolution was over. The AIDS crisis had arrived and was here to stay. Rock Hudson died of AIDS. The star of *Pillow Talk*, and icon of masculinity, was out of the closet. According to the right wing with its 'back to nature' philosophy, AIDS was nature's vengeance on those who tried to violate its laws. AIDS was labelled 'the gay plague'. Promiscuity, whatever your sex, was also blamed and 'safe sex' entered the popular vocabulary. Bizarre billboards appeared. Some portrayed nightmare images such as graveyards darkened by storm clouds and streaked with forked lightning, intended to impress on the public the intimate relationship between sex and death. Others coyly pictured a man putting on a sock, stating that 'Putting on a condom is just as simple'.

But despite the advice for men and women to save themselves by returning to stable monogamous marriages and, of course, traditional conservative family values, apart from the use of condoms there was no noticeable change in sexual practices. Casual sex, serial monogamy, living together, splitting-up, divorce, remarriage and pluralistic attitudes to sex generally, whatever the accompanying problems, were now an intrinsic part of many people's lives. As we see in *When Harry Met Sally*, too many men and women were enjoying their freedom and embracing their similarities as well as their differences. There was no turning back.

Crocodile Dundee (1986)

Directed by Peter Faiman; screenplay by Paul Hogan, Ken Shadie, John Cornell; starring Paul Hogan and Linda Kozlowski

> 'Why do you always make me feel like Jane in a Tarzan comic?'

The release of the Australian film *Crocodile Dundee* in 1986 coincided with the rise of the 'new masculinist' movement in America. Whether the film was influenced by the growing interest in Robert Bly's wilderness retreats, where men, free from the inhibiting influence of women, could be reintroduced to their 'deep masculine side', or whether Australian men had simply never lost touch with their 'inner wild man', the Zeitgeist was in the film's favour. *Crocodile Dundee* was an immediate international box office success.

The heroes of 'noble savage' stories, like the fairy stories of the unnoticed boy who goes out into the world to prove himself, were more compelling if they were orphans or foundlings. In the ancient Roman legend, the twins Romulus and Remus were abandoned in the wilderness to be devoured by wild beasts but instead they were nurtured by a passing she-wolf and later found and raised in the wilds by a shepherd. As a result Romulus attained the kind of superhuman masculine strength suitable for the founder of the great city of Rome. Likewise, as a baby, Tarzan, the lost son of an English aristocrat, was found in the wilds of the African jungle and reared by apes until he grew to manhood, thus elevating the white man to noble savage status. Being a foundling is especially important for a noble savage because it enables him to avoid the problem of his feminine side, or more specifically his having been feminized or made soft by his early dependence on his mother and her domesticity. The only mother fit for the true noble savage is nature or mother earth.

One of the reasons for the rise of the 'new masculinist' movement was the perceived threat of feminism. The Annie Oakley syndrome – 'Anything you can do I can do better' – appeared to many men to have taken hold as more women than ever before were proving their abilities in a man's world. The question posed by *Crocodile Dundee* is, what happens if you pit one of these new 'Annie Oakley' women against a real 'noble savage'? (It's worth remembering that Paul Hogan who stars in the film is also responsible for the story and one of the team of three male writers.)

We don't meet the eponymous hero of *Crocodile Dundee* straight away. Instead, as is often the case in stories where the hero is mythic or larger than life, our curiosity is first aroused by his reputation before we arrive at a suitably dramatic introduction to the man himself. The pre-credit sequence is set in an elegant office in Sydney, Australia, where Sue Charlton (Linda Kozlowski), a New York journalist, is on the phone to her boss in New York. At first Sue appears to be the epitome of the 'new woman'. She's in her early thirties, attractive with a well-groomed, efficient demeanor, divorced, independent, sophisticated, tough and, of course, very successful in a man's world. (Although we soon learn that her boss is also her boyfriend and later in the film we discover that the newspaper she works for is owned by her tycoon father – so behind this successful woman there are two even more successful men!) Whatever, Sue refuses to return to New York until she's investigated just one more story. A man has been attacked by a crocodile a hundred miles from nowhere. A week later he crawled out of the bush, got patched up and promptly disappeared again. Sue is determined to track this man down. Her lovesick boss in New York will just have to wait a few more days to see her.

The credits roll, accompanied by the film's theme tune, evoking the romance and drama of the outback with tantalizing hints of aboriginal tribal music. Sue, our intrepid reporter, in headscarf and dark glasses, flies in a chopper over the rocky escarpments and the harsh deserted wasteland of the Northern

Australian bush. The chopper lands in the middle of nowhere and Sue is met not by Dundee but by Wally, his safari business partner – an elderly man desperately trying to look smart for their important guest. He drives Sue to the Walkabout Creek hotel, which is little more than a bar in a place that is not so much a town as a few buildings dotted randomly in the bare, flat landscape. By mid-evening our hero still hasn't arrived. Instead Sue waits in the hotel bar populated by rough, sweaty, drinking men while Wally rhapsodizes about how Dundee, with half his leg bitten off, 'crawled hundreds of miles through snake-infested swamps on his hands and knees . . .' Every so often he glances sneakily at Sue to check that his story is having the desired effect.

Suddenly a knife spins past her ear and Mick Dundee (Paul Hogan) bursts into the bar fighting furiously with a life-sized crocodile. Pandemonium breaks out amongst the drinking men as Dundee staggers with the crocodile across to the bar and orders two beers – 'One for me and one for me mate' – he indicates the crocodile which, we now realize, is stuffed. He saunters over to Sue, looks her up and down appraisingly and introduces himself. He hands his crocodile to Wally and leads Sue, who he refers to as a 'charming young lady', into a dance. 'Up north in the Never Never where the land is harsh and bare,' he recites jauntily, 'There was a mighty hunter Mick Dundee who can dance like Fred Astair.' He finishes his little ditty with a nifty dance step and grins at her.

Michael J. Crocodile Dundee is blond, middle-aged, his build is slight, his face is tanned and creased like worn leather, he wears a hat adorned with a feather, a necklace of animal teeth and a sleeveless, snakeskin jacket, which shows off the strength of his manly biceps – all testimony to the nature of his outdoor life in the wilderness of the Northern Australia bush. He doesn't know how old he is; he was brought up by a tribe of aborigines and 'they don't have calendars'. So, like Tarzan, he is a foundling who has been reared as a 'noble savage' and he is white, which makes him a perfect role-model for men who yearn to get in touch with their primitive side or 'wild man within' while at the same time retaining the sophistication of Fred Astair. To cap it all, he's also got a sense of humour.

An example of Mick Dundee's wit is when, at the end of his first big scene, he joins the queue of men in the bar who are playing a game that involves punching a gigantic man in the stomach in order to cause a keg of beer he has balanced on his head to fall off. All the men fail except Mick, who goes to punch the man but suddenly kisses him on the lips instead. The big man is so surprised the beer keg immediately topples from his head. In other words Mick is so supremely confident in his masculinity that he can afford to risk laughing at himself and the suckers who fall for his play-acting. He can even risk the ultimate shame for a macho man; kissing another man in public. While the serious point is made – the desire to restore masculinity to its former glory and rebut the assault of feminism – the joke makes it more acceptable to a modern audience. This sets the tone for the comedy in the entire film (although on occasion we are left wondering about the hidden sexual agenda beneath the buddy camaraderie).

The first half of *Crocodile Dundee* follows Mick and Sue's three-day trek alone together through the bush to see the place where Mick was attacked by the crocodile. The implication is that Sue may think she is liberated but she is still 'a Sheila' (Australian slang for a woman). This trek through the wilds will not only put her in her place but also teach her what masculinity is really all about.

On the first day of their trek Sue mostly listens with rapt attention to Mick's stories of his daring exploits in the bush. They then make camp for the night. Sue makes coffee on the campfire while Mick tells her about the aborigines. 'The land is like their mother,' he is explaining when he casually bends down to grab hold of a deadly poisonous snake. 'You see, the aborigines just want to roam the earth and be left in peace,' he breaks the hissing snake's neck and tosses it on the fire. 'Any more around?' Sue asks, clearly terrified. 'Maybe the odd one late at night, but stick close to me and you'll be all right,' he grins. She gingerly climbs into her sleeping bag and moves as close to him as possible, without touching.

Dawn breaks, bathing the swamp and grasslands in pink and then golden light. The incident with the snake is quickly forgotten as Sue grows fed up with Mick's taunts about her only being a 'Sheila' and a city girl who wouldn't last five minutes out here on her own because 'this is man's country'. To prove him wrong she sets off into the bush alone. Mick, of course, discretely follows her. She comes across an idyllic pool and foolishly decides to take a swim. Within seconds she is attacked by a crocodile and Mick leaps to the rescue and knifes the crocodile. Luckily she had a man like him around to save her life. She hugs him and cries while he comforts her. She is finally ready to concede that he was right – 'This is definitely no place for a city girl.'

Sue is now ready for the ultimate lesson in the mysteries of masculinity. Night has fallen. Mick leaves Sue alone by the campfire and goes to investigate a sound he heard in the dark depths of the bush. Suddenly she is again terrified out of her wits, this time when she sees a black aborigine face dotted with white tribal markings watching her through the trees. Mick rushes back to the rescue and, much to Sue's relief, the young aborigine turns out to be Mick's friend. The young man explains that he is on his way home for a corroboree or sacred tribal ceremony – his father, a tribal elder 'would kill me if I didn't turn up'. Sue picks up her camera to take his photograph but the aborigine holds up his hand to stop her. 'You believe it will take away your spirit?' she asks, concerned by her faux pas. 'No,' the aborigine grins cheekily, 'you've got the lens cap on.' The joke is against the gullibility of the twentieth-century tourist, but as always there is a serious point underlying the joke – the aborigine may in some ways be just like you and me but he is also the real thing, a genuine 'wild man' and Sue is suitably impressed. Mick and his friend set off for the tribal ceremony together, leaving Sue behind because 'women are taboo at these events'. Sue, the intrepid reporter, of course follows them discretely with her camera. From her hiding place in the long grass she sees Mick in a small clearing with a group of semi-naked aboriginal men with their faces and bodies dotted with tribal markings, making music and dancing around a campfire. Mick glances in her direction, just to let her know he knows she is there, and she quickly puts her camera away and retreats. She has now learnt the ultimate lesson of 'new masculinism' – there are certain sacred boundaries that men must retain and women must not cross.

The tone of their final day in the wilderness is now quite changed. Dundee takes Sue to Echo Valley, an idyllically peaceful turquoise lake cupped in a safe enclosure of granite cliffs and surrounded by trees and lush vegetation. They swim together (Mick assures Sue that the lake is mineral water, which means it is crocodile-free) and afterwards Sue sits wistfully on the bank watching Mick admiringly while he stands patiently in the water, naked down to his waist, fishing with a spear. He catches a fish and brings it to her on the bank. She looks at him thoughtfully and asks him if he will go back to New York with her: 'It would make a great wrap to the story.' He's disappointed, he thought maybe she was making a pass at him. 'I might have been,' she says, which he takes as his invitation to kiss her.

Despite the beauty and romance of the setting, Sue and Mick's first kiss rates as one of the most passionless kisses in the history of romantic comedy. Luckily their moment of intimacy is interrupted, almost immediately, by Wally who arrives to drive them back to Walkabout Creek. Although Faiman, the director, clearly wants us to believe that Wally's arrival has spoiled a moment of romantic magic, if anything, when Mick withdraws his lips from Sue's, it is with relief rather than frustration. As for Sue, she looks as if she has just kissed a wall.

It's interesting to speculate whether this total lack of sexual chemistry between Sue and Mick is a problem of casting, or the script, or both. As we have seen in earlier films, moonlit nights beneath the stars in the great outdoors often arouse our most atavistic tendencies. This, combined with sexual chemistry, such as that between Clark Gable and Claudette Colbert in *It Happened One Night*, or Cary Grant and Katharine Hepburn in *Bringing Up Baby*, can serve as the most powerful aphrodisiac. But in both these films the heroines were as sparkling, lively and fascinating as their male counterparts – as with all the great romantic comedies, the male and the female characterizations are equally complex and interesting. In contrast Linda Kozlowski's performance in *Crocodile Dundee* is wooden, but Paul Hogan's script gives her little chance to be otherwise. Although the story involves her proving her bravery in numerous challenging incidents, each incident is designed to show off Mick's superior masculinity rather than Sue's bravery. Her role remains essentially one of feminine passivity; she listens, she learns and she admires him. There isn't the rough and tumble and fun of a real relationship.

So, when they finally arrive in Echo Valley, which has to be one of the world's most beautiful and romantic locations, rather than this being a place for them to finally unite as man and woman, it is merely another stunning backdrop for Sue to watch and admire Mick Dundee. The name Echo Valley is interesting, if only by coincidence. In the myth of Narcissus and Echo, Narcissus is incapable of loving another because he is already in love with his own reflection in the water. Likewise, as Mick stands in the lake fishing he is more absorbed with his self-image than he is with Sue. Her role, as was Echo's, is to be a reflection or echo of his ego. As Mick himself told us earlier, the aborigines believe the earth is the great mother. Echo Valley, with its small lake enclosed by rocks and lush vegetation, is the ultimate symbol of female sexuality. Here in Echo Valley man has his idealized mother all to himself; he has no need of real women.

The second half of the film is devoted to Mick's visit to New York and much of the comedy revolves around the fact that this is his first visit to a city, let alone one of the world's great metropolises. But the problem at the core of the film becomes still more apparent: the real love story is not between Sue and

Mick Dundee, it is between Mick Dundee and all the other men in the film. It's these men: the bespectacled doorman of the luxurious hotel where Dundee is staying; the mounted policeman who, when Dundee gets lost in the crowded streets, gives him a lift back to the hotel on the back of his horse; the Italian taxi driver who can 'drink him under the table any day' and takes him on a drinking binge in a rough New York bar; the sharp, powerful black man in the bar who recognizes that in Dundee he is dealing with an equal; the pedestrians in the street who give him a spontaneous round of applause when he knocks out a man who he sees robbing a woman in the street; the black chauffeur of Sue's limousine, who regards Dundee's masculine prowess with ever-increasing admiration; and finally Sue's father, the super-rich newspaper tycoon who knows a real man when he sees one. The one man in the film who doesn't come to admire Dundee for his superhuman masculinity is, of course, Sue's fiancé and boss. This man is quickly established as a weak, effeminate, pretentious wimp and is knocked out, literally, by Dundee on his first night in New York. After punching him in the jaw, Mick turns to Sue with feigned innocence and says, 'You're not serious about this lemon are you?'

Despite the fact that we are now in Sue's home town, her role remains essentially the same as it was in the bush; to admire, respect and learn about Mick's 'magnificent masculine prowess'. Just as he saved Sue from the snake and the crocodile in the bush, in New York he saves her from a gang of black muggers. 'Are you all right?' he asks when the gang have run away in terror at the sight of his superior aborigine hunting knife, which puts their little flick knives to shame. 'I'm always alright when I'm with you,' she breathes happily, 'Why do you always make me feel like Jane in a Tarzan comic?'

The final sequence in the film is brilliant, not because it is the climax of their love story, but because it is the culmination of Hogan's showmanship. Following Sue's fiancé's very public announcement that he and Sue are to be married, Mick dejectedly sets off on 'walkabout' around North America. But

Sue, now realizing that she really loves Mick, dumps her wimpish fiancé and runs after him. She rushes down into a subway station only to find that Mick is jammed into the crowd on the far end of the platform. She calls to him over the heads of the crowd. A black man in a red bandana and a white building site worker in a red hardhat relay her messages to Dundee: 'Tell him I love him, I love you,' Sue shouts. The black man in the bandana calls out 'I love you' to the white man in the hardhat, who in turn calls out to Dundee 'I love you'. Mick looks pleased. He climbs on to the shoulders of the people in the crowd and walks over their heads until he finally reaches Sue. They kiss and everyone on the platform breaks into spontaneous applause.

The joke is that a man effectively shouts, for all the world to hear, 'I love you' to another man. Although, for the sake of the story, the woman is the cipher that sets off this loud declaration of love, the real love affair underlying *Crocodile Dundee* remains his narcissistic love affair with himself and other men's love affair with the kind of masculinity he represents. Sue, who now rashly appears to be ready to devote her life to Mick Dundee, was never rated for being a woman, rather she was admired for her bravery in the face of danger and her ability to do what men can do in a man's world. In other words she was admired for how well she fared in the game of masculinity. Whether women like Sue will really decide that they want to spend the rest of their lives either striving to emulate these masculine ideals, or being a reflection or echo of the masculine ego as represented by Mick Dundee, is another matter.

Working Girl (1988)

Director Mike Nichols; screenplay by Kevin Wade; starring
Melanie Griffith, Harrison Ford and Sigourney Weaver

'She's your man.'

In 1967 *The Graduate* captured the mood of the sixties youth
rebellion against what they saw as the empty values of their
parents' generation. Here in *Working Girl*, released in 1988, just
over twenty years later, director Mike Nichols again captures the
Zeitgeist of the decade – the buzz of success and the making of
money for money's sake. The setting is the corporate world of
mergers and takeovers and high finance. This is a world where in
order to succeed you have to be smart, manipulative, ruthless and
'hungry'. The talk, whether in the office, the boardroom, the
cocktail party or bed is peppered with phrases such as, 'leave your
heart at home', 'go for the jugular', 'grab them by the balls', 'cut
them off at the knees' and 'they'll be eating out of your hands'. In
this world the 'fast track' or 'high flyers' are never 'on another
line', they are 'in a meeting'; you must never let your guard down
because 'today's junior prick is tomorrow's senior partner';
always project yourself as confident, a risk-taker, never afraid to
be noticed because 'one lost deal is all it takes to get canned'.

In this world, power, success and money equals sexy, and
clinching a deal is sexier than any amount of old-fashioned
foreplay. This is an essentially conservative climate, spearheaded
by Ronald Reagan and Margaret Thatcher, where the moral
problem of unemployment and the widening gap between rich
and poor – such as that explored by Frank Capra, however
naively, in *Mr Deeds Goes To Town* in 1936 – have been conveniently swept under the carpet; or neatly dealt with, depending
on your political point of view, by the 'trickle-down theory' of
eighties capitalism.

Just as in the Australian outback of *Crocodile Dundee*, the male-dominated New York money market has its own set of tribal initiation rites and almost as many deadly reptiles lurking beneath the smooth surface of corporate respectability. As a result of feminism, some women have begun to claw their way up to the lower echelons of the male ranks and a few have even made it into the boardroom, but not without learning the rules of the game and not without a momentous struggle. Although, as we see in *Working Girl*, tokenism is alive and well – there may be room for one high-flying woman in the boardroom but is there room for two?

Tess McGill (Melanie Griffith) doesn't look or sound like the female executive she wants to be. Her problem is she's a secretary, and her accent betrays her roots – she's from the wrong side of town. Her make-up is heavy, her skirt is short and very tight and her hair, like her best friend Cynthia's and most of the legions of secretaries in the typing pool, is very big (as was the fashion in the late eighties). It is dyed straw-yellow, back-combed into a lion's mane on top of her head and hangs in long split ends down her back. But despite Tess's appearance, she's very bright and very ambitious. The film opens on her thirtieth birthday but she has no time for a celebration lunch, she's got a speech class. 'What d'you need a speech class for? You talk fine,' her friend Cyn protests in her broad Bronx accent. But Tess is adamant, and she can't do a drink in the evening either, she's got a seminar.

For the past five years she's been attending nightschool where she has recently graduated with honours and, as it soon becomes clear, she knows the complex business of buying and selling stock better than most of the men in her department. Despite this, her application for promotion has again been turned down. As her sleazy boss points out with false sympathy, 'You're up against Harvard and Morgan graduates. What have you got? Some nightschool and secretarial time on your sheet.' As if in compensation, he arranges for her to meet a colleague who is looking for a 'hungry' assistant. The colleague, who Tess meets in the back of his limo, turns out to be a coke-snorting reptile who immediately makes it clear that it's not her business skills but her body he wants. The next day when Tess gets into the office she types furiously on the stocks and shares teleprompter for all the office to read: *Lutz* (her boss) *is a sleazoid pimp with a tiny little dick.* She promptly gets the sack.

So, although Tess has the qualifications, is clearly brighter than her former boss and works in the right building in the heart of New York's financial sector, as a secretary she's not even on the first rung of the executive ladder. Not only is her gender against her, so is her class. As the female employment officer of the corporation points out in exasperation, 'Tess, you don't get ahead in this world by calling your boss a pimp!' But she agrees to switch Tess to another department, mergers and acquisitions, and this time her new boss is a woman.

Katharine Parker (Sigourney Weaver), in a chic grey designer suit and with her coat slung stylishly over her shoulders as she walks past the line of ogling secretaries, is beautiful, elegant, very self-assured and, like Tess, she's just thirty. 'We're practically twins,' she smiles indulgently at Tess. Despite the 'girly' nature of their initial conversation Katharine is quick to establish her innate superiority. 'Dress shabbily and they notice the dress, dress impeccably and they notice the woman,' she advises Tess, quoting Coco Chanel, and suggests tactfully that although Tess 'looks terrific' she might want to 'tone down the jewellery'. Tess immediately heads for the ladies room to peel off her bangles and bracelets and wipe off a layer of make-up. At last she has, in Katharine, a perfect role model for how to be a successful woman and Tess is eager to learn.

Katharine soon demonstrates how power is not just about business skills, it's also about knowing how to turn your sex appeal to your own advantage. At a business drinks party Tess watches, fascinated by Katharine's technique with men: she flirts, but always on her own terms; her style is to give the man her undivided attention, to flatter indulgently and to *appear* to offer future sexual delights *if* she gets a business favour in return. On her way home Tess excitedly sings Katharine's praises to her boyfriend, emphasizing how the most important thing for her is that Katharine takes her seriously, 'There's none of that chasing around the desk crap. It's like she wants to be my mentor which is exactly what I needed.' Her boyfriend is unimpressed. All he wants is for Tess to be like all the other girls in their neighbourhood, to leave her office talk at work and when she gets home to turn him on by wearing his birthday present of sexy lingerie.

Soon Tess is so enraptured by working for Katharine that she decides to entrust her with a business idea of her own (the 'Trask radio deal'). Katharine appears to listen to her idea with serious, if somewhat patronizing, interest and says she will look into it. But a few days later she tells her that she's looked into it and the 'Trask radio deal' is not a goer. Tess bites back her disappointment and kneels at Katharine's feet to help her try on a pair of new ski boots she has bought for a forthcoming trip. Katharine talks happily about how she's planning for her new boyfriend to propose to her. 'I've indicated that I will be receptive to an offer. I've cleared the month of June and I am, after all, me,' she says with breathtaking complacency. 'But what if he doesn't pop the question?' Tess asks. 'Tess, you don't get anywhere in this world by waiting for what you want to come to you. You make it happen . . . Who makes it happen?' Katharine waits indulgently for her pupil and minion to repeat after her, 'I do'. 'That's right. Only then do we get what we deserve.' In the next shot we see Katharine skiing on a snow-covered mountain, careering towards a steep incline. We are left with the sound of her distant scream as she disappears out of sight.

So Nichols has returned to the theme that underpinned *The Graduate* (and so many pre-feminist romantic comedies): the eternal conflict between the good and the bad woman. In *Working Girl*, a female boss may not chase her secretaries around the desk, but this doesn't make all women in power paragons. Women like Katharine have their own, equally insidious methods of exploitation and if they get too big for their boots, which in Katharine's case appear to be ski boots, they should get what they deserve – she's stuck in a hospital bed for two weeks. Tess is now required to handle all her affairs, including going to her home to water the plants and to see to her post.

Tess lets herself into Katharine's home and gazes in awe at the chandeliers and antique furniture – so rather than her mentor's success being hard earned, she was born into wealth and privilege. Like a child in a new playground, Tess tries out Katharine's make-up and vast array of perfumes while idly listening to her private dictaphone. Suddenly she finds herself listening to a message Katharine intended for a man called Jack Trainer regarding the 'Trask radio deal', with an explicit instruction *not* to go through Tess. Tess is still reeling from the shock of discovering that Katharine has stolen her idea for herself when she arrives home only to find her boyfriend in bed with another woman.

This double betrayal gives Tess the psychological (if not entirely moral) justification for fighting back, rather than passively allowing herself to become Katharine's victim. She can now seize the opportunity provided by Katharine's absence to further her own career without appearing like one of those ruthless, cold-blooded women who pursue ambition purely for selfish gain – like Katharine (and most of the men who surround her). Thus Tess can gain brownie points for being the innocent but feisty fighter and retain her position as the good loveable woman, while Katharine is left to be the receptacle for all that we fear about ambitious, selfish women (or the neglectful mother of our primal fantasies).

Tess resolves to take full advantage of Katharine's absence and do the deal with Jack Trainer herself, but not as a secretary, who nobody will take seriously, but as Tess McGill, executive. She uses Katharine's office to book a meeting with Trainer. And then – taking another leaf out of Katharine's book – she decides to inveigle him with her feminine charms on the social networking circuit before hitting him with the proposed deal. For the occasion she raids Katharine's wardrobe and borrows her most expensive little black dress. She hands her awestruck friend Cyn a pair of scissors: 'If you want to be taken seriously you need serious hair,' she tells her. But just to remind us that Tess is not really turning into a super-confident egomaniac like Katharine, after her haircut she panics and Cyn feeds her valium in order to calm her down.

Like Cinderella at the ball, Tess's new look is so effective that when Jack Trainer (Harrison Ford), looking like a somewhat roguish, middle-aged boy scout, sees her sitting alone at the bar of the cocktail party, he is instantly smitten. 'I have been looking for you,' he tells her with his boyish, lopsided smile. 'Why,' Tess asks innocently, having no idea who he is, 'do you know me?' 'No, but I promised myself that when I saw you I would get to know you.' He's either a very practised charmer or an old-fashioned romantic, but Tess passes out before discovering which, or who, he is – tequila and valium don't mix. Jack is forced to take her back to his modest apartment where he undresses her and puts her to bed, although he is very respectful and quite in awe of how pretty she is.

The important thing about their first night together is that Jack falls in love with Tess before he knows anything about her business proposition. His love is innocent, unsullied by the self-interest that becomes central to their relationship the next day when Tess arrives for their official business meeting and pitches her Trask radio idea. After Tess has got over the shock of discovering that Jack Trainer is the man she inadvertently slept with the night before, she is in heaven. Now she has a handsome man almost begging for a relationship with her *and* she's working on her very own deal. She wears Katharine's clothes, uses her office and persuades Cyn to pose as her personal secretary. Cyn enjoys the joke and even hams her part up a little: 'Can I get you anything Mr Trainer; tea, coffee, me?' But she is also worried about Tess's deception – after all, whether Tess likes it or not, she is just a secretary and not the bright, if charmingly eccentric, female executive Jack thinks she is. Tess insists that she will come clean as soon as she's got the deal but, 'I'm not going to spend the rest of my life working my ass off getting nowhere just because I followed rules that I had nothing to do with setting up.'

Tess's statement not only tells us about the moral dilemmas facing women who want to make their way to the top in a man's world. It is also indicative of the moral quagmire of the times. In the mid-eighties financial bubble, lying and cheating in order to seize the advantage from your competitors is the name of the survival game. Jack's plight illustrates this when he begins to panic about the possibility of their losing the deal. There are beads of sweat on his forehead and his stress level is clearly sky high when he confides in Tess that he knows plenty of good men who've got buried, all because of one lost deal and he's worried that she may have found out how he's been 'in a bit of a slump recently'. So, Jack, like Tess, is vulnerable and merely fighting for his own survival in the corporate jungle where it's every man for himself; and that includes women if they want to play too.

Now Jack appears to be as innocent and vulnerable as Tess (well, almost), they begin working together as equals. In order to secure the Trask radio deal they need to bring the powerful conglomerate of Trask Industries on board. Tess has the outrageous idea of pitching the deal to Mr Trask by gatecrashing his daughter's glamorous society wedding. At first her bravado scares Jack but then, when they get to the wedding and Tess appears to be losing her nerve, he becomes even more daring than she and manoeuvres her into a dance with Mr Trask. Tess seizes the opportunity and pitches her idea, using all the skills of flattery and flirtation she learnt from Katharine. The buzz of working so well together is definitely sexy. With only one big meeting with Trask left before they clinch the deal, they can hardly wait to get each other's clothes off and fall into bed.

All the complicated plot strands of the film finally come together in the climactic sequence when Katharine unexpectedly arrives home on the day the deal is due to be finalized. As if that's not problem enough, it turns out that Jack is the boyfriend Katharine was planning to propose to, and now she does, in her inimitable fashion, as soon as she gets the chance. 'Let's merge,' she gushes, as if he's the hottest stock on the exchange, 'and be Mr and Mrs fabulously happy.' Jack looks appalled. But he doesn't have time to deal with her now. He rushes off to join Tess for their crucial meeting. All would be well but for Katharine coming across Tess's appointment book. Hobbling on crutches with her leg in plaster, Katharine barges into the board meeting just as Tess and Jack are making their presentation to Trask Industries and the assembled male heads of various radio stations. Katharine furiously waves her crutch at Tess, almost knocking out the man nearest to her at the table, and denounces Tess as a liar, the thief who stole her idea and worst of all, a mere secretary. 'She's not,' Jack protests in outrage, but he realizes the truth when Tess whispers that she's sorry and leaves in tears. Katharine tosses away her crutches, sits imperiously at the table surrounded by stunned men, and proceeds to take charge of the meeting.

Just as it looks as if Tess has lost everything, as luck would have it, she bumps into Katharine, Jack and Mr Trask as she is leaving the office building with all her things. 'Maybe you can fool these guys with this saint act you've got going,' she tells Katharine furiously, 'but don't you ever talk to me again like we don't know what really happened . . . now get your bony ass out of my sight.' Jack then puts his own career on the line and refuses to proceed with the deal without Tess. 'I'm telling you,' he appeals to Mr Trask on Tess's behalf, 'she's your man.' Trask decides to listen to Tess's side of the story and finally with obvious glee turns to Katharine: 'What was it she said? Get your bony ass out of my sight.' (After two decades of feminism such misogynous insults are definitely unacceptable, but if a woman says it first, particularly a woman who is now 'his man' . . . then it must be all right!)

As the film draws to a close we see Tess, now wearing a brand new 'power dressing' suit of her own – big jacket, padded shoulders, neat little skirt and high heels, grabbing a quick breakfast in Jack's kitchen before she leaves for her first day in her new job as junior executive at Trask Industries. Jack lovingly gives her a present – a child's lunchbox which he has packed with a sandwich, an apple for the teacher, a little cash and a pencil. 'Now remember, play nice with the other kids,' he tells her, 'and make sure you are home before dark.'

As *Working Girl* ends, we are left with the warm glow that accompanies the endings of all the best fairytales. Mr Trask, like the wise old king, has finally seen to it that good overcomes bad. Like a wicked bony-fingered (or in Katharine's case 'bony-assed') witch, Katharine, who was too big for her boots, has finally got her comeuppance. She has been sacked from her job and forced to leave in disgrace. Tess has achieved everything she wanted, she has an executive job and a handsome, loving prince who has proved himself by risking his career to save her and will now look after her for the rest of their life together. But finally the image of the lunchbox Jack has so lovingly packed for her bears a more ambivalent message for men of the future – their traditionally masculine role as protector and provider has now been extended to include maternal nurturing and domesticity.

The message for women is even more ambivalent. Katharine is the manipulative, powerful woman both men and many women fear, whereas Tess is the charming, vulnerable, clever child playing with the idea of power. Tess needs a man to help her achieve what she wants, while Katharine wants a man to confirm what she already has. Tess's vulnerability places her in a more traditional position in relation to men whereas successful women like Katharine, however sexy they may be, are far more threatening than their male counterparts. So long as Tess retains her childlike innocence on her road to success, men like Jack and Trask will be reassured of their manly roles as protectors and providers, and all will be well. But what will happen if Tess decides to grow up, or simply claim her right to equality in the mean and ruthless game of capitalism and power politics?

One token woman in the boardroom is proof of the bosses' largesse towards the opposite sex and their struggle for equality. Two women in the boardroom and it begins to look dangerously as if a 'monstrous regiment of women' is taking over. Is this when the old divide and rule maxim must come into play? After all, hasn't it always been more acceptable for women to compete with each other than to compete with men?

Crossing Delancey (1988)

Directed by Joan Micklin Silver; screenplay by Susan Sandler
(based on her stageplay); starring Amy Irving and Peter Riegert

> 'You are a nice guy . . . maybe I just can't
> handle that?'

According to the eighties popular press 'the man shortage' was a
big issue on the minds of many single women over thirty.
Although statistically speaking there never was a 'man shortage',
nevertheless the myth impinged on the lives of many women at
the time, including the heroine of *Crossing Delancey*, released in
1988. The film was directed by Joan Micklin Silver and written
by Susan Sandler, which itself shows how more women were
breaking through the film industry glass ceiling and adding their
voice to the battle of the sexes debate.

In her book *Backlash,* Susan Faludi argues that 'the man
shortage' was a lie propagated by men, in particular male
journalists, as a reaction against feminism. In other words men
who were hostile to feminism didn't want career women as
partners. On the other hand, as demonstrated in *Crossing
Delancey*, it's doubtful if the myth would have captured the
popular imagination if single women over thirty, including
feminists themselves, many of whom were educated women with
careers, hadn't perceived the 'shortage' in their own lives. Their
problem wasn't a *literal* shortage of males in the population, but
a shortage of 'new men' – that is, the kind of attractive,
interesting, sensitive men many modern women wanted as
partners. The question posed in the film is where are these men
and how do single women find them?

Crossing Delancey also places the issue within a wider
cultural and gender context: how do single people, irrespective
of whether they are male or female, find partners when they are
too old for the social networks provided by youth culture? Their

223

days on the university campus, which was also a fertile dating and mating ground, are over and in the late twentieth century most of the traditional family and community structures for courting have long been abandoned.

For single women in particular the problem of meeting new partners was also exacerbated by the fact that, despite the many opportunities feminism had brought to their lives, one custom remained deeply ingrained. When it came to that all-important first date, women were expected to send out all sorts of covert signals indicating that they were available and interested, but it was men who had to do the manly thing and ask the woman out, just as it was men, not women, who were expected, if the relationship went swimmingly well, to propose marriage. As we have just seen in *Working Girl*, when a woman proposes marriage then alarm bells ring. In this matter it seems that, despite almost two decades of feminism, the old order of passive feminine women and active masculine men remained firmly in place. Although again it is debatable whether the tenacity of this custom demonstrates men's self-interest or whether women have been equally complicit in maintaining it due to some deeply ingrained notions – after all, implicit in the first date invitation and the marriage proposal is the necessity for the man to take the risk of rejection and so prove his bravery and manly worth in the woman's eyes.

The film opens when Izzy (Amy Irving) is serving drinks to the New York literati at a party in the bookshop where she works. Apart from Izzy's fashionably big hair, her appearance in her loose long-sleeved polka-dot dress is somewhat old-fashioned, suggesting that, although she is concerned to appear attractive, her self-image, as a thirty-three-year-old woman, is intellectual and interesting rather than sexy. Although her general demeanour is shy and unassuming there is one man at the party whom she can't help gazing at – Anton, a novelist and Dutch émigré who lives and works in New York. He is in his mid-thirties, separated from his wife, tall, dark, ruggedly handsome, very self-assured and very aware of the effect his charm has on women. When he smiles at Izzy and beckons to her across the crowded room, her eyes light up with hope, only to be disappointed when all he wants is to place his empty wine glass on her tray. Her hopes are raised again when, as the party ends, he hands her a signed copy of his new novel *Cave Dweller* (the title hints at the current interest in the 'wild man' mythology). Outside in the street she reads his personal dedication: 'Izzy dear, it's women like you who make the world liquid and even, still in beauty born.' Anton's charm may seem a little too slick and practised for comfort, but not for Izzy who clutches his precious words to her breast as she makes her way back to her apartment where she lives alone.

According to Izzy being single and living alone is not a problem. She has a wonderful job where she meets interesting people, she has lots of friends including plenty of women who are 'doing tremendous things with their lives and don't need a man to make them feel complete'. But Ida, her widowed bubby (Jewish grandmother) who is lively, warm and devoted to Izzy, doesn't believe her. 'No matter how much money you got, if you are alone you are sick,' Ida insists, wagging her finger pointedly at Izzy. Ida is determined to sort out Izzy's life for her whether she likes it or not and when Izzy arrives on one of her regular visits to her grandmother's tiny apartment in the heart of New York's bustling, working-class Jewish quarter, she finds herself confronted by the local professional matchmaker. The woman is a similar age to Ida, Jewish of course and, with her long bleached hair, heavy make-up and exaggeratedly curvaceous figure, she looks like a cross between a grotesque caricature of an ageing fifties sex goddess and a witch.

Izzy is appalled to learn that this woman has been showing her photograph to single eligible men in the local community and to make matters worse, the man who has chosen to meet her makes and sells pickles for a living! 'You'll put on a nice dress, you'll put on stockings, no naked legs,' Ida instructs her, blithely ignoring Izzy's protests and focusing instead on the problem of her granddaughter's inappropriate attire of denim jeans and trainers. 'Maybe I don't want a husband,' Izzy retorts petulantly, 'and if I did he wouldn't be a pickle man!' That does it for Ida; she angrily puts her foot down. 'Get off your high horse, Miss Universe. This man's just looking, he ain't asking to buy.'

Ida's kitchen table is laden with a delicious spread of food, the witch-like matchmaker is there to officiate over the occasion and Izzy, now dutifully wearing a gingham dress, is seated sullenly at the table when the doorbell rings. Sam, a bachelor in his mid-thirties strolls into the kitchen wearing an open-necked white shirt and a casual suit. Izzy's eyes widen. Despite her prejudices, he is attractive. But then he gives Ida a present, a bag of his best pickles and Izzy turns her head away in disgust. For Izzy the whole occasion is excruciatingly embarrassing and when at last Ida and the matchmaker retreat to another room, pointedly leaving the 'young people' alone to get to know each other, she seizes the opportunity to tell Sam that this whole matchmaking business is 'not my style'. Sam, who has guessed that something is wrong, as she maintained a sullen silence throughout the meal, suggests that maybe she could 'change her style'.

As if to illustrate his point, he tells her a story about a friend of his who 'for years wore a little brown cap with the brim pulled down, you wondered how he could see. Then one day as he was crossing Delancey the wind comes and poof, it was gone.' On Sam's advice his friend bought himself a new hat, 'a grey felt Stetson, a beauty', and as a result he was a changed man. The next day he became engaged to a woman he had had his eye on for a long time but until then 'she couldn't see him – that little brown cap, she couldn't see his eyes'. With his story finished Sam looks enigmatically into Izzy's eyes. For a moment Izzy is intrigued (and so are we, particularly as the story contains the puzzling title of the film), but then her bubby and the match-maker come bustling back into the room and the moment is broken. For Izzy the charade has gone on for long enough. When Sam suggests a date for Saturday night she politely but firmly turns him down, this is not her style. 'Well,' Ida looks angrily at her granddaughter, 'she spoke!'

In the next scene Izzy is back in her chosen world gazing at Anton who is in the bookshop giving a public reading from his new novel. '. . . his body had been very nice,' Anton reads seductively and glances knowingly at the adoring women in his audience. 'She was spreading moisture cream up and down her legs when he came out of the shower. He moved up behind her and bumped against her playfully.' Anton smiles with self-satisfaction as the women in his audience giggle at his sexual innuendo and then sigh with disappointment when Izzy is forced by the bookshop owner to bring the reading to a close, in order to get on with the serious business of selling books.

Anton may be a published writer but his work appears to be dedicated to the glory of himself and his seductive power over women, rather than giving insight into any wider aspects of the human condition. In contrast Sam's story, although it was simply a part of conversation rather than specifically 'literary', can be interpreted in different ways. It could be about Izzy, who is so attached to her style that, like his friend's attachment to the little brown cap, she can't see past it. It could also be about how, in Izzy's eyes, Sam is like the little brown cap – Izzy can't see beyond her prejudice about pickle sellers to the man he really is. Despite Sam's occupation, he knows how to tell a story about real people with feeling, complexity and metaphorical meaning. But Izzy is too infatuated with Anton and the 'real' literary world to see the difference.

Sam doesn't give up. For her birthday he sends her a large floppy hat – a hint that just as the grey felt Stetson changed his friend's life, maybe it's time for Izzy to change hers. Despite herself, the hat, which her friends call an 'Annie Hall' hat, suits her and she is delighted with it. But when she goes to the Jewish market to thank him, the sight of Sam working in his shop, plunging his hands into a barrel of pickled gherkins, is too much for her.

It is only when she decides to take a leaf out of her bubby's book and act as matchmaker by engineering a meeting between Sam and one of her female friends, that Izzy begins to see Sam in a different light. A conversation with her unmarried girlfriends about whether there really is a 'man shortage' or whether it is just a myth gives Izzy the idea. The professional community matchmaker, armed with a bundle of photographs and traditional rules of the game, may be eschewed by the younger, more sophisticated generation but matchmaking itself still has an important role to play, even if the matchmaker has to pretend that the arranged introduction is accidental rather than contrived. As Izzy explains to her girlfriend, at the bar of the restaurant which she has chosen for the rendezvous, 'This has to look very spontaneous, okay? When I fuss with my earring like this, you come over to the table. That's the signal . . . Just stop by, say "hi", I'll introduce you, invite you to sit down, I'll excuse myself. And if the chemistry is good you'll do something about it and if not, nothing missed.' She then goes to greet the unsuspecting Sam.

Izzy's plan might have gone perfectly if Sam hadn't been astute enough to guess what she was up to. But rather than take offence he invites her friend on a date. Izzy is left feeling foolish and, even worse, jealous, particularly when she hears that Sam has taken her friend to the theatre. Not only has she begun to find herself increasingly attracted to Sam but once again he has refused to conform to her stereotype of an uncultured pickle man. Her confusion is further exacerbated when she visits a married friend and enviously watches her breastfeed her young baby. What does Izzy really want? A real relationship and a baby of her own? Or an unrequited love for a man like Anton who flirts with every woman he meets? Finally, with a little more behind the scenes manipulation from her bubby, Izzy decides to accept Sam's invitation for a date.

Wearing a brand new dress for the occasion, she is just leaving the bookshop when Anton turns up, insisting that she come with him to his place – he needs her advice on the new manuscript he is writing. 'Let him wait,' he tells Izzy when she protests that she has a date, 'They love to be kept waiting. Please Izzy . . . you are one of the people I count on.' He looks deep into her eyes and softly breathes, 'Grace. Generosity. Stillness.' This proves simply too much for Izzy to resist. She phones Sam, who is at that moment arriving expectantly at bubby's apartment with a bouquet of flowers. Izzy guiltily tells him she will be late.

At last it appears that Izzy's unrequited love may not have been in vain. Meanwhile poor Sam is left to be entertained by Izzy's bubby with a bottle of wine and not so romantic stories of how she didn't find her husband attractive when she first met him. 'He was just a little man with spectacles that's all . . .' she tells him but, 'Then he says, Ida, I won't move, I won't crawl an inch until you say yes . . . If somebody wanted me so much that he was ready to make a fool of himself, it was easy to see that he would be good for me.' Ida looks meaningfully at Sam and waits for her advice to sink in while she helps herself to another drink.

For Anton, inviting women to sit on his bed and read his manuscript is obviously a tried and trusted form of writer's foreplay and his technique is working beautifully until he decides to tell Izzy that he has arranged to borrow her from her boss at the bookshop. He blithely assumes that she will be delighted to be his temporary secretary, organize his life for him and of course have the added benefit of having sex with him when he feels like it. Izzy can hardly believe how stupid she has been. She furiously rushes out of his apartment and jumps into a cab leaving Anton to shout pathetically from his doorway, 'Let's be honest about this. If anyone's being manipulated it's me.' Anton's self-delusion appears to know no bounds!

It's very late when Izzy arrives at Ida's apartment. In the kitchen the first thing she sees is Sam's flowers lying forgotten on the table. Assuming that he has gone home, she sits on her bubby's rocking chair and cries. 'Go ahead, say "shmuck, what are you still doing here?"' Sam smiles as he appears at the balcony door. (So he has heeded Ida's advice and decided not to move until he gets what he wants.) He makes them both coffee and tells her about Ida's great stories. 'You should write them down, I do.' He produces a small notebook from his jacket pocket and flips through the pages. So, Sam is not only a closet writer himself, but he knows enough about writing to see the storytelling potential in the community where they both grew up. He also cares enough about Izzy to see her potential as a writer, not just a bookshop assistant or a secretary to organize his life for him. In almost every way, apart from selling pickles, Sam appears to be an ideal partner for Izzy. But she is still worried. 'You are a nice guy,' she tells him, 'maybe I can't handle that?' 'Maybe if I abused you, knocked you around a little, I would have a better chance?' Sam retorts, but then he softens. 'You don't know how nuts I was about tonight. I was off the ground. Nobody could talk to me. I made wrong change all day. I was so happy I was seeing you tonight . . . I said a prayer for the planting of new trees.' Persistence finally has its reward. Just as they have their first kiss, Ida wakes up and, as soon as she has made sure that Izzy is out of earshot, she happily begins to make wedding plans.

Izzy and Sam appear to be set to live happily ever after. But whether this ending conforms more to what we would wish for Izzy and Sam, rather than being entirely believable is another matter. In the real world Izzy's infatuation with Anton would probably have won the day. However miserable she may have been as his secretary who also fulfils his sexual needs on the side, the intensity of her unrequited love, his celebrity status and her fantasy projection of him as her ideal lover would simply have been too much for her to resist. As Izzy herself finally admits, she does have a problem with 'nice guys'. But it's too late, in this film anyway, to begin to explore the often-aired problem of why nice women find themselves attracted to not so nice men, or bastards as they are more commonly called – which is another subject that has since become the focus of numerous women's magazine articles and self-help books.

Izzy's story does, however, reflect the growing confusion experienced by many women. She wants the kind of life that will bring her into contact with the glamour and intellectual stimulation of the literary establishment, but she also wants a secure relationship and babies. She wants an exciting, challenging, successful man and at the same time she wants a man who is sensitive, reliable and consistent. She wants to be free, independent and self-sufficient and at the same time she is afraid of 'the man shortage'. She may be content to be alone now but this may not always be the case and what if she finally realizes she's lonely when she's approaching that dreaded age of forty when, according to the popular press, no man will look twice at her and it's too late to have babies.

But finally the message underlying the ending of *Crossing Delancey* is clear. The answer to 'the man shortage' is for women to lower their sights, return to their roots, swallow their pride, appreciate that there is wisdom to be found in the old community traditions, however patriarchal they appear, and to be prepared to compromise. You never know, the pickle man may turn out to be like Sam – a kind, loving, amusing, educated man and a closet writer who knows the difference between mediocre writing and great art – the perfect man to give a woman like Izzy all the intellectual companionship and support that she needs in order for her to be happy and have a career. On the other hand, he may be a nice, homely guy who lacks ambition and simply wants a secure, uneventful family life. In which case Izzy's reservations about him being the right man for her, which she had at the outset of the film, were probably well founded.

It is worth remembering that the film industry, like the corporate world we saw in *Working Girl*, also had a largely male-dominated hierarchy. In order for women writers and directors to break through the glass ceiling they too would have to play their cards close to their chest, be careful not to appear threatening to the male sensibility, be suitably appreciative of the traditional feminine attributes and be seen as 'just the men for the job'. In these complicated 'transition' or 'backlash' years it was in some ways easier, or more acceptable, for male writers and directors to reflect the more threatening aspects of the feminist position than it was for women themselves.

When Harry Met Sally (1989)

Directed by Rob Reiner; screenplay by Nora Ephron; starring
Meg Ryan and Billy Crystal

'We are just going to be friends, okay?'

According to conventional wisdom friendship may be a
valuable part of people's lives, but friends always take second
place to romance. Friends may come and go but true love and
marriage last forever – so the old adage goes. But by the end of
the eighties the reality of many people's lives had changed: it was
now love and marriage that came and went, while friends were
always there. It was our friends who were our confidantes
through the often tumultuous journey of romance, it was our
friends who were our best men and bridesmaids when the big
day came and it was our friends who were still there, waiting in
the wings, ready to help pick up the pieces of our shattered loves.
It's true these friends were usually of the same sex – men had
buddies and women had girlfriends – but in the post-feminist
era, as men and women began to appreciate each other's
similarities rather than always focusing on their differences,
lasting friendships across the gender divide also became more
common.

Is it possible for a long and deep platonic friendship between
a man and a woman eventually to blossom into a romantic
relationship? Or does this fly in the face of all the rules of
romance: love at first sight, the fun of flirtation and the overwhelming power of sexual chemistry? Although many believe
that the prospect of romance lasting is greatly enhanced if our
lover is also our friend, are there certain crucial differences
between lovers and friends that make a combination of the two
roles impossible to maintain? If so are we talking just about
sex, or is sex only one element in the scenario of what is lost

and what is gained? These are the central questions posed by *When Harry Met Sally,* released in 1989.

The romance of great male friendships has always captured the popular imagination. Whether men were probing the boundaries of knowledge, building skyscrapers, fighting crime or risking their lives for each other in war or on the frontier of civilization, the value of the dependable, courageous friend or sidekick has never been questioned. Male friendships have traditionally been about survival. Women may have provided men with a reason to survive, but for this purpose it was thought best if they were left at home with their female friends who gave them comfort and emotional intimacy while their menfolk were away. But in the late twentieth century, just as women were making inroads into the world of men, so the journey was two-way as many men became increasingly curious about the world of women as seen from the inside out, rather than the outside in. One of these benefits, they discovered, was the pleasure and support to be gained from the feminine tradition of emotional intimacy.

Appropriately for a film which sets out to explore the terrain of friendship between the sexes, *When Harry Met Sally* was directed by a man, Rob Reiner, and the sparkling screenplay was written by a woman, Nora Ephron. Their collaboration was enormously successful as the enduring popularity of the film demonstrates.

Harry (Billy Crystal) and Sally (Meg Ryan) first meet in 1977 when Sally gives Harry a lift from Chicago to New York. They are both recent graduates but, as we soon learn, that is about all they have in common, apart from the somewhat tenuous link that the girlfriend Harry is leaving behind was also Sally's friend at university. Sally, with her pretty face and curly blonde hair, is the archetypal suburban girl next door – she's neat, wholesome, prim, fussy, gullible, bright but intensely serious and appears to completely lack a sense of humour. Harry is small and slight with a boyish smile, hair that threatens to recede when he is older and sharp narrow eyes constantly on the lookout for fresh stimulation and amusement, if not with his companion then at her expense. He particularly enjoys playing games with logic and rational argument, being ruthlessly honest (otherwise known as rude) and shocking Sally with his extreme cynicism and black sense of humour. In other words were Harry and Sally to take a compatibility test they would probably rank near zero, apart from one character trait – they are both disarmingly truthful about what they think and feel.

They haven't driven many miles before they are arguing about everything from who has a 'bigger dark side' to whether Ingrid Bergman did the right thing when she left Humphrey Bogart at the end of *Casablanca*. 'You mean you would rather be in a passionless marriage than live with a guy you've had the greatest sex with in your life just because he owns a bar and that is all he does,' Harry sums up Sally's bourgeois position in disgust. 'Yes,' Sally retorts smugly, 'Women are very practical.' 'You obviously haven't had great sex yet,' Harry tosses at her as she follows him into a roadside restaurant. 'It just so happens I have had plenty of good sex,' Sally retorts furiously, before recoiling in embarrassment – the entire restaurant has heard her. She sits down quickly. Harry then stares at her with a mixture of fascination and horror as she proceeds to order her meal: she wants the chief salad with the oil and vinegar on the side and the apple pie, but she wants the pie heated with the ice cream on the side, strawberry instead of vanilla, if they have it, and if not whipped cream but only if it's real, not out of a can, and if not she'll have just the apple pie but not heated. Despite her fussy eating habits, Harry casually tells her she's quite attractive. Sally instantly flies off the handle. As far as she is concerned that was definitely a pass and as her girlfriend's boyfriend how could he even think of such a thing? But he can, and he is still thinking about it in the car when he suggests they stop at a motel. 'Harry,' Sally says firmly, 'we are just going to be friends, okay?' After giving this a little thought Harry announces that 'men and women can't be friends, because the sex part always gets in the way'. Sally disputes this but Harry's powers of argument outwit her and she finally gives up, saying ruefully, 'That's too bad, because you were the only person I knew in New York.' They arrive in New York and part company, supposedly never to see each other again.

Five years later, in 1983, Harry and Sally happen to bump into each other at the airport. At first they both appear to have changed. Sally is now a sophisticated journalist, has a sleek new hairdo, is wearing an elegant business suit and is in a long-term living-together relationship. Harry has become a political consultant, his hair has receded a little but he's also pristine in a smart suit and tie and he's engaged to be married. But, as they both soon discover, they are the same old Harry and Sally underneath. On the aeroplane Sally gives the bewildered air hostess one of her impossibly convoluted orders. And on the travelator Harry launches into one of his equally impossible convoluted arguments about how Sally should have dinner with him, just as a friend of course, because although he stands by his old position that men and women can't be friends, they can if they are both involved with other people, which is 'an amendment to the earlier rule'. He then proceeds to argue himself out of his own position as he remembers that the people they are involved with might be jealous and finally he arrives back to his initial premise, 'Men and women can't be friends, so where does that leave us?' It appears that the traditional difference between the male mindset, which places logical argument on a higher plane than feeling, and the female mindset, which is rooted in experience and common sense, is still alive and well, at least in Harry and Sally. She looks at him witheringly and says goodbye.

Five years later, in 1988, Sally and her girlfriend Marie are browsing in the self-help section of a bookshop, amongst titles such as *Making Your Life Right When It Feels All Wrong*, when Marie quietly mentions to Sally that, 'Someone is staring at you in Personal Growth.' It's Harry. They begin talking and soon learn that both their relationships have recently broken up. They go for coffee together to commiserate. Sally is still reeling from the shock of her partner moving out, all because she wanted to start a family and Harry is equally devastated by his wife leaving him for another man. But despite their delicate emotional states, they appear far more relaxed than they were five years before, both in their dress and their manner. Soon Sally is laughing at Harry's jokes and Harry is apologizing for his past failings – so the effect of broken relationships, it seems, has been to make them both more tolerant and more fun. Sally invites Harry to dinner and he accepts. 'Are we becoming friends now?' she asks. 'Well, yes,' he concedes, 'You may be the first attractive woman I have *not* wanted to sleep with in my entire life.' 'That's wonderful Harry,' Sally smiles happily.

Now the boundaries of their relationship are securely drawn they can enjoy each other's company as friends. And they do. Soon they are constantly on the phone to each other discussing frankly every detail of their emotional lives and how they are each dealing with rejection. They talk about which side of the bed they now sleep on. They analyze each other's dreams. And, as time passes, they discuss the intricacies of their awful dates with other people. Of course, they also argue about everything and their conversation continually returns to sex. They are eating together in a restaurant when Sally decides to take Harry to task on his casual attitude towards the women he sleeps with – he has confessed to her that after sex he can't get out of the door quick enough, anything over thirty seconds is too long. Sally disputes his assumption that the women he has sex with have a good time. How does he *know* they are not faking it? Harry looks at her with amused scepticism: 'You don't think I can tell the difference?' Sally wipes her hands on her napkin and closes her eyes. She then begins to moan quietly under her breath as she throws her head back and pushes her fingers sensuously through her hair. Her moaning gets louder, 'Oh God, Oh God,' she utters passionately. The surrounding diners begin looking at her curiously and Harry grows increasingly embarrassed. Finally she bangs her fists on the table and lets out a loud scream as she 'comes'. She sinks back down into her chair, opens her eyes, looks at Harry and smiles with satisfaction – her point is proved.

For once Harry is stunned into silence. At a nearby table a waiter is waiting for a plain middle-aged woman to give him her order. 'I'll have what she's having,' the woman says, looking enviously at Sally.

What Sally 'is having' is the fun and the intimacy of a totally open and frank relationship with a man she can talk to about everything and anything. What she's not having is sex. And what neither of them are having is a romance. Both Harry and Sally are graphically reminded of this when, at the end of the count-down to midnight at a New Year's Eve party, all the couples surrounding them fall into each other's arms for a passionate kiss. Harry and Sally, in contrast, exchange an awkward and embarrassed peck on the lips. Friendship is many things but it doesn't entirely fill the void of the missing relationship.

They decide to solve the problem by each matchmaking the other with their best same-sex friend. The four meet in a restaurant where Sally does her best to get to know Harry's friend Jess, and Harry struggles equally valiantly to get interested in Sally's friend Marie. But it soon becomes clear that Jess and Marie are more interested in each other, particularly when Marie quotes a magazine article she read somewhere which stated that, 'Restaurants are to people in the eighties what the theatre was to people in the sixties.' Jess is delighted, he wrote that article and, 'Nobody has ever quoted me back to me before.' At the end of the evening Jess and Marie enthusiastically jump into a cab leaving Harry and Sally to commiserate about the failure of their matchmaking venture, at least as far as each other is concerned. Within months Jess and Marie are happily moving in together whilst Harry and Sally are in exactly the same boat as they were before.

The turning point of the story arrives when one night Sally phones Harry to ask him to come over – she has just learnt that her ex is getting married. Harry, as her intimate friend, immediately understands the emotional impact this news will have on Sally and rushes to her apartment to comfort her. 'She's supposed to be his transitional person, she's not meant to be *the* one,' Sally despairs about her ex's engagement and descends into floods of tears – nobody wants to marry her and soon she's going to be forty! Harry gently reminds her there are eight years to go before she is forty. 'But it's just sitting there,' she cries, 'like this great big dead end. And it's not the same for men. Charlie Chaplin had babies when he was seventy-three.' 'Yes,' Harry jokes, 'but he was too old to pick them up.' Sally laughs through her tears and Harry hugs her affectionately. But soon they are kissing and before either of them know what is happening they have made love.

They have spontaneously broken the rule of their friendship. In the heat of the moment all the advice and pop wisdom that Sally has consumed from magazines and self-help books, such as the theory of 'transitional objects', has gone out of the window, along with Harry's endless rational arguments. Desire has smothered talk; feeling has vanquished thought; overwhelming passion has conquered cool detached reason. Sally snuggles up to him and smiles contentedly. But Harry lies with his eyes wide open staring up at the ceiling in blind panic.

They meet for dinner the following evening and both agree they should never have done it. The problem is they did do it. Now they don't know what to say to each other. Harry's whole manner towards Sally has changed; he's now cold and distant. In a long conversation with Jess, Harry desperately tries to rationalize why having sex with Sally was such a bad idea. He concludes that, 'You get to a certain point in a relationship when it's just too late to have sex.' Sally, on the other hand, just feels rejected.

Before long Jess and Marie get married with Harry as best man and Sally as bridesmaid. At the reception Harry approaches Sally – he wants them to resume their friendship as if nothing happened. He tries to give her a list of rational reasons to uphold his position but his arguments backfire. Sally feels hurt and insulted and when Harry thoughtlessly implies that he only made love to her because he felt sorry for her, she smacks him round the face and furiously marches away. As far as she is concerned their friendship is over.

It's Christmas. Harry desperately tries to get through to Sally on the phone but she refuses to return his answerphone messages. On New Year's Eve he restlessly paces the empty streets remembering his car journey with Sally when they first met. He recalls his own argument when he tried to convince her that men and women can never be friends. 'That's too bad,' he remembers Sally saying, 'you were the only person I knew in New York.' He begins to run through the streets to the party where he knows he will find her. She is just leaving the crowded dancehall, to avoid the misery of being alone when midnight strikes. Harry rushes in the door. 'I love you,' he tells her breathlessly. But Sally is still angry with him. 'It doesn't work this way,' she shouts as the countdown to midnight begins. 'Well how does it work?' he shouts back crossly. But then he quickly changes tack.

This time he tells her all the quirky things about her that he loves: the way she's cold when it's hot outside; the way it takes her an hour-and-a-half to order a sandwich; the way she gets a little crinkle above her nose when she looks at him as if he were nuts. He finishes by telling her that he wants to spend the rest of his life with her and Sally melts. 'I really hate you,' she tells him lovingly and they kiss while everyone around them is singing 'Auld Lang Syne'. Harry, true to form, begins puzzling about what the song means. He's been hearing it all his life but he's never understood what it means. Sally listens to him lovingly and smiles, 'Anyway it's about old friends.'

As Sally's line suggests, *When Harry Met Sally* is first and foremost about the value of friendship; mutual trust and the freedom to be both intimate and totally honest with each other. What had at first appeared to be a disadvantage, their being a different gender, became a positive asset, providing them each with an intriguing insight into the other sex's point of view and the opportunity to learn from those insights. Harry's panic when he and Sally made love was about his fear of losing that freedom. Their friendship had provided him with the opportunity to express himself spontaneously and to say all of what he thought and felt without self-censorship. As friends they could tell each other everything – their dreams, fears, their relationship problems. They could even be totally honest about sex and talk about sexual problems free from the worry lovers might have about making each other feel jealous or insecure. As friends they were free because they had nothing to lose by sharing intimate revelations and everything to gain.

The question we are left with is, can they maintain this level of honesty as lovers? Or is total truth a prerogative of friendship? Harry has discovered that it can be easier to be truthful to a friend than a lover. This is the root of his panic after they have made love – he enjoys being able to tell Sally anything. It is liberating to be truthful. If he was in a relationship with her there would be 'all these no-go areas'. Friendship can also provide the benefit of intimacy, at least intellectual and emotional intimacy, without the complications of a romantic relationship. Sex completes the intimacy but it can threaten the honesty. Friendships don't have to be perfect, they just have to be real. The pressure on the romantic relationship to be perfect can be so intense that people are tempted to pretend in order to fulfil their own and each other's expectations. Eventually, in response to the threat of the truth coming out, each person in the couple can become locked into a mutually created climate of unreality.

In my description of *When Harry Met Sally*, for reasons of economy, I have omitted to describe the many short documentary-style scenes that punctuate the film. But these scenes are important to complete our understanding of what Reiner and Ephron are saying in the film. In each of the scenes we are shown a different elderly couple sitting side by side on a couch, talking to camera about their marriage. The accounts they give, sometimes coyly, sometimes proudly, often warily, have one thing in common – each account is their personal myth, their story, or the one which they feel is safe enough to reveal to each other and to present to the world. As for the underlying truth of each of these marriages, that is another story altogether.

When Harry Met Sally ends with Harry and Sally seated side by side on the couch, just like the elderly couples we have seen intermittently throughout the film. They now talk to camera, about their wedding, which took place just three months after we last saw them, and then they go on to talk about how they first met and their relationship. They too have begun to construct their relationship story; one which allows them to feel secure with each other and one which, in their future years together, they will hone into a coherent mutually acceptable narrative about their marriage. Are we to count this as a gain or a loss?

Finally the underlying message of the film is that happiness is about feeling free to be real and friendship provides this. The perfect marriage may promise an even greater sense of fulfilment but the romantic myth can also enslave us in a lie – one that we are ashamed to admit, even to ourselves.

Seven

Fairytales and the Commitment Problem in the Nineties

At the tail-end of 1989 the Berlin Wall was torn down. People throughout the old Soviet Bloc then turned on the vast effigies of the iron men of communism that had for so long dominated their landscape and their lives and toppled them into the gutter of history. The cold war was over. In the West, traditional icons of masculinity were also under attack. The industrial heartlands were littered with the rusting hulks of heavy machinery and abandoned factories that had formerly provided the working man with his income and his identity. Robots and new technology were taking over. Women, with their dexterity and acceptance of flexible working hours and lower wages, were now employed in larger numbers than ever before. The redoubtable image of masculinity as provider and protector, so cherished by Ronald Reagan's generation was now, like Reagan himself, antiquated and surplus to requirements.

Thatcherism had also come to a sticky end. The eighties financial bubble had burst and in the ensuing recession of the early nineties many aggressively competitive, sharp-suited, workaholic young men found that their lifestyles had evaporated. For those whose self-esteem had become dependent on the acquisition of power and the trappings of success the shock was hard felt. On the other hand, the lessons of how to survive in the competitive jungle were now firmly ingrained. Men could no longer expect jobs for life but diversification, enterprise and a willingness to change could save them. The time had come for men to reappraise their priorities, values, lifestyle and while they were at it, their identity as men – the concept of the nineties 'new man' was born.

In 1992, at the age of forty-six, Bill Clinton became the new American president. He had missed the draft, choosing to take up a Rhodes' scholarship at Oxford rather than serve in Vietnam, but with the fear generated by the cold war now quelled, at least for the time being, the leader of the free world no longer needed to wave his war record or project an image of himself as defender of the frontier. Clinton's election campaign was also bedevilled by accusations of sexual infidelity. But sexual attitudes were changing. The opinion polls showed that a majority of voters were 'more likely to accept infidelity in a candidate if the wife had been made aware of it'.[1] For the younger generation and those who, like the Clintons, had been young in the sixties and were now reaching middle-age, lying and hypocrisy were the scourge of the bad old days; openness and being prepared to talk about marriage and relationship problems were the way forward. Bill Clinton and his wife appeared together on national television and Bill admitted his 'wrongdoing' and 'causing pain in my marriage'.[2] Hillary stood by him, although not without some embarrassment, which led her to remind viewers that, 'I'm not sitting here as some little woman standing by my man like Tammy Wynette.'[3] (Afterwards, in response to a storm of protest from Tammy Wynette fans, Hillary apologized for this remark.)

While the new man at the top – with his apparent openness, relaxed manner, willingness to admit to his imperfections and, of course, his youthfulness – was the perfect role model for the New Man, Hillary Rodham Clinton was herself a role model for the 'new woman'. As First Lady, she eschewed the image of glamorous socialite or 'little woman' cultivated by many of her predecessors. Instead she was a feminist and a successful lawyer with political views and aspirations of her own. 'Partner as much as wife' was how *Time* magazine described her. The new first marriage was to be a partnership between friends, confidantes and intellectual equals. But, as the writer Naomi Wolf said of

Hillary Clinton, she also represented 'something at once extremely terrifying and extremely welcome, depending on which part of the American people you represent.'[4] In other words she may have been a role model for some but for others she was the bête noire or the despised 'bad' woman exerting too much power and influence over her man. And as we have seen in previous decades, ambitious women who are perceived to be overly assertive or to threaten their man's masculinity have to soften up or get their comeuppance. Nevertheless, an example of how attitudes generally have changed is *The American President*, a film clearly inspired by the Clinton's relationship where the heroine is just as intellectually astute and strong minded as the president, and her feminizing influence on his policies, particularly regarding global warming, is portrayed as positively beneficial. Far from emasculating the president, the heroine brings a breath of sexual fresh air to the corridors of power.

The new model first marriage was later echoed in Britain when in 1997 Tony Blair was elected prime minister at the fashionably young age of forty-three, while his wife, despite the demands of motherhood, continued to pursue her own brilliant career as a barrister. Although Cherie Blair, careful to avoid Hillary Clinton's mistakes, remained in the shadow of her husband. The ideal marriage was now clearly established as one where both partners were as concerned for each other's careers as they were for their own; and with supportive husbands, women were free to pursue their own ambitions for success, power and influence. The man was no longer required to be aggressive or in control, instead he was caring, nurturing, emotionally open, empathetic and not afraid to appear vulnerable.

Men's magazines such as GQ (which was first published in 1988) became increasingly popular. They were filled with fashion tips, recipes and articles about lifestyle, sex and relation-ship problems – in other words the male equivalent of women's magazines. New Men were eclectic: they could wear their hair short, long, in a ponytail or appear comfortably bald – they were no longer afraid of Delilah emasculating them by cutting off their locks. They could wear make-up. Earrings were no longer a gay man's prerogative. Fitness and the pursuit of a beautiful body for both men and women were an essential part of the new lifestyle and particularly important in a climate that valued youth above everything. Body piercing and tattooing were fashionable for both sexes.

Later in the decade, hard-drinking, football-mad, woman-izing 'Men Behaving Badly' (the title of a popular TV comedy) became the fashionable attitude adopted by 'Lads'. This was both a reaction against the caring-sharing image of the New Man while, at the same time, a celebration of their liberation from (or their deprivation of) men's former roles of power and responsibility. In short, both New Men and Lads (despite their defiant 'attitude') were feminized men – in that neither image provided the power traditionally allocated to men. And girls who retaliated with Girl Power and Laddettes were masculinized women. The gender gap was narrower than in any period in history. The liberation and the confusion experienced by both sexes is portrayed in *Four Weddings and a Funeral* where, typical of many comedies of the decade, it is the woman who is actively striving to get what she wants while the man remains passive, bemused and just out of reach or suffering from the 'commitment problem'.

Post-modernism underpinned the non-judgemental, egalitarian and eclectic approach to life. The post-modernists pointed out how myths and outmoded attitudes regarding politics, race, gender and everything under the sun, were propagated by the way we told stories and the way we used language. It was no longer appropriate to refer to your loved one as 'my husband' or 'my wife': instead, in order to reflect gender equality and sexual tolerance, whether you were married, living together, straight or gay, the correct phrase was 'my partner'. 'The truth' was a trick of the light depending on which belief system you happened to choose and post-modern films, such as *Strictly Ballroom*, were playfully self-reflexive. They fully exploited the emotional power of traditional myths and genres while at the same time using irony and exaggeration to make the audience aware of the storytelling processes and the stories within the story.

But this fascination with traditional myths and, in romantic comedy, fairytales wasn't only a prerogative of post-modern irony, it also expressed a very potent nostalgia for days long gone when both sexes appeared to share the same romantic dream. *Strictly Ballroom* and *The American President* are both reminiscent of Frank Capra's films of the thirties where, just as with the original fairytales, finding true love was intricately bound either to the child's rite of passage into the world of adult love or the moral struggle of goodness against the forces of greed and corruption, or both. On the other hand, in films such as *Pretty Woman* and *Notting Hill* the fairytale appeals to the fantasy we have as ordinary mortals of being propelled by love into the world of the fabulously rich and glamorous. The child's rite of passage and the moral quest are far less evident. The fantasy of rekindling the dream of perfect love – which seems to have got lost somewhere in the distant past when men were men, women were women and love was perfect – is even more explicit in *Sleepless in Seattle*. Meg Ryan suggests the top of the Empire State Building for her romantic rendezvous because that's where the lovers arranged to meet in the fifties romantic comedy *An Affair to Remember*, which was itself a remake of the thirties film *Love Affair*.

Meanwhile in the real world, eligible, single, heterosexual men had retreated into their lonely castles and pulled up the drawbridge, or so it seemed to many single women, particularly mothers who found themselves in a relationship vacuum. One in two marriages were ending in divorce, one in four children were living with a single parent, the vast majority of lone parents were mothers (in Britain 94 per cent), and a quarter of all households were single person households.[5] In a period when traditional family and community support networks were breaking down, more men and women than ever before, either by choice or circumstance, were living alone. After three decades of Gay Pride gay people appeared to have better-established networks of support than straight people. Something appeared to have gone wrong with the state of marriage and heterosexual partnerships. By 1997 even the Clinton's partnership was being severely tested by the Monica Lewinski affair, although the public proved to be more tolerant than the media and their marriage survived.

With so many marriages breaking down many men and women were left angry, confused and bitter. They also found themselves suffering from the 'once bitten, twice shy' syndrome – after being badly hurt trying again can be a frightening experience. *As Good as It Gets* is a controversial exploration of the damage men and women do to each other and the fear, confusion and joy experienced by both gay and heterosexual people as they struggle to learn from their differences as well as their similarities.

Strictly Ballroom (1992)

Directed by Baz Luhrmann; screenplay by Baz Luhrmann;
starring Paul Mercurio and Tara Morice

'To live in fear is a life half-lived.'

Strictly Ballroom was released in Australia in 1992. With
dazzling assurance, dexterity and showmanship, equal to that of
the film's brilliant and innovative dance routines, the post-
modern director, Baz Luhrmann, plays with a wide variety of
stories, myths and storytelling conventions. When interviewed
Luhrmann has called his extravagantly theatrical style 'audience
participation cinema'.[6] He stresses how important it is that the
mythic influences and storytelling references are familiar to the
audience, even if only subliminally, so that, like the pleasure
children gain from hearing the same fairytale over and over
again, the audience has a similar sense that they are participating
in the game of storytelling.

In *Strictly Ballroom* the myth he chose was David and Goliath
– the small individual fighting against immense power and
almost impossible odds. The film also has similarities with
Shakespeare's *Romeo and Juliet* (which was to be Luhrmann's
next film), in that it is a story of how innocent young love is
threatened by the feuding and power machinations of an older
generation intent only on furthering their own self-serving
ambitions. Equally important are the references to the kind of
domestic dramas to be found in contemporary television soap
operas such as *Neighbours*. And the dances, such as the tango
and the passo doble, are themselves romantic and mythic encapsulations of sexual dynamics between men and women. But finally
Strictly Ballroom has all the ingredients of a traditional fairytale.

As we saw in Frank Capra's films in the thirties, the fairytale
is a rite of passage from childhood love to adult love, and the
quest is often hard and difficult, involving a variety of moral

dilemmas and tests of character, which enable the protagonists to learn and change and so earn the happiness they eventually find. Like Capra, Luhrmann uses this fairytale form to attack the corrupt social values of his times. He questions the ethos of greed, blind ambition, the obsession with stardom and winning and reminds us of the much hidden dark side – the fear of losing. He points to the heavy toll moral compromise can take on our lives, our loves, our chances of happiness and particularly our artistic creativity.

Strictly Ballroom opens with the familiar overture of the Blue Danube waltz. A cluster of starry-eyed young couples glide into the dancehall, bow to the panel of judges and a crowd of cheering onlookers and take up their opening positions in pools of spotlight. The overture pauses, the strains of the waltz begin to soar and soon the couples are whirling around the dancefloor; the young men looking sleek and elegant in their black tailcoats with white bow ties and their partners appearing like exotic mating birds, their hair sculpted into elaborate crests laced with spangles, the air rippling through the synthetic feathers of their fluorescent pink and blue and yellow ballgowns. For a few moments we are transfixed by the old-fashioned romance and glamour of ballroom dancing and particularly by the brilliant performance of couple 100, led by Scott Hastings (Paul Mercurio), a lithe and handsome youth with dark smouldering eyes. But suddenly his mother and dancing teacher, Shirley Hastings, a heavily made-up middle-aged woman with enormous dangling earrings, screams harshly from her position in the crowd, 'Come on 100!' The spell is broken.

While the young people dance for all they are worth, Luhrmann introduces us to the drama behind the scenes by inter-cutting mock documentary interviews. Scott's mother, Shirley, talks bitterly to camera about the 'tragedy' that began to unfold that night. 'There was no doubt in anyone's minds,' she insists, that her son and his partner 'would be the next Pan-Pacific Grand Prix Amateur Final Latin American champions. I mean they had worked towards it all their lives. And then came . . .'

Her voice breaks with emotion. 'The samba,' the dancing compere finishes her sentence for her with lascivious glee. We see the tragedy Shirley was referring to. The dancers are gyrating sexily to the pulsating Latin American music, the men now wearing flashy satin suits and the girls stripped down to elaborate bikinis with tiny half-skirts. Scott and his partner are 'boxed in' by a competing couple. Scott, wearing a tight gold lamé costume, deftly ducks under the arms of the couple and defiantly performs a dazzling solo routine, much to the confusion of his partner. The crowd are loving it, particularly the children, but it's *not* the samba. As Len, Scott's coach, a self-important little man wearing an ill-fitting blond toupee, informs us disapprovingly, there's no excuse for resorting to your own 'flashy crowd-pleasing steps'. Barry Fife, President of the Australian Ballroom Dancing Federation, a bloated, middle-aged, power-hungry man who is intent on using his position as chairman of the judges to sell copies of his latest video 'Dancing to Win', is equally scathing. 'You can dance any steps you like, that doesn't mean you will win,' he says with a self-satisfied grimace and awards the prize to the couple who boxed Scott in. Scott bites back his fury and disappointment.

Three days later, during a tango class at the dancing school run by Scott's mother and his coach, emotions are still running high. 'I'm not dancing with you until you dance like you're supposed to,' Scott's dancing partner screams hysterically and walks out. Shirley is distraught – how can Scott win the Pan-Pacifics in three weeks' time if he hasn't got a partner? Scott's fellow dance students turn their back on him in disgust – there's no point in dancing if it isn't to win. It appears that nobody cares about Scott's need to express himself creatively through dancing.

This is the essence of Scott's problem. He wants to innovate but his youthful free spirit is 'boxed in', not only by the formal restrictions of the traditional dance steps, but by the entire ballroom dancing establishment and the unquestioning, sheep-like conformity of his own generation. If Fife is the wicked king of this glittering, superficial fairytale kingdom, Scott's coach,

Len, is the king's ambassador and his mother, Shirley, is the wicked queen – dominating, manipulative, selfish and hysterically determined that her son will win, irrespective of his wishes. Scott's father, Doug, who sneaks away in secret to watch a video he made of his son's brilliant performance, appears to be the only person who recognizes his son's talent. But after years of being emasculated by Shirley, Doug is a pathetic, frightened, broken man. He is no help in this, Scott's hour of need. Scott is left in the darkened dance studio to nurse his wounds.

But he is not quite alone. A second-year student is watching him from her hiding place behind a curtain. In stark contrast to the heavy make-up and artificiality of the girls in the ballroom dancing circuit, Fran (Tara Morice) is an ugly duckling. Her figure, in a sloppy T-shirt and black tights, looks shapeless and ungainly, her hair is tangled and unruly, her skin, scrubbed clean of make-up, appears red and blotchy and her eyes peer myopically through huge round glasses. She is shy, lacking in confidence or any semblance of sex appeal and yet she is a passionate admirer of Scott's innovative dancing. 'I want to dance with you at the Pan Pacifics,' she tells him earnestly, '...when you dance your own steps I know how you feel because I make up my own steps too.' Rather than point out the obvious, that she is simply not pretty enough to dance with him, Scott tries to let her down gently. He points out that she's only a beginner. But Fran won't be fobbed off easily. She angrily accuses him of being just like all the others, 'Scared to give someone new a go because you think they might just be better than you are.' She has a point and Scott recognizes this. Her passion is also impressive. He reluctantly agrees to give her an hour to show him what she can do. At first she appears awkward and ungainly but after a while she nervously shows him some new steps she's been working on at home. Scott is interested. Despite Fran's ugly duckling appearance, artistically they are in tune. Also her courage and her passion could be just what Scott needs in his present crisis.

During the days Scott half-heartedly attends the auditions

Shirley and Len have organized in their desperate quest to find him a new dancing partner. In the evenings, when the dance studio is deserted, he practises in secret with Fran. As she gains in confidence her dancing improves. She also appears more attractive, particularly when Scott suggests that she tries dancing without her glasses (a somewhat hackneyed device for making a plain girl appear more attractive, but it works). When they dance together on the roof of the dance studio, beneath a washing line, a huge neon Coca-Cola sign and the vast night sky, we witness for the first time the genuine romance of two young people dancing, in contrast to the glittering artificiality of the formal dancehall. As Scott walks her home past corrugated iron walls and rusting abandoned cars she teaches him an old Spanish saying – 'To live in fear is a life half-lived' (this saying pin-points the message of the film).

Fran's father and grandmother (her mother is dead) run a decrepit café-bar by the railway tracks. They are first-generation Spanish immigrants who may be poor but they are *not* living in fear. Nobody can take their music and dancing away from them. Their spirit is rooted in the proud flamenco of their homeland. When Scott cautiously reminds Fran that although the Rumba is the dance of love, 'Well, you just pretend to be in love. It's not real,' Fran is desperately embarrassed. No one has taught her how to pretend to be in love, just as she does not know how to pretend to dance with feeling. For Fran and her family dancing *is* feeling; pretending is being afraid of feeling.

This is not the case at the 'State Championship try-outs' (the final hurdle to decide who will dance at the Pan-Pacifics in just a few days' time). Here everyone is afraid of the all-powerful President Barry Fife. His word is God and much to Scott's dismay he has found Scott a new dancing partner, Tina Sparkle – a champion who looks just like all the other artificially pretty girls on the ballroom dancing circuit. Like Cinderella poor Fran arrives late for the ball (her father insisted that she stay at home to prepare for the fiesta he is organizing in his café). In her simple summer dress and discrete make-up Fran looks attractive and womanly. But Shirley is determined that Scott won't miss his chance to dance with Tina Sparkle. While Les drags Scott away for 'a chat with President Fife', Shirley takes Fran to the girl's dressing room.

There, like Cinderella's wicked stepmother, Shirley sets to work on Fran. She is aided and abetted by two girls from the dancing school who, with their ridiculous hair and tinsel finery, look every bit like Cinderella's ugly sisters. 'You're a beginner Fran, what the hell did you think you were doing?' says one. 'And you are really clumsy,' the other adds bitchily. 'You don't want to ruin his chances do you?' Shirley cuts in, oozing with false concern for Fran's well being. She suggests that it would be better if Fran just went home and forgot all about it. Bewildered and in tears, Fran looks up at their three spiteful faces. No, she doesn't want to ruin Scott's chances.

But Scott refuses to be afraid of Barry Fife. He also ignores his mother's protests and the ugly sisters' lies. Like Prince Charming, he rushes to Fran's home to insist that he wants her to dance with him at the Pan-Pacifics. There, for the first time, he is confronted by the impressive figure of Fran's father; a man with black, piercing eyes and the proud demeanour of a Spanish bullfighter spoiling for blood. If Scott wants to dance the passo doble with his daughter, Fran's father tells him, then show him! They retreat to the terrace behind the little café-bar. There, lit by the fiesta lights and the flames of torches, burning as they would in a gypsy encampment on the Spanish plains, Scott and Fran dance. But before long their small Spanish audience begin laughing at them. Fran's father slowly stands, he casts off his jacket, raises both arms, points his fingers forward like the horns of a bull and stamps his feet. The guitar strikes up the distinctive Spanish chords and with Fran's fat grandmother as his partner, Fran's father shows Scott how real dancers do the passo doble. This is nothing to do with showing off, phony emotion or dancing to win, this is the fire in the soul of all great dancing and works of art.

Scott abandons the dance studio to spend all his time learning from Fran's father and grandmother who, although she's fat and old, is also a fine dancer. Fran's grandmother unpacks Fran's mother's precious red flamenco dress for Fran to wear at the Pan-Pacifics. She insists that Fran can be just as beautiful as her mother was on stage, 'You've just not got to be so scared, all right.' Her father contributes to Fran's final lesson in how to be a beautiful swan by teaching her to dance proudly with her head held high. 'Get the focus between you,' he says to the young couple, 'Be strong.' We can see that for the passo doble to work the man and the woman must have equal strength and then it is beautiful. (Although this contrasts with the domestic arena of this Spanish family where her father is definitely the patriarch whom women obey.)

The film's climax is, of course, the Pan-Pacific Championship itself. Barry Fife makes one last evil attempt to get Scott to toe his line. He tells Scott the 'true story' of how his father's dancing career was ruined. Before Scott was born his father had also tried to defy convention and dance new steps at the Pan-Pacifics. As a result his life was ruined and he turned into the pathetic failure he is today. If Scott repeats his father's mistake, Fife warns, 'it will kill your father'.

At first it looks as if this blatant piece of emotional blackmail will have the desired effect. As the competition gets underway Scott is completely torn between his fear of 'killing his father' and his love for Fran. But just as he is about to go on to the dancefloor with Tina Sparkle, his father asserts himself for the first time in the film. He demands that Scott listens to the truth of what really happened. He never danced at the Pan-Pacifics. Shirley refused to dance with him because he insisted on dancing his own steps. She danced with Barry Fife instead. 'Our dancing career was on the line,' Shirley butts in desperately. 'We would never have been able to teach. I couldn't throw all that away for a dream. We had to survive.' She pushes her son towards Tina Sparkle, who is waiting by the dancefloor, and hisses at him to 'win, win, win'. Desperately Scott looks at his father. 'We walked away,' his father says flatly, 'and lived our lives in fear.'

That does it. Scott rushes to find Fran and the two of them reach the dancefloor just in time for the passo doble. Barry Fife attempts to destroy their brilliant performance by pulling the plug on the music and using the megaphone to order Scott and Fran to leave the dancefloor. Everyone in the dancehall is stunned into silence, except for Scott's father who, with tears streaming down his face, slowly claps the rhythm of the passo doble. Fran's father and grandmother join him. Fran and Scott resume their dancing and soon the entire audience are clapping the rhythm for them. This is a people's revolution. As the film ends the ecstatic crowd, including Scott's parents, join Scott and Fran on the dancefloor. Fife, the reigning despot, has been deposed from his corrupt kingdom. The Australian Dance Federation is no longer just for celebrities, stars and poseurs, it is for all the people. *Strictly Ballroom* is revealed as a stunning metaphor for the corruption of popular art forms in our synthetic age.

Although *Strictly Ballroom* is reminiscent of both *The Ugly Duckling* and *Cinderella*, Luhrmann chooses only to borrow aspects for his thoroughly modern fairytale. Like Fran, both Cinderella and the Ugly Duckling were motherless, lonely, were picked on by the others for being different and accused of not being beautiful. Like Cinderella's wicked stepmother and the ugly sisters, Scott's mother and the girls from the dancing school are selfish, spiteful and superficial. They believe they are beautiful in their glittering clothes, jewellery and horrifically manufactured hairdos yet, as both fairytales suggest, real beauty is not a superficial veneer, it is a reflection of a good and therefore beautiful soul. Finally, Prince Charming and Scott both recognize this. Although it did make a difference that when Prince Charming first fell in love with Cinderella she had been magically transformed by her fairy godmother for the ball. And in the final scene of *Strictly Ballroom* Fran has been similarly transformed by her grandmother's loving restoration of her mother's red flamenco dress. But there is a crucial difference between Fran's story and that of Cinderella, which reflects

Fran's position as a woman of the nineties and the influence of feminism. Fran does not sit at home by the cinders waiting for a fairy godmother to help her out or for her prince to come looking for her. She is active, not passive. Despite her shyness and lack of confidence she fights for what she believes in and this is why she gets her reward in the end.

Luhrmann may use his film to make ironical comments on many storytelling conventions – including romantic comedy itself – which is the essence of post-modernism, but finally his own passionate message shines through with an almost old-fashioned revolutionary zeal. We feel joyful that Scott and Fran have found each other and are dancing their own steps. We are pleased that Barry, the power-hungry manipulator, has met his comeuppance. We are reminded that it is possible for goodness to win and for true passion to prevail over fake emotion. It is possible to return the authentic world of dance to the people from whence it came. Luhrmann's ironical comment has somehow freed us from sentimentality and liberated us to feel honestly.

Four Weddings and a Funeral (1994)

Directed by Mike Newell; screenplay by Richard Curtis; starring
Andie MacDowell and Hugh Grant

> 'Maybe I meet the right girls all the time. Maybe it's
> me?'

The concept of the New Man was a response to the need many
younger men felt for reappraising their identity as men. So what
were the priorities, values and lifestyle of the New Man? Who
was he now? What did he want? How did he relate to women?
And how did he distinguish between who he was and who
women wanted him to be?

Four Weddings and a Funeral, directed by Mike Newell, was
released in Britain in 1994. Its success catapulted its star, Hugh
Grant, to stardom. In the eyes of many younger women he
became the epitome of the eligible, middle-class New Man; just
the kind of man they believed they wanted as a lover, partner in
life and father for their children. In the film Hugh Grant's screen
persona, Charles, is not at all aggressive or controlling, he is self-
effacing, gentle, childlike in his playfulness and endlessly polite.
Even his boyish good looks have a feminine charm. Beneath his
thick, unruly brown hair, his face is most finely sculpted with
large, forlorn, quizzical eyes, a refined Roman nose and shapely,
slightly pouting lips. Like the classical ideal of a beautiful woman
he is effortlessly, almost innocently, attractive to the opposite sex,
not least because of his apparent lack of guile, his feminine
passivity, his innate vulnerability and his amazement that he
should be the cause of arousing so many women's passions.

He is the kind of man who would never hurt a woman, not
deliberately anyway. The problem is that his girlfriends do keep
getting hurt, which he finds eternally bewildering. It appears that
the very character traits that women find attractive about him
are what lead them to their downfall. Like female counterparts

to the sailors who were tempted by mythical sirens on to the rocks, Charles's girlfriends find themselves continually flailing against his ultimate inaccessibility. Charles, in common with many New Men, has a 'commitment problem'. And he is as baffled by this as are his many ex-girlfriends. Is it because he hasn't met the right woman yet? Or do its causes run deeper?

Like many single people Charles has a close-knit group of friends, most of whom, like him, are in their mid to late twenties. The film opens in Charles's modest flat in London where he is blissfully sleeping while his friends, in their respective households, are getting ready to go to a wedding. Tom and Fiona, minor aristocrats, hurriedly help themselves to a breakfast served by their housekeeper. Tom is shy, stuttering and totally lacking in confidence. His sister Fiona is beautiful with a sophisticated air of ironical amusement, tinged with tragedy (which we discover later is due to her secret, unrequited love for Charles). In a considerably more modest house we see two more of his friends: Gareth, plump, ebullient, theatrical and gay and Matthew, Gareth's sensitive and reserved lover, are also hurrying their breakfast. Charles suddenly wakes, looks at the time, panics and rushes to wake up his flatmate Scarlett, a tiny, bubbly, tom-boyish woman with short spiky hair. Charles and Scarlett's platonic domestic arrangement, although a little unusual, appears perfectly comfortable, particularly because Scarlett's quirky personality doesn't pose any sexual challenge. It also introduces Charles as a non-threatening man who likes women, at least enough to share a flat with one.

By the time Charles and Scarlett arrive at the church the first wedding is about to begin. (As the title suggests, the film is structured around four weddings and a funeral.) 'So sorry I'm late. I will be killing myself after the service if that's any consolation,' Charles, who is best man, apologizes with self-deprecating charm to the anxious groom. As they take their seats Carrie (Andie MacDowell), a strikingly beautiful American looking stunning in a white jacket and huge black hat, rushes into the church and walks purposefully to her seat. She is watched by everybody in the congregation, including Charles. After the wedding, as the guests mingle on the lawns where the reception is being held, Charles's interest in Carrie grows. But just as he manages to introduce himself he is interrupted by an old school acquaintance. 'How's your gorgeous girlfriend?' Charles politely enquires. 'She's no longer my girlfriend,' the man replies. 'Oh dear. Still, I wouldn't get too gloomy about it,' Charles tells him amiably, 'Rumour has it that she never stopped bonking old Toby, in case *you* didn't work out.' The poor man, looking totally deflated, informs Charles that, 'She's now my wife.' Carrie bows her head to conceal her amusement at Charles's faux pas and discretely walks away. A few moments later she notices Charles, consumed with guilt, banging his forehead against a marquee post.

Later, in a desperate attempt to make his best man's speech amusing, Charles's blundering indiscretions threaten to wreck still more marriages. His friends are reduced to helpless laughter while the older generation sit in shocked silence. He finally ends with the heartfelt words, 'I am, as ever, in bewildered awe of anyone who makes the kind of commitment Angus and Laura [the newlyweds] have made today. I know I couldn't do it and I think it's wonderful they have.' Carrie looks distinctly disappointed, as does his friend Fiona who is listening equally intently.

As Newell, the director, skillfully observes, weddings generate strong and strangely unsettling emotions in the guests. Those who are married find themselves recalling their own wedding with nostalgia, confusion or both, depending on their ensuing marriage. Singles find themselves questioning their single status, battling with feelings of longing and wondering anxiously if they will ever find the right partner – which is perhaps why so many people meet their future spouses at weddings (as is mentioned later in the film). For others, like Charles, weddings are disturbingly threatening occasions, which only serve to reinforce their ambivalence about the institution itself. Not that their ambivalence diminishes their desire for love, at least for the night ahead.

It's late, the bride and groom have left and the reception is beginning to disintegrate. A few lucky singles have found a partner for the night, or even longer. Charles's friends are gathering to go back to Tom and Fiona's nearby castle. Charles, who is of course expected to join them, is despondently drinking his beer alone when Carrie coyly approaches him. 'Hi,' she says with a stunning smile, 'I was just wondering where you are staying tonight . . . I'm staying at The Boatman.' Charles is too surprised or dithering to seize the moment. But on his way to the castle he realizes what a fool he's been and changes course for Carrie's hotel. There, once again, his dithering politeness lets him down as he becomes ensnared in the bar by yet another old school acquaintance. Carrie skilfully saves the day, or the night. She pretends to be his wife and sends a waiter with a message for Charles to come up to their room immediately. Almost as soon as he enters her room she sets about seducing him. Charles happily succumbs.

Carrie is clearly the kind of woman who doesn't hesitate to use her initiative to get what she wants. Although if she wants a man like Charles, who has just publicly confessed that he could never commit to marriage, what can even a woman as charming and beautiful as Carrie do about it? After a night of blissful sex Charles wakes to find her packing to go to America. She looks at him with wide, serious eyes and asks when they will be announcing their engagement: 'I assumed that, since we slept together and everything, we would be getting married. What did you think?' Charles gulps back his terror and attempts to talk his way out of it, before suggesting hopefully, 'You're joking?' Carrie laughs, although somewhat ambivalently. But Charles is reassured. 'For a moment there I thought I was in *Fatal Attraction*,' he says, breathing a sigh of relief. 'You were Glen Close and I was going to get home and find my pet rabbit . . .'

This reminder of *Fatal Attraction*, the infamous eighties film about a man who finds himself stalked and terrorized by a woman he initially found attractive, suggests that for Charles the fear of the dark side of woman's power and the ever-present possibility of entrapment is never far beneath the surface. On the other hand, Carrie's strangely unsettling joke, if it were a joke, suggests that she may be toying with the idea of marriage, if not testing the water. 'I think we both missed a great opportunity here,' she tells him wistfully. As if a part of her knows that Charles is a hopeless case and, wisely, she's not prepared to become another sacrificial victim on the altar of his commitment problem, she picks up her bag and leaves.

For Charles the second wedding is even more disturbing. At first he is delighted to see Carrie again, but then she introduces him to her new fiancé, a suave and confident Scottish politician. (So marriage was on her mind!) Mortified, Charles retreats and despairingly tells Mathew, his gay friend, that he's seriously worried about himself; why is he always at weddings and never the one getting married? Mathew gently suggests that maybe he hasn't met the right girl yet. Charles isn't convinced, 'Maybe I meet the right girls all the time. Maybe it's me!'

If Charles has been meeting the right girls all the time he has certainly made a mess of things. At the reception he is forced by the place settings to sit at a table which is almost entirely surrounded by his very attractive ex-girlfriends. As the conversation develops it gradually emerges that they all have Charles in common and, much to Charles's humiliation, they begin to swap bitter-sweet stories about their respective relationships with him. Soon after the meal Charles bumps into yet another ex, Henrietta (known to her friends as Hen and to her enemies as Duck Face). At the merest sight of Charles she bursts into tears. Charles half-heartedly tries to comfort her but Hen's friend furiously tells him to leave her alone, 'Haven't you hurt her enough?' Charles guiltily decides that his best course of action is to disappear upstairs until the coast is clear and he can go home. Even there Hen manages to track him down.

At first her concern appears to be for his future rather than her own. She earnestly tries to get him to understand that he can't go on like this, having one girlfriend after another but never really loving anyone because he will never let them near him. 'You don't have to start a relationship thinking I must get married,' she tells him, 'But you mustn't start every relationship thinking I mustn't get married.' Charles tries to explain that most of the time he just doesn't think at all, he just potters along. Whether it is in response to his ineffectual words or his hang-dog helpless expression, something sets Hen off again – she throws her arms around his neck, smothers him with tears and then runs off down the corridor crying. Carrie, with her usual impeccable timing, appears further down the corridor and seizes the moment to once again, charmingly, take the initiative. Her fiancé has left for Scotland, maybe Charles would like to come back to her hotel for a nightcap?

The contrast between the two women is palpable. Hen's problem is that she has guilelessly allowed herself to run aground on Charles's 'commitment problem' and consequently she's lost her dignity, her charm and her power to attract him. By getting engaged to another man Carrie has made herself as ultimately unattainable as Charles. She has effectively kept their relationship on an equal footing and saved herself from the possibility of her turning into another Hen or any of his other ex-girlfriends – although marrying the wrong man could be a high price to pay for keeping Charles on his toes. When Carrie and Charles wake up after their second blissful night together they gaze lovingly into each other's eyes but neither of them speak. Instead Carrie watches him silently from the bed while he dresses. As the proverb goes, you can lead a horse to water but you can't make it drink. It is clearly up to Charles to make the next move but this requires a decisiveness on his part that he singularly lacks. He smiles ruefully and leaves.

Charles meets Carrie just one more time before her wedding. He's out shopping for her wedding present when she happens to bump into him in one of the shops on her wedding list. (If it weren't for Carrie's charm one might be forgiven for thinking that she is stalking him.) Charles is looking particularly soft in a loose floral patterned shirt and baggy shorts; Carrie's wearing a man's check shirt and casual trousers. As if to emphasize even further how, in life as well as in fashion, the gender differences appear to be increasingly overlapping, over coffee Carrie lists all 33 of the men she has slept with in her life. She rates each of them according to their sexual performance; from a bent little finger for 'can't get it up', to having slept with the father of one of her boyfriends. Charles is number 32, she tells him wistfully, and 'he was lovely'. She also insists that once she is married (to number 33) she intends to be a totally faithful wife.

So the new woman of the nineties knows what she wants and she wants everything. Not only has she moved into the traditionally masculine territory of promiscuity but she also insists on the traditional wife's right to faithfulness. Could this be one of the reasons why men like Charles appear to have retreated to a position of passive bewilderment?

They are by the river in the drizzling rain when Carrie reluctantly says goodbye. Charles has at last realized that this is his last chance to tell her how he feels. But how does he feel? His speech becomes increasingly muddled as he battles with his fear . . . of what? Of commitment? Of the enormity of what he is saying? Of her? '. . .in short,' he stammers, 'to recap . . . in the words of David Cassidy, in fact while he was still with the Partridge family, I think I love you, and er . . . I . . . er . . . I just wondered whether or not you wouldn't like to er, no of course not, I'm an idiot . . . lovely to see you, sorry to disturb you, better get on.' Carrie kisses him on the cheek and gives him a final appealing look. She clearly wants him to say more, be more decisive, more direct, do something! But he can't. And she has done everything except say what has to be said for him.

Carrie's wedding is in a small Scottish church, followed by an impressive reception in a local castle. The friends are all there, as usual. Gareth, in particularly ebullient mood, observes that none of them are married and he would like to go to a wedding of someone he loves for a change, 'so go forth and conjugate, find husbands and wives'. As if to set them an example he joins in the Highland fling with gusto. Charles is naturally forlorn but puts on a brave face as he listens to Carrie make her wedding speech.

She finishes with the disarming words, 'Oh, by the way, someone here told me confidentially that if things didn't work out with Hamish [her new husband] he would step in. I just wanted to say thanks, I will keep you posted.' The guests of course laugh. Charles looks perturbed. Carrie's new husband, who is from the older generation which still thinks men are the ones who should be in control, immediately counters confidently with his own speech: 'Anyone involved in politics for the last twenty years has got used to being upstaged by a woman. I didn't expect it to happen on my wedding day, however . . .' As the assembled guests roar with laughter at his associating Carrie with Margaret Thatcher, Gareth collapses on to the floor.

Gareth's funeral takes place in a church on a dilapidated housing estate in London. In the packed church Gareth's working-class parents battle to come to terms with the loss of their son and his wide social network of friends, many of whom are gay. Charles, Scarlett, Tom and Fiona sit together. Carrie sits alone in another part of the church having postponed her honeymoon to be there. The congregation listen in silence as Mathew makes his speech about Gareth, their love and his feelings of loss. He finishes his speech by quoting the words of 'another splendid bugger', W. H. Auden: '. . . He was my North, my South, my East and West/ My working week and my Sunday rest,/ My noon, my midnight, my talk, my song,/ I thought that love would last forever: I was wrong.' Tears run down the faces of each of the friends as they listen. For the first time in the film we are hearing words which really do capture the meaning of the reality of love.

Funerals, like marriages, provoke strong feelings about love and loss and often cause people to review the course of their lives and what they want. After the funeral, as Charles walks with Tom to the river's edge, he suggests that if the service shows anything, 'It shows that there is a perfect match.' Tom disagrees. He thinks what appears to be a perfect match is the outcome of an altogether more practical arrangement. For instance, he's just looking for a nice girl, not the thunderbolt. Charles ruefully concedes that maybe he's right, 'Maybe all this waiting for the one true love gets you nowhere.'

Ten months later the wedding invitation announces Charles's wedding. (The identity of his bride is withheld until the last minute.) While Charles is nervously waiting in the church for his bride to arrive, Carrie appears. She is looking vulnerable and appealingly feminine in a long grey mackintosh. Her marriage is over already. 'It's absolutely the last time I marry someone three times my age,' she tells him. (So the failure of her marriage was Hamish's fault for being a traditional man?) She goes on to comment sadly on the bad timing that has beset her relationship with Charles. This, of course, is guaranteed to throw Charles into panic. By the time Hen, his bride, is walking towards him down the aisle, his panic is so acute that it appears as if he will succumb to his usual passive inertia and go through with the ceremony out of politeness. Charles now appears like the classic fairytale damsel in distress in need of a knight in shining armour to rescue him. His deaf and dumb younger brother steps into the role. All Charles has to do is passively translate his brother's sign language for the vicar and assembled guests. 'He says I suspect the groom is having doubts . . .' Charles translates, parrot fashion, 'I suspect the groom loves someone else . . .' 'Do you love someone else?' the vicar asks. Charles is silent. Eventually he says, 'I do.' Hen suddenly throws a powerful left hook, punching him in the face. Charles collapses on to the floor and she runs from the church in tears.

The effect of this gender reversal is remarkable. By behaving in a traditionally masculine fashion and punching Charles in the face, Hen appears to be a bad woman and as such she deserves what she gets, or in her case loses. While Charles, who has been really bad by standing her up at the altar, now appears in the more traditionally feminine role of helpless victim and so he is neatly vindicated. In the final sequence of the film Carrie and Charles stand together in the pouring rain. '. . . Do you think you might agree *not* to marry me,' Charles asks in his usual convoluted fashion, 'And do you think *not* being married to me might be something you could consider doing for the rest of your life?' Carrie says, 'I do.' Behind them a thunderbolt of forked lightning streaks through the darkened sky. The film ends with a non-wedding photo of Charles and Carrie happily cradling their new baby.

So what were the causes of Charles's 'commitment problem'? For the entire course of the film Carrie has been the active one; she makes all the moves and Charles passively responds, or doesn't respond. Could the underlying message be that for a New Man, like Charles, the 'commitment problem' is the only safety net and recourse to power at a time when men appeared to have relinquished or lost so much power in other aspects of their lives? Similarly with almost all the other male characters in the film, it is the women who spot them, chase them and eventually win them. The days are over when men were thought to be the prime movers, or gallant knights in shining armour required to prove their masculine worth in order to win the woman they love. In the nineties men have been happily feminized, or unhappily emasculated (depending on your point of view). The result is confusion and fear for both sexes. Men like Charles are confused about who they are and what they want. They are also afraid of losing their identity still further. And they are afraid of women's power. Women who were once afraid of traditional men's power now want New Men like Charles. But they are confused by his confusion. And their old fear of men has been replaced by a new fear; they are now afraid of losing him or not quite having him to lose.

On the other hand, if we are to believe the ending of the film, Charles never had a 'commitment problem'. He simply hadn't met the right woman until Carrie came along and he was struck by a thunderbolt, although he didn't realize this at the time. His problem wasn't commitment but his fear of the institution of marriage. And Carrie was a sweet vulnerable woman all along, the perfect future mother for his children. Believe that if you like!

The American President (1995)

Directed by Rob Reiner; screenplay by Aaron Sorkin; starring
Annette Bening and Michael Douglas

'She threatened me, I patronized her . . . but I
thought there was a connection.'

Frank Capra's *Mr Deeds Goes to Town* was a fairytale response to
the major issue of the thirties, the depression that blighted so many
people's lives. Similarly, *The American President*, released in 1995,
is a fairytale response to what continues to be one of the major
issues of our time – climate change as a result of global warming
and the kind of leadership required to avert a future world
catastrophe. And of course, the most powerful leader in the world,
the American president, is the modern equivalent of a fairytale
king. But even fairytale kings are often troubled, particularly when
their power is under threat (which is much of the time) and when
they don't have a queen to share their problems or their happiness.
The American President (a forerunner to the 2000 TV series *The
West Wing*, also written by Sorkin), has transposed this familiar
fairytale dilemma into a hypothetical problem for the hard-nosed
and cynical political climate of the mid-1990s.

The question the film poses is: How does a widower who also
happens to be the president of the United States, whose every
action has to be vetted for its political expediency and whose
every move is watched by the media hawks, find and woo a
girlfriend? Or to look at the question from the woman's point of
view: What kind of strength of character would his girlfriend
need if she is not to be completely overwhelmed by the immense
seductive power intrinsic in the glamour and status of his
position? As Rob Reiner made brilliantly clear when six years
earlier he directed *When Harry Met Sally*, for a relationship to
be ideal at the end of the twentieth century it must first and

foremost be a friendship and a partnership between equals, even if one of the partners does happen to be the American president.

The eponymous hero is President Andrew Shepherd (Michael Douglas), a handsome, youthful, middle-aged man. (His surname is significant; it's a name we associate with benevolence and the Christian ideal of a leader who is concerned primarily with peace and the safety of his flock.) We first meet Andrew Shepherd on a normal Monday in the White House. As he strolls along the luxurious corridors of power he appears to be supremely relaxed and comfortable with his role as the most powerful man in the world. But he is soon assailed by his speech writer, a young liberal idealist, who is very upset with a speech the president has made declaring that, 'Americans can no longer afford to pretend they live in a great society . . . and then nothing.' According to the speech writer, the president dumped the 'whole kick-ass para-graph on handguns' and put nothing in its place, leaving the press-pack wanting to know what he was talking about – what *is* wrong with American society? The president blithely reminds him that in an election year prudence is everything.

Prudence is also his priority when he decides on his response to the environmentalists at the 'Global Defence Council' who are blaming his presidency for the lack of action on global warming and demanding a twenty per cent cut in fossil fuel emissions. As A.J., the president's friend and chief political adviser points out, they will never get twenty per cent through congress. 'How do we know we won't get it through if we haven't tried?' the speech writer despairs as he sees yet another ideal slipping away. But Andrew Shepherd has made up his mind – a ten per cent cut is the most they can offer. His dictum is: 'We've got to fight the fights that we can win.'

In other words the president may once have had ideals and a vision for the future of his country but now he makes speeches that set out to say something and then fizzle into nothing. The pressures of office have worn him down. Now the only thing that matters is the kind of political expediency necessary in order to get re-elected.

Just as there is emptiness in the heart of his speech, there is also a vacuum in the centre of his life. Andrew Shepherd is a widower. He is very fond of his twelve-year-old daughter Lucy, but the fact remains, he is lonely. It is this that is preying on his mind when late that night he walks back to his private apartment accompanied by A.J. who briefs him on a meeting that is due to take place with the Global Defence Council the following morning. The environmentalists have brought in 'a hired gun', A.J. tells him, a female lawyer called Sydney Ellen Wade, an experienced lobbyist who has had a lot of success getting congressmen elected. 'Maybe we should steal her,' the president jokes. He then tries to put work behind him and turn their conversation to more personal matters. He reminds A.J. that he is his friend, not just his official adviser, and it would make him feel better if A.J. called him Andy, not 'Mr President'. But A.J. just smiles, and says 'Goodnight Mr President'. It appears there is nobody willing or able to see beyond his official position and relate to him as a normal man.

We first meet Sydney Ellen Wade (Annette Bening) the following morning when she arrives for her meeting in the White House. She's in her early thirties, bright, smart, with very short red hair and a mischievous elfin smile – her personality, like her name, is an intriguing mixture of masculine feistiness and feminine charm. 'This is my first time at the White House,' she tells the security guard with undisguised excitement, 'I'm just trying to savour the Capra-esque quality.' 'He doesn't know what Capra-esque means,' her jaded colleague mutters at her impatiently. But the security guard insists that he does and lists *It's a Wonderful Life* and *Mr Smith Comes to Washington* to prove it. So Sydney is not just a smart ambitious woman, she also loves Capra's fairytale comedies – which suggests that she is an idealist at heart and believes that people should fight the fights that matter, *not* just those they can win.

In her meeting with A.J. she very quickly demonstrates her 'hired gun' reputation: 'The president has critically misjudged reality,' she says with her eyes glinting as she launches her attack, 'if he thinks the environmental community is just going to whistle a happy tune whilst rallying support around this pitifully lame mockery of environmental leadership just because he's a nice guy, then your boss is chief executive of fantasy land.' She ends with a triumphant smile, little realizing that Andrew Shepherd has quietly entered the room while she was in full flight. 'Let's take him out back and beat the shit out of him,' Andy says good humouredly. Sydney is mortified by the impression she has made. She stammers her apology, becomes even more flustered and is convinced that she has blown it when Andy tells her he wants to talk to her in private. She waits nervously in the daunting surroundings of the Oval Office, like a child about to be carpeted by the headmaster. But instead of the expected dressing down she is amazed when Andy offers her a deal. If she can get twenty-four senators to vote for a twenty per cent fossil fuel reduction then he will promise her full White House support. 'Do I have your word on that, sir?' Sydney gasps. 'Absolutely,' he says. His voice then softens, 'Listen, are you hungry . . . do you want to have a donut or coffee or something?' Sydney's eyes narrow suspiciously. 'Sir, I'm a little intimidated by my surroundings,' she says with all the professional dignity that she can muster, 'And yes, I have gotten off to a somewhat rocky and stilted beginning, but don't let that diminish the weight of my message.' She goes on proudly to insist that if he doesn't live up to his side of the deal the environmentalists will 'go shopping for a new candidate'. With that she attempts to make a dignified exit but, much to his amusement and her humiliation, she chooses the wrong door and has to be redirected.

Andy is not bothered by the deal he has made. As he tells A.J. over a game of pool, it is merely a clever piece of political manipulation – he is quite sure Sydney will never be able to come up with twenty-four votes and by showing goodwill he will maintain the environmentalists' support for the coming election. He then confesses that his interest in Sydney is more personal than political. As he puts it, 'She threatened me, I patronized her.

We didn't have anything to eat but I thought there was a connection.' In other words he likes her but how does a president go about dating? A.J. suggests that if the president wants 'female companionship' he could find a girl willing to be smuggled in for the night and in that way ensure total privacy. But that's not what Andy has in mind. He wants a real woman not a bimbo, and he wants to take her out on a proper, above-board, old-fashioned date despite the risk of adverse publicity and the possible detrimental effect on his rating in the polls.

Sydney, wearing a boyish pair of pyjamas, is working in her sister's living room when the phone rings. She pauses for a moment when she hears Andy's voice and then decides it must be a friend playing a joke. 'I'm so glad you called,' she replies with heavy irony, 'because I forgot to tell you today what a nice ass you have . . .' She hangs up leaving Andy looking at the phone in bewilderment. He tries again. By the time he manages to convince her that it really is him she is nearly in tears of humiliation. But then he asks her to be his date at the official state visit of the president of France. Her eyebrows pucker as she silently tries to take this in. She finally rises to her feet and, in her pyjamas looking like a child who is playing soldiers and has just been given a very exciting assignment, she beams with pride: 'Mr President, you have asked me to join you in representing our country. I'm honoured. I'm equal to the task. I won't let you down, sir.' 'Sydney,' Andy reminds her, 'this is just dinner, we won't be doing espionage.' But when he hangs up we can see he's excited too – he's done it, he's invited a woman on a date and she's said yes.

Their first date is literally the stuff of fairytales. The entire political and social elite of Washington are there in full evening attire, eager to witness the pomp and ceremony of the American president entertaining his distinguished French guests. Sydney gamely keeps the conversation going as she and the president walk arm in arm down the main staircase into a barrage of photographers' flashbulbs. After the dinner, as she dances with Andy, she asks him how he does it. 'Two hundred pairs of eyes are focused on you right now with two questions,' she says, 'Who is this girl? And why is he dancing with her?' Andy points out that the two hundred pairs of eyes are not focused on him, they are focused on her. And he is right, of course. The following day a picture of Sydney dancing with the president is plastered on the front page of all the newspapers.

'Did you sleep with him?' her boss shoots at her when she arrives in her office for work. Sydney is offended. That is none of his business. But her boss insists that it is. 'Politics is perception,' he says, reminding her of her own mantra as a political lobbyist. He hired her reputation. He hired a grown-up, a major player, a person capable of running a national campaign. If this relationship with the president doesn't work out, he warns her, 'the amount of time it will take you to go from being a hired gun to being a cocktail party joke could be clocked with an egg-timer.' Sydney is experienced enough in politics to know that he is right, but extracting herself from an affair with the president is more difficult than she bargained for. Each time she tries to tell him it will never work out something comes up. Soon she finds herself helping his daughter with her homework and then, when Andy gives her what he calls 'a twenty-five cent tour of the White House', this inevitably leads to their first kiss.

'And then what happened?' her sister demands in alarm when Sydney tells her about the kiss. 'He had to go and attack Libya,' Sydney replies, frowning, 'I've got to nip this in the bud. This has catastrophe written all over it.' But, as her sister so astutely points out, 'He's the leader of the free world, he's brilliant, he's handsome, he's funny, he's an above average dancer. Isn't it possible our standards are just a tad high?'

Sydney's sister is right. Andy Shepherd does appear to be the perfect combination of the New Man mixed with all the best attributes of the traditional man. Andy Shepherd (like President Bill Clinton who was in office when the film was made) is a post-war child and has never done military service. In the eyes of many traditional men, this is a weakness; it means he somehow escaped the Vietnam draft which is a serious flaw in his masculine image. But as Reiner takes care to show us, President Shepherd is man enough to bear the burden of the enormous moral responsibility of bombing the Libyan Intelligence HQ. And he is caring enough to insist that the attack takes place at night when the fewest people will be in the building. (Given the constraints of the romantic comedy genre we are unable to assess the wider political arguments behind this decision.) The point is that Andy Shepherd does 'What a man's gotta do' (as John Wayne has reputedly uttered in many a John Ford western) and so proves that a nice New Man can at the same time be a tough traditional man – both essential requirements for a hero at the end of the twentieth century.

Likewise women at the end of the twentieth century also have to prove themselves. They have to show that they are equal to men in the world of work – a world that remains dominated by men in the higher echelons of power – but at the same time they can be as feminine and attractive as a traditional woman, if and when they choose. The next time Sydney arrives at the White House she is determined, however, to put her personal feelings to one side and act in her capacity as an experienced professional. 'Hi,' she tells him brightly, 'I just came over to tell you why I can't see you any more.' She points out that if she were on his staff she would tell him that the worst thing he can do is open himself up to character attacks by having an affair in an election year. Andy watches, rather than listens, and when she has finished her speech he suggests that her problem is 'sex and nervousness'. He goes on to explain why. First Ladies, he tells her, are not nervous about having sex with presidents because they were not presidents when they met them, but that is not the case here. 'Ah,' Sydney says wonderingly, as if he has just divulged one of the secrets of the universe. She then asks if she can be excused, she wants 'to freshen up'. While she is in the bathroom Andy fixes them drinks and continues to talk in the same reassuring vein. He has a plan, he tells her: they are going to slow down, 'and when you are comfortable, that's when it's going to happen'. Sydney appears at the bathroom door wearing nothing but one of his white shirts. She looks sexy, beautiful and challenging as she tests the firmness of the bed. 'Are you nervous?' Andy asks nervously. 'No,' Sydney replies frankly. 'Good,' he says, 'My nervousness exists on several levels. One, I haven't done this in a long time. Two, any expectations that you might have, given the fact that I'm . . . you know . . .' Sydney approaches him smiling: 'The most powerful man in the world,' she suggests as she takes the wine glasses from his hands in order to lead him to the bed.

So Sydney has now proved that she is the perfect heroine for the end of the twentieth century: equal to any man on the work front, sexy and feminine in the bedroom and yet unafraid to take the initiative sexually, when her initiative is required, which in this case it is. Andy may be president but beneath his official persona he is a mere man with real fears; such as whether he can perform well enough in bed, a task made even more daunting by his fear of her high expectations given his superman status. We are also reminded of an old truism that Andrew Shepherd seems to have forgotten – some women may find power intimidating but for many it is an aphrodisiac.

Their relationship is now the number one news item with headlines such as 'The Girlfriend Factor' and 'Day 15 of Sydney Watch – is the world's most eligible bachelor off the market?' Sydney is followed everywhere she goes by press photographers. The president's enemies in the Republican Party, led by Senator Rumson, a short, balding weasel, go into action to use Sydney to discredit the president's character. They even dig up an old FBI photograph of Sydney in her student days burning an American flag in protest against South African apartheid. The president's aides are worried. His opinion poll ratings are falling and they want Andrew Shepherd to fight back. But he refuses to comment, even when on national television Rumson suggests that Sydney may have traded sexual favours for votes in her home state of Virginia. Rather than risk the political ramifications of defending Sydney's honour, Andy remains convinced that 'no comment' is the wisest form of defence.

The final crunch between Sydney and the president comes, not because of his falling ratings or anything Rumson does, but because of Sydney's work. With a disarming mixture of feminine charm and emotive argument, such as, 'Think like a grandfather for a second – wouldn't you like your grandchildren to be able to take a deep breath when they are thirty?' she has persuaded twenty-four senators to vote for the twenty per cent reduction in fossil fuel. She has lived up to her reputation as a brilliant political lobbyist and now has enough votes to get the Fossil Fuel Bill through congress. Andy, on the other hand, is failing to get enough votes for his Crime Bill. His solution to this problem, which he doesn't disclose to Sydney, is to promise three senators with a heavy interest in the petro-chemical industry that he will bury the fossil fuel legislation if they will vote for his Crime Bill. In other words he betrays Sydney's interests in favour of his own and he breaks the promise he made to Sydney when he first met her. He again places short-term political expediency before the long-term interests of the nation.

When he returns to his private apartment he finds Sydney furiously packing the clothes she has left there during the course of their relationship. She's been fired, she informs him bitterly, for not achieving the objectives of her job. '. . .You know those prickly environmentalists,' she tosses at him, her voice heavy with irony, 'if it's not clean water it's clean air they want. Like it's not good enough that I'm on the cover of *People* magazine . . .' He tries to explain that it is the environmentalists who got screwed, not her personally. But she's not having it. As far as she is concerned he has put an emasculated Crime Bill that won't make any significant difference to the state of crime ahead of important environmental legislation that affects everyone's future simply in order to get re-elected. 'Sydney, I don't want to lose you over this,' he tells her calmly, still not fully aware of the seriousness of the situation. 'Mr President,' she says with passionate earnestness, 'You have got bigger problems than losing me. You have just lost my vote.' With that she leaves.

The choice before the president is clear. He can either stick to his pragmatic policy of only fighting the battles he knows he can win. Or he can act like a heroic leader, or fairytale knight in shining armour, and risk fighting a battle he might lose. But at least he will be fighting for the honour of the woman he loves and for the force of good against the evil implicit in inaction. Blinkered short-term objectives don't take into account the future of the planet, which is now in his hands.

The film ends with Andrew Shepherd unilaterally taking the decision to make an impromptu speech to the assembled press corps. His White House aides and advisers watch with astonishment and growing excitement. He talks about freedom and what it means to an impoverished mind like Senator Bob Rumson's 'who is only interested in two things: making you afraid of it, and telling you who is to blame for it. That's how you win elections.' He accuses Rumson of telling lies at Sydney's expense: 'You want a character debate Bob (Rumson), you better stick with me because Sydney Ellen Wade is way out of your league . . . I have loved two people in my life. One I lost to cancer, the other I lost because I was so busy keeping my job I forgot to do my job. That ends right now!' He finally announces that he is 'presenting the Energy Bill to congress requiring a twenty per cent reduction in fossil fuel over the next ten years. By far the most aggressive step ever taken in the fight to reverse the effects of global warming.' With his speech finished he goes back to his office and sets about the task of trying to borrow a car. He intends to go and find Sydney and get her back, whatever it takes. But at that moment Sydney rushes in to hug him – she heard his speech on the radio.

Whether Andrew Shepherd wins the election or not we shall never know. But in true fairytale fashion through fighting for Sydney and her honour he has also proved that he can act with the courage, goodness and vision necessary to change things for the better in a corrupt world. Just as we saw in Capra's *Mr Deeds Goes to Town*, both Longfellow Deeds and Andrew Shepherd attempt to change the world they live in by making a great speech and thereby win the woman they love – the preferred arms for the knight's glorious battle are words not weapons. Of course, it was Sydney's moral conviction that the environment was worth fighting for above all else, combined with the contemporary ethos of equality, friendship and partnership between men and women, which gave him the necessary courage and vision. Sydney has proved herself to be the new fairytale princess for the twenty-first century.

In contrast to *Four Weddings and a Funeral*, with its underlying message that a New Man is essentially an emasculated man who can only hint at his need for power by withdrawing his commitment, *The American President* portrays a New Man who is both feminized and powerful. The philosophical position of the film is that power is not bad in itself. The moral issue is what you do with your power when you have it. By creating a female heroine whose strength is equal to that of the president and showing how his world view and his actions benefit from his partnership with such a woman, the underlying message of the film is that the feminization of society, far from being a threat to masculinity is its necessary counterbalance.

As Good As It Gets (1997)

Directed by James L. Brooks; screenplay by Mark
Andrus and James L. Brooks; starring Helen Hunt
and Jack Nicholson

'She's evicted me from my life!'

As the twentieth century draws to a close many family and
community support networks are breaking down and more
adults than ever before are living alone as if in a state of siege.
People are guarding their physical and psychological boundaries,
allowing in only the trusted and familiar, intent on defending
their values and identity from what is felt to be a hostile outside
world. The question posed by *As Good As It Gets*, is: How can
love find its way through such well-constructed defences?

In 1979 James L. Brooks wrote the screenplay of *Starting
Over*, which explored the question of how a decade of feminism
was changing relationships and particularly men's sense of their
own identity. In *As Good As It Gets*, released almost twenty
years later, Brooks, as co-writer and director, portrays a middle-
class society that has become more feminized but finds that the
state of gender relations and particularly our concept of
masculinity has become even more confused. An alternative title
for the film might be *The Taming of Melvin*. In *The Taming of
the Shrew* Kate is a woman consumed by fury to the point of
madness. She is so wild, egocentric and bad that it would appear
impossible for any man to love her, let alone be loved by her in
return. In *As Good As It Gets* Brooks takes a similar theme but
reverses the genders. It is the man who rages against what he
perceives as the feminized, politically correct, caring, sharing
world that threatens the identity of men like him. And it takes an
equally strong woman, who is able to assert her feminine
character traits, to 'tame' him.

When the film opens Melvin Udell (Jack Nicholson), middle-aged with a large, manly physique, a creased, lived-in face and strikingly volatile eyebrows, is caught in mid-temper tantrum in the smart communal hallway of the apartment block where he lives. The object of his loathing is Verdell, his neighbour's tiny long-haired dog, who glances up at him innocently while proceeding to pee against the wall. Melvin leaps on the dog, holds it at arms length in disgust and shoves it in the trash chute. 'This is New York,' Melvin mutters darkly as the dog slides down into oblivion, 'You can make it here, you can make it anywhere.'

You may be pleased (or not so pleased depending on your predisposition) to learn that Verdell is safely returned to his owner, Simon, by the janitor who found the dog in the basement garbage 'eating diaper shit'. Simon, Melvin's nearest neighbour, is a serious and talented young artist. He's also an unself-consciously attractive man in his late twenties; blond, blue-eyed, sensitive, gentle, charming, polite – in short he appears to be endowed with all the likeable character traits that Melvin lacks. The only drawback, from a woman's point of view, is that he happens to be gay.

This is also something of a problem when he knocks on Melvin's door to complain about Melvin's treatment of Verdell: he is met with a homophobic diatribe about how he is *never* to disturb Melvin when he is working (Melvin is a writer of romance fiction) even if 'some fudge-packer that you date has been elected the first queer president of the United States and he's going to have you down to Camp David and you want someone to *share* the moment with, even then, don't knock . . . Do you get me sweetheart?' Simon blinks in bewilderment: 'Yes,' he replies politely, 'it's not a subtle point that you are making.' As a well brought-up white, middle-class American, Simon is intimidated by his neighbour's heavy sarcasm. But Frank, his sophisticated, gay African-American art dealer, who 'grew up in hell', is not. Just as Melvin settles back down to his work – he is trying to think of a definitive definition of love to complete his latest novel – Frank knocks on his door. He grabs the terrified Melvin by his shirt collar and orders him never to abuse Simon or touch his dog again. 'I hate doing this,' he finishes, frustrated by the low level of humanity a man like Melvin has reduced him to, 'Have a nice day.' His point made he skips back to Simon's apartment leaving Melvin in a near hysterical state of shock.

Melvin is a classic misanthrope – his aggressive cynicism is not restricted to homosexuals and blacks, the whole of mankind is fair game for his scathing attacks. He also suffers from a psychiatric condition known as obsessive-compulsive disorder. His bathroom cupboard is filled to the brim with bars of medicated soap, which he uses once and then throws away. Whenever he enters or leaves his apartment he is compelled to lock each of the numerous locks on his front door – only then does he feel safe. He swerves unnervingly when he walks down the street in case he should tread on a crack or line on the sidewalk. He wears leather gloves to prevent his skin inadvertently coming into contact with others'. In short Melvin's obsession with control is out of control. His entire life is ruled by routine, repetition and the warding-off of disorder, to such an extent it is difficult to imagine how he could submit to an out of control passion such as love. It is equally difficult to imagine how any self-respecting woman could bring herself to love a man like Melvin.

On the other hand, Melvin is a successful writer of popular romance fiction. This tells us that somewhere tucked away in the safe cocoon of his imagination, protected by his encrusted outer shell, he nurtures an idealized vision of love as the guiding light to a perfect world. Secretly he longs for love, even if the secret is so well kept he is hardly aware of it himself.

There is one exception to Melvin's contempt for the human race: Carol (Helen Hunt), a tall, shapely, disarmingly direct waitress in her mid-thirties who works in the restaurant he routinely frequents. Of course, he always has to sit at the same table, so when he arrives to find some other people sitting there his behaviour sinks to an even darker level of obnoxiousness.

'I've got Jews at my table!' he announces, shocking the entire restaurant clientele. Carol, like a capable mother dealing with a recalcitrant child, points out that, 'It is not your table, it's the place's table. Behave!' She places her hands firmly on his hips and moves him out of her way. Melvin looks momentarily suitably chastized, and bewildered by the fact that she has actually touched him, but he's soon back to his old ways. When Carol lightly reminds him that he will die soon if he continues to order fries, he launches into a diatribe about how 'We are all going to die soon, I will, you will, and it sure sounds like your son will.' This time he has gone too far, even for Carol. He has blundered across an invisible boundary into her personal life and she is hurt and angry. 'If you ever mention my son again you will never be able to eat here again . . . Do you understand me? You crazy fuck!' Melvin looks shocked – not only has she touched him physically, she appears to be the only person who can get through to him mentally and, if only for the briefest of moments, make him aware of the feelings of others.

Even with a minimum of make-up Carol has a beautiful face, with high cheekbones, dark intelligent eyes and light brown hair which she wears casually pinned out of the way, but she also looks tired and careworn with all the responsibilities of a single mother. She's struggling, with the help of her own loving mother, to bring up a small son who has a dangerously severe asthmatic condition and an immune system that fails whenever he gets an infection. She's also lonely. But as we soon realize when she brings a man she is dating to her crowded little apartment, sex on the sofa with her mother sitting in the kitchen wearing earplugs and her son being sick in the bedroom is not many men's idea of a good time. Carol's chances of finding a relationship appear almost as hopeless as Melvin's, particularly as she is not the kind of woman who is prepared to risk hurting her son or her mother for any man.

Melvin, Simon and Carol would appear to be three entirely incompatible individuals. Their lives are on such separate trajectories that even though their paths occasionally cross they have very little, if anything, to offer each other. But Melvin, like a man trying desperately to plug the holes in a leaking dam to save himself from drowning, is fighting a losing battle. He needs help, although he would be the last person to admit it. Luckily life has a way of seeping through even the most formidable of barriers and in the most unexpected ways. The first barrier is broken when Simon is viciously attacked by two young male prostitutes (friends of his life model) who he catches robbing his apartment. Simon is rushed to hospital, leaving the problem of who will look after Verdell. Frank, in his inimitable way 'persuades' Melvin to take on the task. 'I own this guy . . . trust me,' he reassures Simon in hospital; he's not to worry about the dog.

One of Melvin's carefully constructed boundaries has now been breached. No living creature, apart from Melvin, has set foot in his immaculate apartment since he moved in, but little Verdell now sits appealingly on his carpet waiting to be fed. Contrary to all expectations Melvin begins to soften. He reluctantly gives the dog a bowl of roast beef and plays the piano while Verdell eats. Soon he has completely incorporated the dog into his daily routine, even taking it to the restaurant with him and smiling with pleasure when some children pet the little creature. Carol watches in amusement. But it will take more than a dog to change Melvin.

A second crisis impinges on Melvin's carefully sealed world. Carol stops working at the restaurant. Melvin is so upset he bribes a waiter for her home address and confronts her on her doorstep with the words. 'I'm hungry. You've ruined my whole day. I haven't eaten.' By way of an explanation he adds, 'This is not a sexist thing. If you were a waiter I would be saying the same thing.' Carol stares at him in disbelief. 'Do you have any control over how creepy you have allowed yourself to get?' she asks. 'Yes I do,' he replies, 'To prove it I haven't gotten personal, you have.' For a moment she is ashamed of her personal attack, before she remembers this is Melvin, the king of rudeness, making her feel bad about herself. But her son is too sick for her to waste time worrying about how Melvin makes her feel, he needs to be rushed to the emergency room and Melvin's visit proves useful as she is able to commandeer his taxi.

Soon afterwards Carol receives a visit from a private doctor, a specialist in childhood allergies, who offers to cure her son. All expenses are to be paid for by Melvin. Possibly as a result of taking care of Verdell, Melvin has begun to feel some concern for others, although he would be the last person to admit it. Whatever the reason for Melvin's generosity, Carol is so overwhelmed she gives the doctor a hug. It is only after he has left that she begins to panic. By the middle of the night she is so worried about her obligation to Melvin that she makes her way through the pouring rain to his apartment. 'Why did you do this for me?' she demands, suddenly noticing that her T-shirt is drenched and quickly covering her breasts with her hands. 'So you would come back to work and wait on me,' Melvin replies bluntly. Carol is staggered by the egocentricity of his reply. Assuming that his hidden agenda must be sex, she tells him, equally bluntly, that, 'I am not going to sleep with you. I am never going to sleep with you.' She then turns and leaves. Melvin is now so disturbed that he can't sleep. He needs to talk and the only person he can talk to is Simon.

Since Simon came out of hospital his life has been in constant crisis. His handsome young face is so badly scarred he can hardly recognize himself in the mirror, his arm is in plaster and he can't hobble across a room without a stick. Also due to his lack of medical insurance he's broke. But perhaps most humiliating of all, his life has become uncomfortably bound to his homophobic neighbour by Verdell. Not only has the dog become attached to his new master and his roast beef dinners, but Melvin has grown so fond of Verdell that he actually cries when the time comes to give him back to Simon. (He is alone, of course, when he cries. For a man like Melvin it would be impossible to cry in front of another man.) Despite Melvin's usual blundering insensitivity, Simon has no alternative but to ask Melvin to walk the dog and Melvin is delighted by the opportunity. So when Melvin comes knocking at his door in the middle of the night to talk about his problems, Simon is surprised to say the least.

They sit awkwardly side by side on a hard seat just inside Simon's front door. Melvin talks about how he hasn't been sleeping, he hasn't been clear in his head and it's not just the tiredness, he's in trouble. 'When everything looks distorted, and everything inside aches and you can barely find the will to complain,' Simon suggests, suddenly identifying with his neighbour's depression. 'Yes,' Melvin says, surprised that his gay neighbour appears to understand how he feels, 'I'm glad we did this. Good talking to you.' He stands awkwardly and leaves. Simon looks utterly confused, which is understandable – Melvin omitted to mention that the cause of his depression was his growing attraction to Carol. For a man like Melvin, talking about his emotional life is such a rare activity, particularly to another man, that what he thinks has been an intimate sharing conversation is for Simon an encounter that's barely begun.

Women, on the other hand, have traditionally found it easier to talk to each other about their feelings and Carol also needs to talk. Now that her son, Spencer, has been cured by the doctor, for the first time in years she has time to think about herself. Melvin is so used to only thinking about himself that thinking about other people is disturbing. Carol has the opposite problem. As she tearfully tries to explain to her mother, '. . . I'm feeling this stupid panic thing inside me all the time. I just start thinking about myself and what good does that ever do anybody?' She goes on to confess that she's lonely, she's beginning to see couples everywhere and she envies what they have. She's even found herself feeling bad that Spencer's doctor is married, 'Which is probably why I make poor Spencer hug me more than he wants to. As if the poor kid doesn't have enough problems, he has to make up for his mum not getting any.'

Frank once more inadvertently acts as the catalyst, or an instrument of change, in other people's lives when he persuades Melvin to drive Simon to Baltimore. Simon has lost his ability or will to paint and so has no alternative but to visit his estranged parents and ask them for money. Melvin is of course reluctant to do this but, with a little nudging from Frank, he can see how the trip could be an opportunity for him to get closer to Carol if he can persuade her to come along. Carol is appalled by the prospect of a trip with Melvin, but after what he has done for her son how can she refuse his invitation?

So the unlikely threesome set off for Baltimore. From Melvin's point of view the trip rapidly turns into a disaster. Carol and Simon naturally like each other. They are similar; they are both warm, caring, empathetic human beings. Carol shows a maternal concern for Simon's horrific injuries and is genuinely interested in Simon's problems with his homophobic father and consequently his estrangement from his mother. Melvin reacts to her interest in Simon like a jealous spiteful child and finds himself firmly put in his place by Carol who insists on pulling over so she can give Simon her full attention. But by the time they check into a hotel for the night, despite Melvin's compulsive rudeness and social ineptitude, Carol has begun to suspect that there may be a complex and acutely sensitive man trapped beneath his abrasive exterior; a man who is struggling to reach out to her.

Melvin takes Carol to an expensive restaurant. His behaviour is as awkward and erratic as ever but he finally manages to settle down during their romantic dinner. He tells Carol how he hates taking pills for his 'ailment' (his obsessive-compulsive disorder) but that night when she told him she would never sleep with him, he started taking the pills. 'You make me want to be a better man,' he discloses with disarming honesty. 'That's maybe the best compliment of my life,' she replies and kisses him fully on the lips. She explains that the kiss wasn't because of what she owes him – the very first time she saw him she thought he was handsome. She goes on to whisper, 'It's OK, if you ask me I'll say yes.' The physicality between them is electric. But Melvin is terrified. As usual he uses talk as his way to defend himself and to escape from his fear. He blunderingly tells her that the reason he brought her along, among other things, was because he thought she might have sex with Simon – which is not only ridiculous, but it is also insulting from Carol's point of view. She walks out.

Back in the hotel she moves into Simon's room, as a way of being sure not to see Melvin when he returns. With the prospect of seeing his parents and his painting career apparently in ruins, Simon is terminally depressed. But the sight of Carol sitting on the edge of the bath with a towel draped around her, looking like an Ingres painting, arouses his artistic instincts. He is entranced. 'You are beautiful, Carol. Your skin, your long neck, your back, the line of you. You are why cavemen chiselled on walls.' He reaches for his sketchpad and for the first time since his injuries he is inspired to draw again. By the time Melvin returns the room is covered with beautiful line drawings of Carol. Melvin jealously demands to know if they had sex. 'It was better than sex,' Carol tells him defiantly, 'What I need, he gave me.' Simon laughs and says, 'I just love her.' Simon, as a sensitive gay man, appreciates and understands Carol's femininity in a way Melvin can barely comprehend. And Carol needs that, it makes her feel good about herself. But Simon can't give her all she needs, as Carol knows only too well. On the other hand, neither can Melvin, or so she believes.

Now Simon can draw again, he no longer needs to see his parents. He insists that they return to New York where he can work his way out of his financial crisis. For their entire return journey Carol remains angry and Melvin sulks. When they arrive in the city she tells him straight, 'I don't think I want to know you any more. You make me feel bad about myself.' She goes home alone.

Simon, who has been evicted from his apartment, is living in Melvin's spare room when Melvin again turns to him for advice. 'I'm dying here,' Melvin tells him. 'Because you love her,' Simon suggests. 'No . . . she's evicted me from my life,' Melvin insists. And in a way she has. It is Melvin's fear of losing the safe, if barren, life he knows, for an unpredictable, out of control future with the woman he loves, that is holding him back. For him the next step is huge, but prompted by Simon he takes it.

Despite the fact that it is four in the morning, Melvin goes to visit Carol in a last effort to tell her how he feels. 'Why can't I have a boyfriend who doesn't go nuts on me?' Carol cries out in despair when he greets her on the stairwell of her apartment block. Her mother, who has been listening at the door, hopeful that Melvin may be offering her daughter a chance of happiness, apologetically appears in the hall: 'Everyone wants that dear,' she reminds her daughter, 'It just doesn't exist.' Melvin suggests they go for a walk.

As they wander through the deserted night streets, Carol, still in her nightdress, grows increasingly afraid of what she might be letting herself in for, particularly as Melvin still zig-zags erratically trying to avoid walking on the lines. But he does try. In a final speech (perhaps a contemporary equivalent to Kate's big speech at the end of *The Taming of the Shrew*), he tells her why he loves her. And we listen, as Petruchio listened, and like Carol now listens, on tenterhooks, hoping that he really has changed, that he won't mess up, but hardly able to believe that it's possible. He tells her that he might be the only person on earth who knows that she is the greatest woman on earth. He might be the only one who appreciates how amazing she is and all the amazing things that she does: how she is with Spencer, how she says what she means and almost always means something that is about being straight and good, how he's watched her waiting on tables, bringing food and clearing it away, and the people in the restaurant just don't get it, 'And the fact that I get it makes me feel good about me . . . Is that something that it's bad for you to be around?' He finishes with a hopeful smile – at last he has learnt to focus on her, only mentioning his own needs and feelings last, instead of first. Carol is moved. She thinks carefully about his question. 'No,' she says – it's not bad for her to be around. They kiss. A nearby bread shop opens and they go to have a hot roll. With Carol holding his hand, Melvin manages to walk straight, no more zig-zagging to avoid the terrifying lines.

Just as Kate's madness in *The Taming of the Shrew* can be understood as her sense of identity being endangered by the strict controlling confines of the male-dominated world she inhabited, Melvin's madness can also be interpreted as his response to his masculine identity being under threat in the more feminized climate at the end of the twentieth century. The need to be in control or to have things under control is a masculine characteristic, just as the feminine is often associated with sharing, empathy and a tolerance of emotional disorder or chaos. The taming of Melvin takes place because, like Petruchio, Carol refuses to compromise who she is for Melvin's sake. She and Melvin are equally matched in their battle of wills. Carol refuses to let Melvin use or abuse her. Like Kate, Melvin has to learn not to be rude and intolerant; he has to learn to control his temper and his madness; he has to learn to be a proper rounded human being before she will love him. Carol also has a lot to learn. She too has to discover how to come out of her safe world, where she was living through her child and had forgotten how to live for herself. She has to learn to take risks, to give life and happiness a chance.

In the romantic comedies of earlier decades, there was frequently a splitting of woman between the good – the virgin or maternal, nurturing wife, and the bad – the temptress, whore, or selfish mother. In *As Good As It Gets* man is split between Melvin – the mad, bad masculine man, the heterosexual who is unable to properly relate to women – and Simon, the good feminine man, the caring, empathetic homosexual who relates well to women but is unable to make love to them. The splitting of woman has caused no end of confusion in both women and men. For women the confusion is about who they are and who they want to be and how they can bridge the divide, be both good and bad, in order to experience themselves as whole. For men the splitting of woman has also caused confusion as men often want or desire both kinds of women, despite all the life complications that entails. The contemporary tendency to split men into the good, feminine man and the bad, masculine man may well give rise to further confusion. What kind of man does woman want? What kind of man do men want to be? How can women have both and how can men be both? These will perhaps be the most pertinent questions for the next round of romantic comedies in the twenty-first century.

Finally, Carol, like Melvin (and Simon as an artist), always insists on the truth of things. One of the most important lessons they learn is that their separate truths are not necessarily the same. The underlying message of *As Good As It Gets* is that men and women need to learn to feel secure in their differences and to love and respect each other for who they are, not to try to convert each other into mirror images of themselves. This is perhaps the second big challenge for the romantic comedies of the twenty-first century.

Epilogue

So we have arrived at the beginning of a new decade, the first of not just a new century but, more weightily, a new millennium. It's certainly too soon to know what will be the dominant themes. As we have seen, sometimes the particular identity of a decade was clearly emerging at the outset: this was particularly apparent in the forties as a result of the effects of the Second World War; other times, such as in the eighties, the distinctive characteristics of the decade emerged more slowly.

It may be more satisfying if we could conclude that, as we journeyed through the romantic comedies of the twentieth century, each passing decade saw a new generation progressing towards a more enlightened understanding of sexuality, gender, love and relationships and so was moving closer to that elusive thing called happiness. But, of course, there was no such linear progression. The two world wars, which were hardly in themselves signs of enlightened progress, brought about unexpected developments such as precipitating a greater sexual freedom for both sexes. In contrast it was the depression years of the thirties and the relatively peaceful and prosperous fifties that saw the revival of traditional gender roles and conservative sexual morality accompanied by the fairytale vision of the one great love, which, if we are lucky and good, will strike us like a thunderbolt from the blue leading inevitably to our living happily ever after.

It was to take the sixties sexual revolution and the upheaval brought about by feminism in the seventies to once again open people's minds, and to allow them to admit openly that the struggle to conform to traditional gender roles and the romantic quest for the one great love could in themselves be forms of enslavement. Love didn't always last for ever. Sexual desire and love needn't be the same thing. Love could be a matter of free will or a conscious decision we make about the kind of life we want to lead in our pursuit of happiness. Masculinity and femininity weren't necessarily located in two separate genders but our individual temperaments may contain aspects of both. Love that challenged social conventions wasn't necessarily bad and to be hidden away like a guilty secret. The hypocrisy of secret affairs and the double standard – what is okay for men but not for women – were finally out of the closet. And marriage, built on the cornerstone of life-long sexual fidelity, itself became the problem. Increasing numbers of people began to want everything: a secure, lasting, equal relationship with both partners pursuing separate stimulating careers and a fulfilling domestic life, as well as the freedom to explore the full range of their sexual desires, without resorting to lies and hypocrisy.

But just as it began to seem as if the more open, honest and liberal our attitudes to sexuality and gender, the closer we would be to achieving our goal of happiness in love, so there was also a growing sense that something was missing. The nineties saw a hankering for the return of the fairytale romance and for more clearly defined and separate gender identities, which may be equal but are also distinctly different. Could it be that this was another swing of the pendulum, another backlash by men attempting to hang on to the last bastions of their power, as feminists continued their inexorable struggle for equal rights? Or could it be that this nostalgia for something lost is, in itself, an essential concomitant in the quest for happiness? Are there certain in-built and irresolvable contradictions in the human condition when it comes to matters of sexual desire and lasting love, or of what we want and what we need? After all, the linchpin of all comedy romance is the eternal double-act between men and women, or masculinity and femininity, in which, to borrow a phrase from *The Beast in the Nursery*, 'something that can never be known is always at stake'.[1]

According to a recent survey of 168 scattered world cultures eighty-seven per cent 'recognize in themselves "the madness of love"'.[2] The term madness implies that the love they recognize is not, or does not feel as if it is, a rational experience. Love, like madness, is out of control. It can be heaven but it can also be hell. It can overwhelm us and sweep us off our feet, bringing joy, fun and magic to our lives while at the same time afflicting us like an illness, bringing with it agony, misery, anger, despair, a desire to be rid of it and a terror of losing it.

We can search for explanations for the roots of our affliction by delving into our unconscious needs and desires formed in childhood relationships. And we can sift through the multitude of cultural influences, such as the myths and fragments of fairytales we have discovered lurking beneath the surface of many of these twenty-eight films, encapsulating as they do archetypal situations, characters and relationships, which, at least in our wishes and projections, we strive to emulate. We can ask ourselves, as Shakespeare did, whether lasting happiness is founded in 'the madness of love' or in a partnership based on calm reason and suitability. Shakespeare's sonnets leave us in no doubt that he himself was captivated by 'the madness of love'; although not because it brings lasting happiness but because it exists and repressing such powerful passions would be a violation of life itself.

The pleasure to be gained from romantic comedy, whatever its form, is not necessarily rooted in our desire for insight into ourselves and our lives. We also crave an escape from our everyday reality. Romantic comedies allow us to be secretly transported into how we would like the world to be and how we would like to be in the world. They provide us with an opportunity to imaginatively transform our real selves into our dream selves and to feel the warm glow of pleasure in that transformation, free from guilt or current 'politically correct' restraints. They allow us to transcend the contemporary debate and re-engage with the age-old battle of the sexes.

This in essence is the fantasy that underlies *Bridget Jones' Diary* (released in 2001, although the book was written in the nineties). Bridget is a (slightly) overweight, out of control, fallible, flawed single woman with just the kind of bright and feisty personality many women can easily identify with. She also finds herself in the enviable position of being torn between two men: Darcy who, like his namesake in *Pride and Prejudice*, is stunningly handsome, virtuous, faithful and morally upright; and Cleaver, her boss at the publishing house where she works, who is equally handsome but a thoroughly disreputable, sexually exciting philanderer. Both men become besotted with Bridget and sexual jealousy plays its inevitable hand. A duel, or at least a fist-fight ensues, in order to see off the competition in the time-honoured masculine way. What more could any woman want?

Finally, I am mindful of Adam Philips' elegant summary of Freud's response to a patient who wanted to be given a brief 'didactic' insight into his analytic technique: 'To be suspicious of clarity and to value what catches our attention. To find the plausible always slightly absurd. And to be in awe of the passions.'[3] Likewise, when it comes to our quest to understand ourselves, our pursuit of love and what makes us happy, there are no simple methods or solutions. If there are any lessons to be learnt from this book it is that romantic comedies can be far more complex than may at first appear to be the case. The battle of the sexes, or the double-act between the masculine and the feminine, will continue unabated because we don't want it resolved; we enjoy it too much. We may all be on a quest for that elusive happy-ever-after but at the same time we don't want the story to end.

References

Introduction

1. *Uses of Enchantment*, Bruno Bettelheim (Penguin, 1978: p. 145).
2. *The Taming of the Shrew*, (New Penguin Shakespeare, 1968, edited by G. R. Hibbard: p. 19).

Chapter One

1. *Terrible Honesty, Mongrel Manhatten in the 1920s*, Ann Douglas (Farrar, Straus and Giroux, 1995: p. 4).
2. Ibid., p. 20.
3. F. Scott Fitzgerald quoted in *Two Views of the Twenties*, Kevin Rayburn (http://www.louisville.edu/-kprayb01/1920s-remark-page.html; p. 1).
4. *Twentieth-Century Sexuality, A History*, Angus McLaren (Blackwell, 1999: pp. 51, 52).
5. *Divided Lives, American Women in the Twentieth Century*, Rosalind Rosenberg (Penguin, 1993: p. 81).
6. *I Remember the Thirties*, John Steinbeck. Originally published in *Esquire*, June 1960 (http://homepage.mac.com/cfarley/slhs english/thirties.html; p. 1).
7. *Washington Post: The FDR Years, On Roosevelt and His Legacy*, William E. Leuchtenburg (Harvard University Press, 1988 and Washingtonpost.com, p. 6).
8. *Divided Lives*, op. cit., p. 90.

9. *From Reverence to Rape, The Treatment of Women in the Movies*, Molly Haskell (University of Chicago Press, 1987; p. 21).

10. *Washington Post: The FDR Years, On Roosevelt and his Legacy*, op. cit. p. 8.

11. Ibid., p. 10.

12. Ibid., p. 12.

13. *Twentieth-Century Sexuality*, op. cit., p. 57.

14. *The Uses of Enchantment*, Bruno Bettelheim (Penguin, 1978).

15. Ibid., p.111.

16. Ibid., p.111.

17. *Romantic Comedy in Hollywood, from Lubitsch to Sturges*, James Harvey. (De Capo Press, 1998: p. 307.

18. *From Reverence to Rape, The Treatment of Women in the Movies*, Molly Haskell (University of Chicago Press 1987; p. 108).

Chapter Two

1. *The Woman I Wish I Knew, Tabloid: The Bulletin*, Charles Hornberger. (pp. 2–3, 19 Feb 1998, www.tabloid.net).

2. Obituary in *The Times*, 1995.

3. *Time 100: Leaders and Revolutionaries*, Doris Kearns Goodwin. www.time.com/time/time100/leaders/profile.eleanor.html.

Chapter Three

1. *Divided Lives*, op. cit., p. 148.

2. I*bid*., p. 156.

3. Ibid., p. 147.

4. Ibid., p. 153.

5. Ibid., p. 154.

6. *The International Film Encyclopedia*, Ephraim Katz (Macmillan,

1982).

7. *Variety Movie Guide 1999*, Ed. Derek Elley (Boxtree).

8. *The International Film Encyclopedia*, op. cit.

9. *Ways of Seeing*, John Berger (BBC and Penguin, 1972: p. 45).

Chapter Four

1. *Twentieth-Century Sexuality*, op. cit., p. 176.

2. *Divided Lives*, op. cit., p. 192.

Chapter Six

1. *Backlash, The Undeclared War Against Women*, Susan Faludi (Vintage, 1992: p. 342).

2. Ibid, p. 342.

3. *What a Man's Gotta Do*, Anthony Easthope (Routledge, 1992: p. 39).

4. *Divided Lives: American Women in the Twentieth Century*, Rosalind Rosenberg (Hill and Wang, 1992, p. 253).

5. Ibid., p. 121.

6. Ibid., p. 21.

Chapter Seven

1. *The Seduction of Hillary Rodham*, David Brock (The Free Press, 1996: p. 254).

2. Ibid., p. 255.

3. Ibid., p. 264.

4. Ibid, p.262.

5. *Men Don't Iron, the New Reality of Gender Differences*, Anne and Bill Moir (HarperCollins, 1999: p. 241).

6. Interview with Graham Fuller in the *Observer Review*, 19 August 2001.

Epilogue

1. *The Beast in the Nursery*, Adam Phillips (Faber & Faber, London, 1998), p. 117.

2. *Falling in Love: A History of Torment and Enchantment*, Susan Sullivan (Macmillan, London, 1999), p. 3.

3. Phillips, op. cit., p. 118.